BUILDING OR BUYING
THE HIGH-QUALITY HOUSE
AT LOWEST COST

A graduate engineer and writer with wide experience in the field of housing, A. M. Watkins is the author of *How to Judge a House* and co-author of *Insulate and Air-Condition Your Home*. He has been a sales engineer in the building industry, an associate editor of *House & Home* and *Architectural Forum* magazines, and has written many articles for *Harper's Magazine, Better Homes & Gardens, The American Home, House & Garden,* and others. He lives in a roomy, sixty-six-year-old Victorian house in Piermont, New York, with his wife, two children, and a dog.

BUILDING OR BUYING
THE HIGH-QUALITY HOUSE
AT LOWEST COST

A. M. Watkins

DOLPHIN BOOKS
DOUBLEDAY & COMPANY, INC.
GARDEN CITY, NEW YORK

Building or Buying the High-Quality House at Lowest
Cost was published simultaneously in a hardbound edition
by Doubleday & Company, Inc.

Dolphin Books edition: 1962

DEDICATION

To Jo, Davy, Anne, and Toddy Watkins, who were closely
associated with the writing of this book.

ACKNOWLEDGMENTS

A portion of this book was originally published in a booklet called *How to Judge a House*. This book is, in a way, a greatly enlarged and expanded version of the booklet and contains much new and additional material.

Some of the material is excerpted, in part, from previously published magazine articles by the author. The author wishes to thank the following magazines for permission to re-use such material:

The American Home, for sections in the chapters on "Buying an Old House," "Shopping and Negotiating for a House," and "Should You Use a Real Estate Broker?"; *Better Homes & Gardens* and *Harper's Magazine* for sections in "What's Wrong With America's Houses?"; *House Beautiful's Building Manual* for material in "What Is Good Construction?" and "Heating."

Credit is also given to *New Homes Guide, Home Modernizing,* and *Today's Home* for the occasional use of research material originally used for articles published by each and to the New York *Herald Tribune* for permission to reprint the excerpt from an article by Terry Ferrer.

And thanks to John Tiffany Elliott for helpful advice and guidance.

CONTENTS

WHAT THIS BOOK IS ABOUT

Before you build, buy, or remodel a house, do you know the basic rules for judging the floor plan and room arrangement, the kitchen, bathrooms, and other rooms? Do you know:

The five most common causes of high upkeep in houses and how to avoid them?

How to get top-quality heating, wiring, flooring, roofing, counter-top surfaces, among other things, that actually cost less in the long run than the ordinary products in most houses?

The unwritten rules for negotiating and bidding for a house which can save you more money than almost any other saving possible when you buy a house?

Which is best for your family: one-, 1½-, two-story, or a split-level house?

"What is probably the most costly and common mistake" in building a house, according to government experts?

The biggest reason for buying an old house, as well as the nine widespread flaws to watch for in old houses?

When brand-name construction products are of superior quality and when they are not?

Who can check a house for you, as well as the kind of "expert" to beware of?

How to shop for the cheapest mortgage?

That you can be charged an additional $250 to $750, sometimes more, in closing costs when you buy a house, but not everybody pays this much?

That the paying of discount "points" can cost people from 2 to 12 per cent of the FHA or VA mortgage amount, over and above the price of the house?

What the FHA can and cannot do for you?

The surprisingly helpful services sometimes provided by real estate agents; as well as how to avoid the most common gyp-broker tricks?

The answers to these questions—given in down-to-earth, non-technical language—are typical of the content of this book. Here, in other words, is what you should know before you build or buy a house today, and in many cases before you fix up or remodel your present home.

Importance of Good Design and Construction

The high price of houses is probably the biggest single problem in home building today. You not only have to pay a high price for a new house, the bills keep coming in long after you've bought it. Quite aside from mortgage payments and taxes, maintenance and upkeep turn out to be painfully high every year, as any number of buyers have learned to their dismay.

The central troubles are poor design and poor construction. While costs have been steadily rising, the quality of new houses seems to slide steadily downhill. The chief complaint of most buyers is that their houses are too small and pinched for space. But space costs money and the lack of it is not necessarily the fault of the builder. As noted later in this book, a lot of people want a $30,000 house for $20,000, an act which requires a magician, not a builder.

But where the builders do fall down is in the basic design of houses. Often floor plans and room arrangements are singularly ill conceived. There is little storage space. Doors and windows are haphazardly located. The house itself is poorly placed on its lot. Virtually no consideration is given to such crucial factors as the house's position in relation to the hot sun, the best view, drainage, privacy from neighbors, and protection from street noises. And it is rare indeed for a builder to provide for expanding the house later at minimum expense.

If our houses were properly planned, the buyer would get a bonus of 10 to 20 per cent more use from the same space. Consider, for instance, the kitchen, a particularly important room since women spend so much time there. The

Small Homes Council of the University of Illinois examined the kitchens in more than a hundred housing deveolpments. More than 90 per cent of them had insufficient base cabinet storage, 77 per cent had insufficient wall cabinets, 67 per cent had constricted counter space—these being three of the most important aspects of kitchen planning. A good many of the kitchens also were found deficient in thirteen other specific needs, and more than 50 per cent of them had four to six architectural planning flaws. The Small Homes Council concluded that kitchens in small houses are "generally inadequate and poorly arranged."

In addition to poor design, many builders use the cheapest quality doors and windows, lumber, flooring, plumbing, heating, and wiring, and the cheapest construction methods they can get away with. Building-supply dealers will tell you that development builders in particular are notorious in this respect. In brief, minimum standards prevail and the home buyer is left holding the bag.

Builders can get away with it, since even the shoddiest doorknob looks bright and shiny when a house is new. After the builder packs up and goes, leaving a happy couple in the full flush of new-home ownership, it does not take long for disillusionment to set in. They learn that the cheapest materials turn out to be the most expensive in the long run.

On the other hand, the structure, per se, of a lot of houses today is much better than many critics charge. Houses tend to be structurally sound in their 2 × 4 "bones," in their beams and rafters. A salesman will point out to you enthusiastically, for example, the strong double 2 × 6 "headers" (horizontal supports over windows), and the extra bracing at wall corners. These things are practically standard now in most houses largely as a result of the FHA's uplifting influence. But they're not enough.

It is in certain other crucial elements, as the mechanical and electrical systems, where there is still great room for quality improvement. Here are, for example, seven of the most glaring causes of dissatisfaction and high upkeep expenses in houses today:

(1) *Shoddy heating systems,* which heat poorly, cause excessively high fuel bills, and wear out quickly.

(2) *Skimpy electric wiring.*

(3) *Short-lived water heaters*—the separate little heaters which provide hot water for your kitchen and bathroom.

(4) *Token insulation,* with the smallest permissible amounts spread over your ceiling and little or none used for the walls.

(5) *Cheap roofs* good for ten to fifteen years on the average, after which many an owner has to spend from $300 to $750 for a new roof. (Ironically, the well-heeled buyers of many $50,000 houses also get the same kind of cheap roofing used on the lowest-priced houses.)

(6) *Cheap plumbing, piping, and bathroom fixtures,* resulting in noisy, inefficient operation, quick deterioration, and expensive repairs.

(7) *Poor waterproofing,* which opens the way to such widespread problems in houses as moisture condensation, wood rot, exterior paint peeling, wet basements, and even termites (which thrive on wetness). The lack of waterproofing and moisture control is one of the most bothersome problems in American houses today. But doing something about it after a house is finished requires so much trouble and expense that it is usually hopeless.

Each of these glaring examples of dissatisfaction in houses is dealt with in detail in this book, along with information on how to avoid each. Tips on avoiding other common design and construction errors are also sprinkled liberally through the following pages.

You need not worry so much about getting a really good house if you hire a top-flight architect to design one for you and a good builder to construct it. But most of us think that we cannot afford an architect and cannot afford the time, expense, and worry to have a house built to order. Most of us are limited to buying a ready-built house or a used house. This book, therefore, presents fundamental guides about design and construction so you can thoroughly judge the caliber of the new or old house you buy.

How Much Extra Cost for Quality?

This book also puts great emphasis on high-quality construction. Naturally, when a house is built with first-rate materials, compared with the usual minimal-quality materials, its cost goes up. But the extra cost is less than you may think. Significantly, the use of quality materials throughout a house will raise the total construction cost of your house only 5 to 7 per cent more than the cost of the usual, cheap, minimal-grade products normally found in houses. This is simply because it costs just about as much money for the labor to *install* the cheapest product as it does to install a top-grade version of the same product.

The extra expense goes almost entirely for extra quality in the products themselves. The cost of an ordinary $20,000 house is raised by perhaps $1000 to $1400 in all when quality products are used. Your mortgage payments go up about $7 a month. But you get dividends—large annual savings as a result of the low-cost upkeep and maintenance that go hand in hand with high quality. As noted in the chapter on heating, a mere $50 more (approximately), spent for a really good heating system, will return this money to you countless times over in reduced fuel bills every year and in equipment with a longer life.

Many of the same fundamental principles apply when you buy a used house, which we define as any house from one to 250 years old. In addition, a used house raises special questions due to age and possible neglect. These are answered in the special chapter on buying a used house.

Another Savings Principle

It is axiomatic in building that the cost of adding a special feature to a house is nearly always cheaper if it is done when the house is being built, rather than providing the same feature after the house is finished. We tend to cut out all but the most essential things when we build or buy a house. We figure that we can add the other things later. This is a normal reaction when we are confronted with the cost figures for a variety of "extras" we might like in a new house.

But putting certain things off will often cost you much more money in the long run. As noted later, it is downright foolish not to insulate the walls of a new house at 6 to 8¢ a square foot, when its cost automatically jumps to 20¢ or more a square foot as soon as the walls of a house are closed up; adding a second bathroom may cost only about $800 when a house is being built, yet the very same bathroom put in later may cost $1200 or more. The same principle applies to a variety of other features in houses, specifically mentioned in the following pages. You should judiciously seek them out and, if at all possible, have them provided in the beginning. Your mortgage payments, to be sure, will go up, but you will be far ahead of the game, considering the expense of adding the same things later.

Certain things, of course, will not cost any more later. One example, mentioned in Chapter 19, is a finished recreation room. It is often provided in new houses mainly because it impresses prospects. You can almost always turn raw space into a recreation room later at little or no extra expense, so let *it* wait; get the builder to give you, say, a second bathroom instead, or whatever else you need that counts more.

The Perfect House?

Unfortunately, there is no perfect house. Every house is a compromise. This book strives to present the ideal rules for getting the best possible design and construction. We give absolute standards on the principle that the higher you aim, the higher you will land. You should know, however, that virtually no house will ever conform to all or even most of the ideal design and construction standards given in these pages.

Most houses have flaws. You have to accept them. You need not, however, tolerate the most glaring flaws. Choose another house. In fact, houses are more prone to built-in errors and flaws than almost any other consumer product today. As you read this book and later go shopping for a house, you should remember not to turn down a house because it breaks, even flagrantly, a few of the fundamental standards you have read about here. A major-league ball player only needs to hit three out of every ten times at bat to become one of the few leading 300 hitters. A good batting average among houses is not much higher, painful as it may sound. (What can be done about it is discussed in the Part 7 on America's horse-and-buggy housing industry.)

One way to approach the ideal house is by hiring a good architect and building your own. Then you can specify the best quality design and materials. If you can afford this, fine. This book then should be of even greater help.

How to Use This Book

To simplify things, the book is divided into separate sections on design, construction, and so on, as listed in the Contents. It is not necessary to read the various sections consecutively, but this can be useful. However, you may skip those chapters which do not apply to you personally—Chapter 20 on "Building a House," for example, if you are buying an old house. This will be obvious. And at the end, a summary check list is included which you can take out or copy and carry with you when you look at houses. It sums up the most important things to check, based on the over-all contents of the book.

By necessity, occasional repetition occurs in various chapters. This is unavoidable in order to make each chapter self-sufficient. Certain considerations in buying a used house obviously are duplicated when you buy a new house. Rather than refer you back to the original section for guidance, we have often repeated important points.

PART 1

HOW MUCH HOUSE AND WHERE?

These are the first key questions to resolve when you decide to build or buy a house. Here, unfortunately, is where your dreams meet the realities of the market place. Most of us would like a $30,000 house for $20,000. Perhaps you can pay more. The aim of this section is to help you decide how much you can afford to spend, based on your income and family expenses. It also offers guides for judging the amount of house you can get for your money, choosing between a new or old house, and deciding where to live—i.e., choosing a good neighborhood, one of the most important considerations of all.

CHAPTER 1

PRICE, SIZE, AND NEIGHBORHOOD

The price obviously should be within the bounds of your income. It also should be a fair figure for the amount of house you get. In general, it should not exceed two to two and one-half times a man's annual income. This is an old rule of thumb and still makes sense. It's best not to include a working wife's salary, especially if she expects to quit work and have children. A $6000-a-year family can afford up to a $12,000 to $15,000 house; with $10,000 a year you can go as high as $20,000 to $25,000.

If you are a young couple with children, a fixed income, and a tight budget, it's best to stay on the low side. If your job prospects are good and your income on the rise, you can use the upper limit and even stretch it a bit. If you have a nest egg that permits a sizable down payment, it can make possible a step up to a higher-priced house at the same or even lower monthly payments than required for a cheaper house.

Another general rule is that most of us can afford up to 25 per cent of our income for housing expense—roughly one week's pay a month. But remember that housing expense is more than just monthly mortgage payments and taxes. You will also have regular bills for such things as insurance, heating operations, and the inevitable repairs. Don't let the prospect frighten you, but don't ignore it, either. A good idea of what you can afford for a house can be had by drawing up a personal balance sheet of current expenses versus income, as shown here. But be realistic. Fudging the figures to make them look better can bring on deep woe later.

BUDGETING FOR A HOUSE

1. Determine how much money you can spend for housing

TOTAL MONTHLY LIVING EXPENSES OTHER THAN HOUSING

Food $_____

Clothing   _____

Life Insurance   _____

Average medical bills   _____

Installment payments (Washer, drier, TV set, etc.)   _____

Automobile upkeep and insurance   _____

Commuting   _____

Entertainment & recreation   _____

Children's school or college expenses   _____

OTHER SAVINGS

Books, records, hobbies $_____

All other, including contributions, membership fees, summer vacation, etc.   ======

Total Living Expenses other than housing $_____

MONTHLY INCOME

Gross monthly pay $_____

Minus all deductions (income taxes, social security, others)   _____

Net take home pay   _____

Less Total Living expenses other than for housing (above)   ======

MONTHLY INCOME AVAILABLE FOR HOUSING $_____

2. Determine money available for monthly mortgage and interest charges.

Total monthly income available for housing (from above) $_____

Minus taxes, insurance, and upkeep @ $3–$4 a
month per $1000 of house price. (Figure from $3
in small towns up to $4 in large towns or metro-
politan areas.)

TOTAL MONEY AVAILABLE FOR MORT-
GAGE PAYMENTS (including principal and
interest): $_____

This last is the figure to know. It is a guide to the maximum mortgage you can take on, including interest. Monthly
carrying charges for mortgages are given in the chapter on
financing, Chapter 24.

The average cost of $3 to $4 a month per $1000 of
house for taxes and upkeep means $30 to $40 a month for
a $10,000 house, $60 to $80 for a $20,000 house, and so on.
It is an approximation for a typical house based on:

$18 to $20 a year per $1000 of house price for taxes;

plus $3 per $1000 for insurance;

plus $15 to $25 a year per $1000 for upkeep and repairs.

Thus a total of $36 to $48 a year per $1000 of house.
This figure may be higher or lower according to local conditions. A telephone call to tax officials, board of assessors,
town or city clerk can tell you about taxes. Also ask about
impending tax increases, and possible new assessments for
roads or schools. If you buy an existing house, the seller
should show you recent tax bills.

Location and Neighborhood
*"The value of thy property dependeth upon thy neigh-
bors."—Confucius*

Real estate experts may be less philosophical than Confucius, but, to a man, they rate the neighborhood the greatest single influence on the market value of a house. It ex-
erts a major influence on the mortgage terms you get and
is of prime concern in maintaining house resale value.

A house should conform in size and price to its neighborhood. The location should be in an established neighborhood not likely to go downhill and should not be in the path

of commercial or industrial growth. Best test for this is the "zoning" (the word for local real estate codes or laws). It should be zoned strictly for one-family houses. The local building inspector or a zoning-board official can tell you if it is or is not. If zoned for multi-family houses, commerce, or industry, watch out. Also ask if any down-zoning changes are ever likely. And stores, schools, shopping center, churches, and transportation facilities should be nearby.

A $25,000 house is a bad buy in a $15,000 neighborhood. This also means not to plan on putting so much money into fixing up a house that it will become overpriced for its neighborhood. A Midwestern man learned this the hard way. He bought a charming $25,000 old house in a neighborhood of $25,000 houses, then poured in another $7000 for new roof, heating, screened porch, and a modern kitchen. Later he had to sell the house and took a hefty loss. He wanted $32,000, which was fair enough, but the house went begging for over a year. He had to drop the price down almost to $25,000 before he could sell it. People who were willing to pay more backed out because of the neighborhood.

What About the Schools?

This is important not only because many people want their children well educated but also because the caliber of the high school counts enormously for college entrance. A student may have top grades, but these will be discounted by college admission officials if he comes from a high school with mediocre teachers and low standards. Don't accept a real estate agent's offhand judgment that local schools are outstanding. This is usually unfounded opinion, if not plain nonsense. Check for yourself.

Unfortunately, there is no national rating system that will tell you the caliber of a local school district. (Some colleges reportedly have such ratings, but they are kept secret.) Determining how good the schools are may take much time and effort. It demands more than a casual investigation and more than a few words of advice, according to Dr. Carroll F. Johnson, Superintendent of Schools, White Plains, New York. He presents a check list for appraising the schools where you may move. Though rather detailed, it is given here so that those who want to know may use it (excerpted from an article by Terry Ferrer in the New York *Herald Tribune*):

1. Before looking for a house, locate the communities with the highest levels of education among their citizens. This can be obtained from U. S. Bureau of Census studies, available at any good library. [See section on Population Characteristics for your area.] The Census districts may not coincide with school districts but such information is a good guide. The higher the general education level of its citizens, the greater effort a community will make to maintain and improve its schools.

2. How much does the school district spend a year per child for all expenses? There is no one correct answer and a wide variation from state to state. In one part of the New York metropolitan area including some of the better schools, total average expenditure in 1959–60 was $712 per pupil. It may be considerably higher or lower in other places. So make a comparison of what it is for the various school districts in the area where you may live; the higher the figure, the better.

3. How well is the school staffed? How large are the classes? Better schools have a wide variety of specialists and enough supervision, while still maintaining relatively small classes. Studies indicated that classes of twenty-five or smaller approach the ideal in this respect.

4. What is the median teaching salary? How does it compare with neighboring districts? This indicates if a district is paying high enough salaries to attract and hold good teachers. [A high turnover rate, however, does not necessarily indicate poor schools. It can mean that a district that makes a practice of hiring good young women teachers, say, finds itself competing with young men who find the teachers equally attractive for wives which keeps turnover high.]

5. Does the school system sponsor trips out of the local area to recruit the best teachers available? Better staffs represent the best teachers in the country—those who are willing to come to a particular school district.

6. What is the local record in recent years on local budget and bond issue elections? One should think twice before settling down in an area in which school budget requests are consistently turned down. Even the best school districts lose some requests but consistent rejections are a bad sign.

7. What is the percentage ratio of "capital and debt service" to total expenditures? Capital and debt service represent money spent to improve the physical plant. It includes principal and interest on bond issues. It is estimated that debt service can run as high as 25 per cent of total expenses and still reflect improving quality. If debt service exceeds 25 per cent, watch out. It will put heavy pressure on the over-all school budget when times are bad and everything will suffer as a result of pinched expenditures.

8. What percentage of total school expenditures is borne by the property tax on single-family houses? It can be hazardous if too high, compared with other nearby districts. (It can be obtained from the local school-board office.)

9. Are any of the schools on double sessions? If they are, what plans are there for correcting the situation?

10. Are the schools responsive to new thinking? A good system is responsive. PTA's and other citizen groups are encouraged, even though policy is set by the Board of Education.

11. What provision is made for pupil transportation? If school buses are not provided, public transportation should be available and convenient.

12. Tour the promising districts and examine both schools and communities. Ask local people what they think of their schools. Ask if the junior and senior high schools are considered as good as the elementary schools. Ask about the superintendent and the Board of Education. Is the superintendent regarded as an educational leader? Are the board members respected members of the community?

Finally, get permission from the school principal to enter classrooms. The school should be a place where the visitor is welcome. This is the crucial test of any school. Note: If the Board of Education balks at answering questions or if the principal is not co-operative about visiting, look for another place to live. [A good administration is careful about not upsetting the routine in the school—but a good routine allows for visits.]

Of course, people who live in an area generally know how good their schools are. Those you respect can shed light on the subject. A real estate agent, however, is not likely to be the most reliable informant.

New or Old House?
Which is better? Consider the new house first.

Perhaps its most important practical advantage is that it is easier to finance. Obtaining a mortgage is less trouble and the down payment required is considerably lower than when buying a used house. This makes a big difference to many buyers.

In addition, a new house is fresh and clean, requires little scrubbing and painting to start with. The equipment is new, and a major breakdown or expensive repairs is much less likely. Ideally, a custom-built house or, better still, an architect's design just for you and your family is best of all.

A new house, however, is not all peaches and cream. Windows stick and doors may warp. The heating ducts may be clogged with debris which will fly into the house when the furnace is first turned on. Such bugs are inevitable. The first year or so will be a shakedown cruise during which work will cry out to be done. (This is why it is important to buy from a builder with a good reputation for service and workmanship. You can count on service.)

With many new houses you have to cope with little or no landscaping. You painstakingly try to grow grass, and often the streets are unpaved when you move into a new development. And the details involved in getting a new house built can be maddening.

The Case for an Old House—Any House Over a Year Old

The biggest single advantage of an old house is usually more space for the money. Often an older house is loaded with twice as much interior space as a new house at the same price, not to mention such things as the charm of high ceilings. There are trees and few landscaping problems. You can move into an established neighborhood and move in at once. Taxes are more likely to be stable. Commuting to work is probably quicker and less expensive, often a chore and expense never to be ignored. Because older houses are harder to sell than new houses, you are put in a better bargaining position. It is virtually assumed that the owner will nearly always come down in price, sometimes quite a bit.

On the other hand, many an old house is located in a run-down neighborhood or in the path of spreading blight. (But first appearances can be deceptive here, since more and more formerly run-down neighborhoods, particularly in big cities, are making a strong comeback, as people find great bargains in such areas. En masse, they remodel and fix up. On the west side of New York's Greenwich Village, for example, block after block of formerly ramshackle houses have been bought up by bargain seekers and are being remodeled into extremely attractive houses. As a result, the whole section is on the rebound.)

Financing an old house may be tough, since a stiff 25 to 40 per cent cash down payment is often required. An old house also may demand expensive modernizing as well as interior painting and redecorating; major repairs are a strong possibility and the older the house, the more likely. Serious structural defects are easily overlooked; this makes it essential to have a used house checked out by an expert before you buy. If defects are found, a price adjustment sometimes can be made to allow for them. How to buy an old house and suggestions on the most common defects to watch for are discussed in Chapter 18.

What Size House?

The number of bedrooms is a widely used guide for choosing house size. At least three bedrooms are recommended even if you do not have children. A two-bedroom house is hard to sell. Like a two-seater car, its resale value is small. Besides, you can always turn a spare bedroom into a study or sewing room or, for that matter, install a pool table in it.

Try for at least three bedrooms. A large family should consider four or perhaps five. Adequate bedrooms can alleviate crowding and allow for occasional overnight guests. Even more important is the size of a house in total square feet of finished floor area. This is *the* key figure today for determining building value. It is generally far more important than the number of rooms or cubic volume. Two nearby houses each may have six rooms. But one has a total of only 1200 square feet because of small, cell-like rooms, whereas the second may contain 1600 square feet, its rooms much larger and abundantly more livable.

At first glance you may favor a $14,000 house, say, over

another priced at $15,000. Breaking it down to price per square foot may show that the cheaper house is actually more expensive per square foot of space—i.e., that the higher-price house actually offers much more value in *space per dollar*.

The minimum-size house needed for a typical family of four is approximately 1350 square feet, a 30 × 45 foot house. This includes all finished rooms with heat plus halls and stairs. It does not include garage, basement, attic, or unheated space to be finished later. Every builder has this figure on the tip of his tongue, but unfortunately you will generally draw a blank from a real estate salesman on this score.

Ask for the house area in square feet or figure it yourself. Measure the outside dimensions less garage and multiply. A 25 × 40 foot house gives a tight 1000 square feet; a 30 × 50 a more ample 1500. Double the area of the first floor for a two-story house. Floor by floor areas have to be figured separately for 1½-story houses and split levels; omit the basement.

Costs for building a new house today generally range from about $10 to $15 a square foot, excluding the lot, and up to $20 or more per square foot for custom houses. The actual figure you pay depends mainly on local building costs. These vary greatly across the country, as shown in the FHA cost chart for different cities in Chapter 20. Since building costs were considerably less in past years and used houses offer more space for the money, used-house prices often break down to less than $10 per square foot.

Next Step?

When your over-all objectives are brought into focus— approximate house size and price, new or old house, and where you wish to live—how do you judge the house it-self? The first and perhaps foremost aspect to evaluate is the over-all design, its fundamental suitability for living and for your family in particular.

PART 2

HOUSE DESIGN

Design has to do with how well a house is planned, its overall shape, as opposed to how its flesh and bones are put together, its construction. Design is deceptive. A house that may appear to be perfectly charming at first glance can turn out to be impossible to live in. Like beauty, design is more than skin-deep.

The following chapters tell you how to judge the floor plan and room arrangement, and give you fundamental guides for judging style and appearance.

Here also are minimum rules for adequate storage (avoiding jam-packed "Fibber McGee" closets), how to choose among the four main kinds of houses (one-, 1½-, two-story, and split level), how to tell if a house is placed properly on its lot, and the crucial, though much overlooked, importance of good exposure—the proper orientation of a house and its rooms in relation to the sun and prevailing winds.

CHAPTER 2

WHAT IS GOOD DESIGN?

Good design has to do with how well a house *works* for you and your family, not fancy gimcracks and useless ornamentation. It means design for efficient and convenient living, working, sleeping, playing, entertaining, and just plain relaxing. It means that people can work or play without clashing with others involved in different activities.

It means that a house should be cheerful with plenty of light and a feeling of openness, that it is warm in winter and cool in summer, that it is designed for good living with privacy and is not cursed with built-in noise, frustration, and inconvenience.

A house should have a good floor plan and room arrangement. Each room should be designed well for its particular purpose. The house should be located properly on its lot and turned properly in relation to the sun. It should have adequate storage space of the right kind in the right place. Like a pretty woman, it should be pleasing to look at and live with.

All of this may sound like a large order but it is not. It is fundamental. This is why a good architect is required to lay out a house, even if it is a development house. That's why good builders use architects. But you, too, should understand each basic requirement. When you aim high it is surprising how much you attain. For good design pays off in delight and pleasure every day in countless ways that most people never know until they experience the sheer joy of living in a really well-designed house.

Zoning

Good houses have three main zones: living, sleeping, and working. Each zone should be clearly separate from others, yet properly related to the others, the street, the sun, and the outdoors. This is one of the first things an architect tackles when designing a house.

Are the bedrooms separated from the noise of work and play? Can you entertain guests without waking the children? A buffer zone, not just a mere partition, is needed between bedrooms and the rest of the house. This can be a hall, bathroom, or adroitly placed closets. Can unfinished laundry be left as is without being in view of a chance visitor? It depends on the zoning.

The two-story house is a good example of natural zoning between the second-floor bedrooms and the kitchen and living areas on the first floor (but its disadvantages must be considered, as pointed out in Chapter 5). Even better is a house laid out like an H, the living and sleeping zones at opposite ends of the house neatly connected down the middle by the kitchen and utility work zone, and all on one level. Though ideal in design, this costs more to build because of the large wall area. Much the same effect can be had in a more compact plan through careful design. Good zoning also goes hand in hand with room arrangement and good circulation (which in this case refers to the movement of the occupants within the house).

Six Tests for Good Circulation

How can you tell a good floor plan? The main routes in a house, the ones used over and over again, are the key. You can spot them by six tests:

1. *Does the family entrance lead directly from garage or driveway to kitchen?* This is highly important. The main entrance for a family is usually through the kitchen. The garage and driveway should be near the kitchen for quick entry and swift grocery unloading. The garage-to-kitchen route should be sheltered from rain. Travel through the kitchen plainly should not run smack through the kitchen work area (where food is prepared).

2. *Is the kitchen centrally located?* This, too, is crucial. From the kitchen a woman should have control over the entire house. She should be near the front door and family

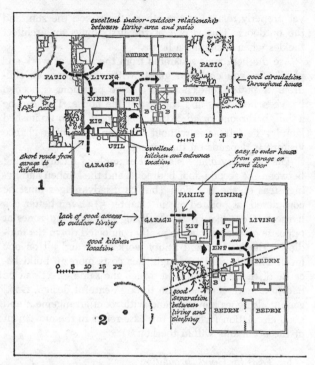

Figs. 1, 2, 3 Diagrams illustrate good and bad features of typical houses. They point up the importance of good circulation of traffic within the house, and good zoning between living, working, and sleeping areas.

entrance. She should be able to watch children playing outside, and also be near the dining room, living room, and outside patio. The kitchen should be a command post, not a foxhole. The remote, isolated kitchen is a widespread offense. It probably leads to more wear and tear on people, particularly mothers, than any other planning defect.

3. *Does the front door (main entrance) lead directly to the center of the house?* Guests enter here. A center hall or foyer will help greatly. It will shield people inside from

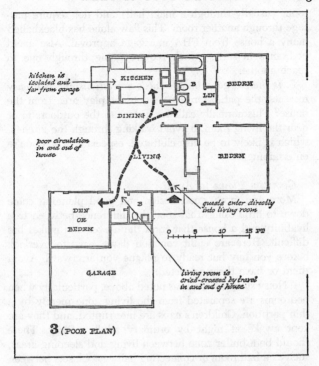

kitchen is isolated and far from garage

KITCHEN

B

BEDRM

LIN

DINING

poor circulation in and out of house

LIVING

BEDRM

guests enter directly into living room

DEN OR BEDRM

B

0   5   10   15 FT

GARAGE

living room is criss-crossed by travel in and out of house

3 (POOR PLAN)

casual visitors, and protect you from the inrush of wind, snow, and rain. The main entrance should be close to the driveway and street. A clothes closet near the front door is essential.

4. *Is the living room shielded from cross traffic?* It should not be a main highway for people going in and out of the house. It should be a dead end, so you can read, talk, watch TV, or entertain guests in peace without kids running through every few minutes.

5. *Is there good room-to-room circulation?* Can you go from any room to any other room without passing through a third room (except the dining room)? From any entrance to any room without walking through a third room? The main bathroom in particular should be accessible from any

room (usually through a main hall) and not require passage through another room. This flaw alone has blackballed many a house from FHA mortgage approval. Also avoid bedrooms in series which require going through one to reach another.

6. *Is there a good indoor-outdoor relationship?* Is it easy to reach the patio, terrace, or outdoor play area from the house? This normally calls for a door to the outdoors in or near the living room to avoid walking through the kitchen, which is likely to be dish-cluttered, especially when you're entertaining.

Common Flaws to Avoid

More and more, good design and good planning come down to little things that spell the difference between true livability and a house that frays the nerves and makes life difficult. Here are eight common flaws, easy to overlook before you buy but ready to plague you afterward. Avoid them or have them corrected:

· Noisy sleeping areas, as noted above, particularly when bedrooms are separated from the living zone merely by a thin partition. Children's naps are interrupted, and they are kept awake at night by ordinary adult activity. There should be a buffer zone between living and sleeping areas, such as a bathroom or connecting hallway. Closets between the two areas are another good idea, or bookcases on the common wall. Acoustical ceiling tile for the bedroom hall also can reduce noise travel to the bedrooms.

· Exposed bathroom, visible to other rooms, or squarely in view from the living room or from the head of the stairs when its door is open. It's embarrassing from both sides.

· A picture window in front of a house. Quite common, it is senseless nine times out of ten. You have to cover it with drapes or blinds for privacy. Or all you see is passing traffic —and it sees you. A picture window will do far more good at the side or back facing a private patio, terrace, or good view.

· No front-door glass or window next to it that lets you see who is at the door when the bell rings.

• No outside basement door to get such things as screens, storm windows, and garden tools in and out without lugging them through the house. An outside basement door also provides a separate entrance for children playing downstairs, so people upstairs are not bothered. It should be at least thirty-six inches wide for ease in carrying things through.

• A basement-stairway door that opens *toward* the basement. This is hazardous. It should open the other way.

• Walls so cut up by windows and doors that furniture placement is limited.

• No room for expansion, particularly in the great number of two-bedroom houses built after the war, and in many tight little 1½- and two-story houses. Sometimes the house itself is impossible to add to. Sometimes there isn't enough land around, and sometimes, worst of all, local zoning restrictions bar an addition (because the house falls too close to street or lot lines). Avoiding this flaw requires an advance check of local zoning restrictions. Will they permit a new garage, a room added on, or other expansion?

CHAPTER 3

ARE THE INDIVIDUAL ROOMS
PROPERLY DESIGNED?

Much surface appeal is put in the kitchens of new houses so they *seem* new and modern. Don't be misled, for the kitchen that looks most glamorous at first glance often turns out hopelessly inadequate. A good kitchen meets three main requirements: It conforms to the all-important work-triangle principle; it provides adequate storage and counter space; and it is pleasant to work and eat in—i.e., it has plenty of light and air. These are in addition to a central location, the importance of which has been emphasized.

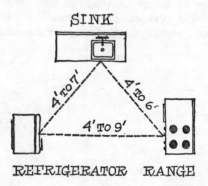

Fig. 4 Basic kitchen requirement is proper work triangle formed by refrigerator, sink, and range. Shortest to longest distances recommended from one to the other are also given. Two of the three fixtures may be on same wall.

The work-triangle principle means proper relationship of the refrigerator, sink, and cooking range. According to a famed research project at Cornell University, the distance from refrigerator to sink to range should form a triangle of between twelve and twenty feet, from left to right in that order for most women. (A left-handed woman may prefer a right-to-left arrangement.)

The average size of the work triangle for women will fall between sixteen and seventeen feet around the triangle—about 6½ feet from the center front of the refrigerator (or refrigerator-freezer) to center front of sink; about five feet from sink to center front of range; and about five feet from range back to the refrigerator. The space near the refrigerator is often called the mix center. The refrigerator door plainly should open toward the sink. A handy counter-top space at least thirty-six inches wide is needed next to the refrigerator for chopping, cutting, and rolling dough.

The sink center, for both preparation and clean-up, is the core of the kitchen and an active area. Dishwasher, garbage disposer, and some supply cabinets go here. Counter space at both sides of the sink is essential. The range or cooking center also requires counter space on both sides plus cabinets. Some people say the sink should be placed under a window but this is desirable, not essential, especially if it disrupts the kitchen plan. A separate oven can be located in a less important area. It, too, should have counter space on one side at least (for putting down hot dishes).

Minimum Kitchen Size

Cornell recommends a total kitchen work area of at least ninety-six square feet (8 × 12). There are L-shaped kitchens, U-shaped kitchens, corridor types and the everything-on-one-wall kind. The University of Illinois found that minimum work area for an efficient U-shaped kitchen is 8 × 10 feet. With a separate oven and a dishwasher the minimum is 112 square feet (9⅓ × 12). These are minimum rules; try for more.

Regardless of shape, the vital work triangle should conform to the above rules. As food is prepared it should move toward the dining center where you will eat. A serving center, last stop before the table, is optional but a help. The work triangle itself, a busy place, should be clear of obstacles such as tables and chairs. Be sure it is not criss-crossed by people coming in and out of the house, a maddening flaw.

Common Flaws to Avoid

According to a University of Illinois study, the three most widespread kitchen flaws are skimpy cabinet storage, not enough counter space, and no counter at all next to the range. Here are Illinois' minimum standards:

At least five to 8½ feet of wall cabinets.

At least eighteen inches of counter space on each side of the sink, on at least one side of the range, and on the open side of the refrigerator. The refrigerator door should open toward the sink.

With no dishwasher, at least thirty inches of additional counter space near the sink for draining and drying.

You can't tell about counter space by looking. Shiny new kitchens all look marvelously spacious. Fill one up with the assorted bowls, pans, tools, and foods for one meal and the space dissolves.

The quality of kitchen cabinets and drawers is important. Good wood cabinets require kiln-dried, treated wood or warping may be a problem. Steel cabinets should be made of bonderized, cold-rolled steel of at least twenty-two-gauge thickness (the lower the gauge number, the thicker). Do drawers move in and out smoothly? This generally requires metal slides and nylon rollers which permit pulling a drawer all the way out without sagging and sticking. Look also for magnetic latches and adjustable shelves. The best cabinet finish on steel for low upkeep and long life is a baked-enamel finish applied in a factory, which calls for factory-made cabinets.

Kitchen Counter-Top Surfaces

New counter-top surfaces may shine handsomely, but how long will they stay that way? Are they easy to clean, stainproof and rotproof? It depends on the materials used. Here is a rundown of counter tops in the order of preference:

A plastic laminate such as Formica wipes clean with one

swipe, will not stain, rot, or fade, and has good heat resistance to spilled boiling water. Very hot pans can mar it and knives cut it, but it should last at least twenty years, particularly if it is the high-pressure kind ($\frac{1}{16}$ inch thick), not the low-pressure kind ($\frac{1}{32}$ inch thick).

Sheet vinyl, lower in cost than a laminate, is easy to clean and lessens dish-clanking noises. Its chief limitation is poor resistance to heat; hot pans will stick to it or melt it and boiling water can damage it.

Linoleum is colorful, attractive, inexpensive, and heat-resistant but is susceptible to stains, scratches, and knife cuts and will rot due to water penetration. It should not be used anywhere near the sink.

Stainless steel, increasing in popularity, is highly durable, stainproof, heatproof, easy to clean, and surprisingly resilient. But it is hard on knives, naturally, and will show scratches.

There are also ceramic tile, marble, and wood. Chief feature of the first two are their heat resistance and durability, but both are hard on dishes and glassware. Tile will not stain but marble will. Both are easy to clean. Wood is best for a chopping center, it does not chip, crack, or dent, but does stain easily. It will show heat rings unless kept rubbed down with a good sealing agent (hot mineral oil).

The ideal kitchen, therefore, would have a combination of materials: tile, marble, or stainless steel where hot pans are put down (range center); wood for your chopping and food-preparation (mix) center; plastic laminate or vinyl for good looks and easy cleaning elsewhere and particularly around the sink. You may rarely find such a combination in a house, but it can pay to ask for it. The proper surface in the right place will not only mean less upkeep and longer satisfaction, but is also a decided plus feature if you put the house up for sale after a few years. Then the kitchen will still look new.

The Third Kitchen Requirement

To be bright and cheerful, the third design requirement in a kitchen calls for good exposure, plenty of air, and ample lighting. Ideal exposure for kitchen and dining room is on the southeast side of a house. This will give you bright morning sunshine all year around. A kitchen facing the south gets less morning sun, especially in summer, but more afternoon sun. A kitchen on the north gets little morning sun except in summer (which may be fine if you live in the South) and is exposed to cold winds in winter. A kitchen on the west or southwest is probably worst of all; it gets the worst onslaught of sun in late afternoon which can make it furnace-hot in summer.

Plenty of air, or ventilation, calls for an exhaust fan or, even better, a range hood with a built-in fan. Its location is crucial. Best location is in the ceiling directly over the range. Next best is high on the wall behind the range, not low. Other locations will mean inefficient removal of smoke, cooking heat, and airborne grease; other kitchen air is pumped out instead. Minimum-size fan to accept is one with an exhaust capacity of at least 300 cubic feet per minute of air (c.f.m.). More capacity is needed for large kitchens. Check for quiet operation—noisy fans are a widespread nuisance. A good idea here is locating the fan at the end of its outlet air duct, not at the beginning over the range. The grease filter, however, goes at the kitchen inlet side.

Good lighting calls for a light shed over the sink and the main work surfaces, particularly deep under kitchen cabinets. A central kitchen light fixture is not enough. A woman standing at the sink, for example, ends up working in her own shadow. A light is needed over the sink but carefully wired to avoid water hazards. Extra illumination, often with short fluorescent bulbs, should light up counter-top areas. There also should be at least two or three well-placed electric outlets along the wall behind the dry counter-top area for small appliances such as mixer, toaster, and broiler.

Living Room and Bedrooms
There are several tests for each: Is it big enough? Are there good places for furniture? Is there good traffic circulation within? Is it bright, cheerful, and pleasant with adequate light and air?

Living-room size depends much on personal requirements. The feeling of size can be enhanced by a high ceiling, a sloped cathedral ceiling, or the judicious use of a lot of glass (but not the foolhardy picture window in front). The living room not only should be free of cross traffic but also should have at least two exposures, and its design should permit your furniture to face the three main focal points—fireplace, TV set, and outside view. It's a great nuisance when furniture has to be switched around every time you watch TV, enjoy the fire, or merely sit with guests, looking out the window.

Bedrooms for adults should be large enough to hold a desk and chairs as well as bedroom furniture. A child's bedroom needs space for study and play. Windows should be large enough to let in ample light and air. Windows in at least two different walls formerly were mandatory for cross ventilation but are less important now if you plan on air conditioning. A common drawback is the use of high "ribbon" bedroom windows for privacy. People feel just as compelled to draw curtains or shades over them as over large windows. They are also particularly imprisoning in children's bedrooms, hard to see out of, and hard to get out of in case of fire.

The Family Room

This is an optional room, basically an informal living room largely for children and their toys. It is also a handy place for such things as a film projector. It has grown increasingly popular in recent years because of the explosion in the average size of American families.

Ideally, it should go next to the kitchen where the mother can keep an eye on small people, and preferably on the opposite side of the kitchen from the living room. It should have access to outdoors. In small houses part of it can double as your dining room (or without a family room, the living room inadvertently ends up as the playroom). It should have plenty of natural daylight and not be too small and cramped. A good size is about 14 × 20 feet, minimum size about 12 × 14.

The need for a family room depends most on your family size and living habits. In a split level house the lowest level area sometimes can double as a family room but not always. In a cold climate this level is often so cold and poorly heated that it is off bounds in winter. A basement playroom is also a poor substitute. It is not practical for young children, and because of the poor light and ventilation characteristic of so many basements, parents as well as older children do not use it as much as they had expected. Still, a clean, reasonably comfortable play area can save much wear and tear on good furniture, and parents. The family room, incidentally, has been called merely an upgraded, modern version of the famed "whoopee room" of the Roaring Twenties—a special basement room used as a playroom for children as well as a party room for parents.

Bathrooms

Bathrooms should be large enough to accommodate two people at once; they should be properly located, provide plenty of storage, and have the proper fixtures and accessories sensibly located. Minimum size recommended is 6 × 8 feet. Sometimes a 5 × 7 bath will do if planned well. A half-bath or powder room can be as small as 3 × 4. One bath is adequate for a one-story house of up to about 1000 square feet, or in larger houses with only two or three people in the family. Most larger houses should have a bath for every two bedrooms. A two-story or split-level house should have a half-bath on or near the ground floor.

Bathroom Location

Ideally, the master bedroom should have its own bath. But a common mistake in two-bath houses is isolating this bath off the master bedroom so guests cannot use it. They end up in the children's bath, which is often a mess. Locating the master bath off the center hall instead and making it off limits for kids avoids conflict. It also obviates the hectic cleanup of the children's bath when guests are expected any minute or, unhappily, arrive unannounced. An interior bath location also makes sense; not every bath requires wall windows or a choice outside-wall location. Equipped with an exhaust fan and an overhead skylight, it can be relegated to less valuable interior space.

The three essential fixtures are, of course, lavatory, toilet, and tub. The best lavatory is one with a built-in storage cabinet below. Plenty of counter-top space next to the sink is a boon. A 20 × 24 inch lavatory (or the equivalent built-in) is the minimum size recommended, especially if you like to wash your face without splashing water on the floor.

There are four kinds of toilets: the usual round, washdown type which is the cheapest, noisiest, and hardest to keep clean; the elongated bowl or siphon-jet model which has a larger bowl, makes less noise, is easier to keep clean, and is the least you should settle for in a new house or when you remodel; the de luxe, quiet-flush model, considerably more expensive and found chiefly in expensive custom houses; and the quiet-flush, wall-hung model which is installed on the wall, not the floor, and makes cleaning chores much easier.

Location of the bathtub can be critical. It should not be under a window where an acrobat is required to open or close the sash. Most bathtubs are thirty inches wide and five feet long. A wider, thirty-two-inch tub is gaining popularity. It is much more convenient, especially for bathing children. Ask if the tub has an acid-resistant enamel finish. All colored tubs do as do almost all steel tubs, but not all cast iron ones. This acid-resistant factor protects the finish from washing off if the wrong detergent is used. Extra cost is only a few dollars more. Colored fixtures, by the way, cost about 10 per cent more than standard white ones. They have grown popular in recent years but this may be a fad that will die out. They can be good-looking or they may be garish. They limit redecorating possibilities somewhat but with the proper accessories are attractive.

Like toilets, bathtubs and lavatories vary in quality. The cheapest and poorest grade ones are most commonly found in big housing developments. You can tell a good kind by looking for the manufacturer's name or trade-mark on it.

Almost all big manufacturers make a low-quality model, but none puts his name on these, his cheapest line. If you do not see it, you can make the obvious conclusion.

A good bathroom will contain plenty of storage for towels, bathroom-cleaning materials, and a soiled-laundry hamper, as well as storage for medicine, cosmetics, and so on. The medicine cabinet should be at least 20 × 30 inches with built-in lights (so you can see your whole face without shadows) and a built-in electric outlet (*which should be well out of reach of the bathtub for safety*).

Other good bathroom features are a clothes bin, linen rack, built-in towel and soap racks, clothes hooks, shower nozzle that is both adjustable and high enough to clear your head, hand grips, full wall tile around the tub and shower, shut-off valves at each fixture which means you will not have to shut off the main water supply to the house just for a minor repair, and a small exhaust fan, recommended but not essential, for blowing out steam and odors.

The Laundry

Like other rooms, the location of the laundry is important. Ideally, it should be near the kitchen and the bathroom, which will save steps for a woman. A location near the bathroom eliminates steps in gathering soiled clothes and putting away clean ones. It also eliminates the need for clothes chutes and requires little additional plumbing cost.

In a two-story house a first-floor location gets the nod over a basement location. It makes laundering much simpler, and a woman is not burdened with the chore of getting a clothes basket up and down the basement stairs. Putting the laundry in the kitchen has become a popular idea. But it draws fire from women who dislike the idea of soiled clothing in an area where food is prepared. A hall location is also increasingly popular but too often it is small, cramped, and lacks adequate light and ventilation. An old-fashioned pantry or back kitchen often serves nicely; a utility room in a new house is worth considering. The total amount of space needed for a laundry depends on your equipment. The smallest space recommended with an automatic washer, drier, and ironing area is about 6 × 12 feet.

There should be a cabinet or shelves for storage of soap, detergents, iron and so on, counter space for sorting, and a space for a clothes rack, no longer so important for drying but a convenience when ironing.

Equipment Arrangement

The equipment should be arranged for all movements in one direction toward where clothes are dried: from hamper, to sorting counter, washer, drier, and ironing center. The normal sequence for a right-handed person is right to left, which means the drier should be on the left of the washer when they are side by side. This puts special emphasis on having the doors of the washer and drier open in the right direction. For the recommended right-to-left washer-drier location, the washer door should be hinged at the right or at the bottom, the drier door at the left or at bottom. The opposite is required for a left-handed woman. Check this when appliances come with a house or when you go out to buy them—and remember to check also for what the doors may open into . . . other doors, for instance.

The drier should be located near an outside wall to permit easy venting to outdoors. Be absolutely sure it is vented. Otherwise much moisture, heat, and lint will be blasted into the house. Some drier brands, however, have drainpipe attachments for carrying away their exhaust; they do not need an air vent.

An excellent Laundry Planning booklet is available for 15¢ from the University of Illinois' Small Homes Council, Urbana, Illinois.

CHAPTER 4

DESIGN, STYLE, AND APPEARANCE

You should look at many houses to become familiar with good design. Style, of course, is a matter of personal preference. You have a right to your own likes and dislikes, to traditional or modern design, colonial, Georgian, or simple Cape Cod. But remember that certain old traditional houses were contemporary design during their period. They came about as a result of former living needs and building materials available when they were built.

The original Cape Cod is a classic example. It had a tight, compact plan and many small rooms built around a large central chimney. Rooms were small and windows were tiny, chiefly because central-heating systems had not been invented. That is why the *true* Cape Cod house, however quaint it may seem, is an obsolete house today.

New structural techniques have eliminated the need for a central chimney to hold up the house, and we can have fireplaces elsewhere. Because of central heat, insulation, and storm windows, we can enjoy larger rooms and big windows. Acoustical tile permits open room planning with reduced noise. We have moved the barn up from behind the house, attached it, and call it a garage. And we can, if we wish, eliminate a big hole in the ground below the house, since modern heating units are small and no longer need a coalbin (though a basement can be great for storage).

These are the reasons for the trend today toward contemporary houses which take advantage of ideas unknown in the past (including even the extreme all-glass houses that in their daring also serve a purpose, as do the experimental cars with which Detroit auto makers try out their most imaginative ideas).

In short, do not fear a contemporary house just because it is new. But there are splendid contemporary houses and there are monsters. On the other hand, do not be swept off your feet by a house just because it seems strikingly modern at first. Apply the same stiff design criteria to it as to any house, to its interior as well as its exterior looks, and to its heating and insulation as well as its window orientation. Regardless of the particular style you like, a few general guide rules apply to all houses:

1. A simple rectangular or L-shaped plan gives more house for the same money than a house broken up with jogs and offsets. A simple plan is cheaper to build. Every time you add a corner to a house, building costs rise and interior planning is made tougher.

2. A continuous roof line makes a house look bigger. A broken roof line, changing to a lower level for the garage, for example, makes a house look chopped-up and small.

3. The tops and bottoms of all windows should line up, each conforming to one long horizontal line across the house. Small windows should line up with the top or bottom half of large windows. When the tops of exterior doors also line up with window tops things will look even better.

4. There should be a minimum of different exterior wall materials. The use of banana-split fronts embodying a mixture of brick, stone, and wood is a trick often used "to achieve variety." But after a while such gingerbread will become tiresome. The house that looks good over the years is one with a simple, coherent exterior. Yet a house may be so simple it is plain and dreary. Here is where the choice of exterior texture and color can make a big difference. In general, stay with simplicity and classic design, whether traditional or modern.

5. The roof should extend (overhang) past the house itself. When it overhangs the exterior wall two to four feet, it is almost always a sign of a well-designed house. Overhangs give a house a distinctive and handsome appearance. They protect windows and walls from snow and rain. Wall paint lasts longer; rain will not pour in an open window. The earth around the house next to the foundation is

shielded from rain, which means less chance of a wet cellar. Overhangs can also shade windows in summer.

6. Roof color is important. A dark color makes a house look taller and less wide. It is best for long, low one-story houses. A light color emphasizes the horizontal, making a house look broader and wider. It is generally best for small houses and two-story houses. Roof color should also contrast nicely with the rest of the house. A roof that is almost the same color as the house gives a wishy-washy effect.

7. A house should conform to the slope of the land around it. When the ground slopes away and part of the house sticks up in the air it looks as awkward as a sore thumb. Similarly, a split level perched on flat ground may be ungainly. Splits should take advantage of sloping ground.

Other good features to look for (or plan for) outside are: exterior electric outlets for porch and patio; outside lights for garage, driveway, and front entrance; an outside water connection for a hose; outside gas, electric and water meters, enabling utility men to read them without disturbing you inside; a short driveway with space enough to turn around or park a second car without blocking the garage; and a roofed-over main entrance to shield you from rain when you're fumbling for the key, and to shield waiting guests as well.

Basement or No Basement?

The chief reason often given for having a basement is that it offers much bargain space for little extra cost. This is only part of the story. It is not always usable space.

A basement is cheapest in a cold climate where foundation walls must go down at least three to four feet into the ground to get below the frost line. The cost of extending them deeper for a basement is comparatively small. You can virtually double the over-all space of a one-story house for about one-tenth over-all cost. It is additional raw space, to be sure, for storage, in addition to housing the heater, workshop, and so on. But in a warm climate the foundation walls need not go so deep, a reason why basements are often omitted in the South and in California. The heating plant and coalbin, were the original overriding reasons for basements in the North.

But the trouble with basements is that they can be dark, gloomy, and damp, if not downright wet, and clearly not satisfactory for fun and play. They are unwise in an area with very wet ground or a "high ground water table." Waterproofing costs are high, and even when the job is done well you can never tell when the water will break through. Good waterproofing is essential even in ordinary ground, and it should be applied to the outside of the walls (as discussed in Chapter 14). It must be done during construction because of prohibitive cost if left till later.

Getting full value from a basement calls for plenty of ribbonlike windows to let in light and air, and the more windows that face south, the better. The heating equipment and stairway should be located against a wall, not in the center where they will prevent full use of the remaining space. If a house is built on sloping land the basement can be opened up with large glass windows on the downhill side—one possibility that can turn a basement room into one of the best in the house. And it is a good idea to have the necessary wiring, lighting, and heating outlets installed in advance if you plan to turn the basement into extra living or working space later.

The Case for No Basement

For one thing, the flooring, finished walls, extra heat, wiring, lighting, and so on (on top of waterproofing expense) cost as much underground as they do above ground. For another, the opening for the basement stairs not only subtracts from usable space upstairs, but it can greatly complicate upstairs room planning. For roughly the same money you often can get the equivalent usable space upstairs, with natural light and ventilation to boot.

Without a basement, a large utility room or area, the basement equivalent, is essential above ground. It should measure from 8 to 12 per cent of house living area. Best location is off the kitchen where it can be expanded to serve as a laundry, children's play area, and for storage as well.

Without a basement, this space should be mandatory, especially with no attic to take up the slack in storage needs.

About the only remaining reason for a basement is for those who have hobbies or businesses necessitating them, for those who like basements, and for resale purposes in areas where people think they are necessary. But if there is a basement equivalent above ground this can be discreetly pointed out along with the good reasons for not having a basement.

CHAPTER 5

ONE-, 1½-, TWO-STORY, OR SPLIT-LEVEL?

The chief advantage of a one-story house is its glorious lack of stair climbing. This makes a one-story house a boon for mothers with small children and for elderly people.

But one-story living without good zoning (room and internal traffic arrangements) can drive a family to distraction. It puts a damper on entertaining at night because you may wake the children. Or noisy children playing at your heels are less than a blessing when you need privacy. So double-check for good zoning. Is the living room at the opposite end of the house from the children's bedrooms? Is there a good "buffer" zone between the two? Is there a place for parents to flee for privacy?

Another big advantage of the one-story house is its aptness for what magazines call indoor-outdoor living, since every room is at ground level. This feature works best when doorways permit direct access to the outdoor patio or terrace. The house should be built close to the ground with few or no steps from inside to outside. Steps discourage travel in or out and also cause accidents. Stairs are a special problem when there is a basement and the house is built several feet above ground level. A one-story house should hug the ground; the closer it is to the ground, the better it looks.

The 1½-Story House

The 1½-story house is often a Cape Cod with an expansion attic. Some people feel that the second-floor rooms are a delightful bonus, extra space for little extra money. But this is deceiving. The 1½-story house is more likely to be an incomplete two-story house. Its main advantage, much publicized by builders, is initial economy. Start with a small house, they say, and add second-floor rooms as you need them. But if the upstairs rooms are small and cramped, window area limited, the ceilings low, and the walls chopped-up, it's dubious economy.

Two other problems are rampant in 1½-story houses: The upstairs rooms under the roof tend to be torrid in summer and hard to heat in winter. After all, this is converted attic space. So insist on extra-thick insulation upstairs and good ventilation under the roof. A regular two-story house is usually lower in cost and better in the long run. If you get a 1½-story house, make sure the heating plant has ample capacity for the future rooms upstairs, have the heating ducts or pipes installed up to the second floor and capped until they are needed, and have plumbing pipes installed and capped if you plan on a future upstairs bath.

The Two-Story House

The two-story house not only offers natural zoning between the upstairs and the downstairs rooms, it also crams the most living space onto a small lot and provides much space for comparatively little cost. And many people like the privacy and safety that go hand in hand with bedrooms on the second floor. On the other hand, it is cursed with the need for tiresome stair climbing (which should rule it out for older people and is a consideration for hard-working young parents); the space given over to the stairs and landing is wasted (it could give you another room); the upstairs bedrooms and play rooms are shut off from direct access to outdoors, and it lacks design flexibility (especially for expanding the house).

The stairway location is crucial in a two-story house; poor stairway location is a common defect. The stairs often slice through the middle of the house separating the living room and dining room like a knife. This prevents convenient use of the dining and living room together.

Good stairway location usually calls for stairs on the opposite side of the living room from the dining room. Or the kitchen, living room, and dining room should form a long rectangle with the stairs parallel to its long side. The stairway location also determines whether the upstairs hall will be short and efficient or long and wasteful. Remember that if the dining room and living room are next to each other, it is most convenient, though this is often hard to get, especially in old houses.

The Split Level

The split-level or multi-level house shines best on hilly land, its different levels arranged to conform with the land slope. Many, however, are built on flat land, which can be a blunder. Part of the house ends up below grade, and much of the house is stuck above grade, which calls for a maddening number of steps. A poor indoor-outdoor relationship also results.

A good split level takes advantage of hilly ground by having the lowest level open up on the downhill side (giving direct access to outside), the next level turned around so that it opens out on the uphill slope, and the third or top level facing downhill and giving you full advantage of the view that goes hand in glove with height. This is the case for what is called the front-to-back split level. Observed from the street, it has each of its floor levels extending the full width of the house from right to left. It is therefore a natural for land that slopes up or down from the street.

There is also the side-to-side split. Observed from the street, it has its floor levels stacked in tiers to the right and to the left of the center of the house. The garage, for example, may be on the right of the house and at the lowest level; the next level will be higher than the garage and on the left side of the house; the next level after that will be over the garage on the right side; and so on, back and forth. The side to side split is a natural for a hilly street—i.e., when the lot slopes up or down parallel with the street.

Disadvantages of the Split Level

Many claims are made that the split-level offers much extra space for a minimum of building cost. When such space is achieved, it can be a good buy. But the split is often done at the expense of good interior planning, particularly in small splits. Room arrangements are a jumble, and often every room is on its own level, necessitating going up or down a few steps every time you pass from one room to another, or from one part of the house to another. Avoid this split at all costs, unless you are athletically inclined.

Poor heating is another widespread charge against splits. The lowest level, often a play area, is cold in winter, the floor is icy, and it is impossible to heat. This space is the equivalent of the basement in other houses; thus it requires special wall insulation below ground, and well-designed heating (either hot-water baseboard radiators around the exterior baseboards or warm-air outlets at exterior floor locations, *not* at or near the ceiling).

The room over the garage, generally the master bedroom, also tends to be chilly (largely because of little or no insulation at the garage ceiling). And the bedrooms at the highest level are too hot, chiefly because of the natural rise of warm air from below; they are often appallingly hot in summer. For these reasons, split levels generally require zoned heating controls—a separate thermostat for each level.

A final note about all multi-level houses—1½- and two-story and split-level houses: a half-bath or powder room on the first floor is a boon for avoiding stair climbing.

CHAPTER 6

IS THERE ADEQUATE STORAGE?

Most houses today have the usual bedroom closets, coat closet, linen closet, and cabinets for kitchen storage, but people still yearn for more storage space. Things are less cramped if there is an attic and a basement, a big step in the right direction for space. But an attic is sometimes hard to reach, and because of mildew you must be careful what you keep in the basement. The hard fact is that cramped storage space, the result of poor planning, is one of the biggest single, frustrating drawbacks in houses today.

What to look for is simplified when you break down your storage requirements into two parts: "live" storage for the things you use from day to day and "dead" storage for things like trunks, screens, sleds, and garden equipment which are used seasonally or infrequently.

Live storage requires chests, drawers, closets, and shelves, but each should be sized and planned for a particular need and located at the proper places. Dead storage often calls for special facilities, too, and a basement or attic is a boon here. An attic, however, should have a drop-down staircase or ladder at least.

In general, each person should have a closet at least twenty-four inches deep and forty-eight inches wide, or eight square feet per person. A family of three or four requires at least forty square feet of total closet space, sixty is even better. Full width and ceiling-high closet doors are best, since you can see everything inside at a glance. Look also for an inside light, adjustable shelves, and the closet floor raised about two inches to keep out dust.

Built-in Storage

Built-in storage is growing more and more popular because it is both practical and space-saving. For example, the space under a built-in window seat can double as a chest for children's toys. The dead space inside of partition walls can be reclaimed by building in shelves and cabinets. Storage walls are superb for this. They are special ceiling-high wall cabinets with shelves and drawers which also serve as a partition between two rooms. They are not in general use, however, so you will have to ask for them.

Storage needs vary from room to room. There should be places in the living room for books, magazines, records, card tables, and fireplace wood, a place in the dining room for linen, silver, and dishes, a place in the family room or playroom to hide the clutter of toys that do not stay put in the children's bedrooms, and space in or near the garage for garden tools and bikes. Such storage can be built after you move into a house, though you seldom catch up. It is best to provide it before you move in, even if it means a few extra dollars in original building cost.

It should be repeated that storage will be critical in a house without a basement, the bane of literally millions of people who have moved into such houses since World War II. This calls for the basement equivalent above ground as already mentioned. Also specify an extra-wide or extra-long garage for additional utility space. One or two large outdoor closets can be built at the rear of the garage or house for conveniently holding outdoor furniture or equipment such as a lawn mower. Not all of us, naturally, can afford all of these features; some may sound like luxuries. But a house without ample storage is like a coat without pockets.

Ten-Point Storage Summary

According to a study by the Southwest Research Institute, here are minimum rules for good storage:

1. Is there a coat closet near the main entrance?

2. Is there storage in the living room for books, records, card tables, fireplace wood?

3. Are there adequate kitchen cabinets (as specified in Chapter 3)?

4. Is there storage near the dining room for linen, silver, and dishes?

5. Is there a place in your utility area for ironing board, soap, laundry necessities?

6. Does the bathroom have built-in storage for towels, soap and soap dishes, and toilet paper, as well as a medicine cabinet and laundry hamper?

7. Is there a big enough closet in each bedroom?

8. Is there a convenient place for trunks, boxes, sleds, screens, and similar things?

9. Is there a place near the outdoors for lawn mower, garden tools, and summer furniture?

10. What is the total floor area of all general storage, excluding closets noted above? Under thirty square feet is poor, over fifty is good.

CHAPTER 7

IMPORTANCE OF LOT AND SITE

Poor location of a house on its lot is "probably the most costly and common mistake" made in houses, according to one government housing agency. To understand good site planning, consider the land around a house as divided into three zones: public, service, and private.

The public zone is the front lawn in public view. The

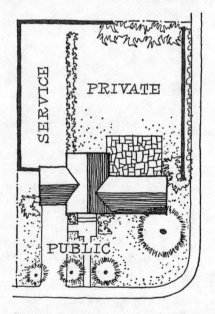

Fig. 5 Visualize the site of a house as divided into three zones, shown above. This facilitates a quick judgment of site planning. House here faces the rear for maximum use of lot.

service zone includes sidewalks, driveways, clothes-drying and trash-storage areas. The private zone is for the patio, play, and garden. Sheer logic calls for giving over as little of your land as possible for public and service use and retaining a maximum for private use.

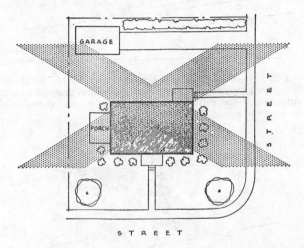

Fig. 6 Poor site planning: The lot is cut up with wasted land, has a lack of privacy, and both a long driveway and a separate service entrance are required.

Ideally, therefore, a house should be set forward on its lot toward the street with small public and service areas in front and on the side, thus opening up the rear of the lot for maximum private use. There will be a minimum of front lawn to be mowed, driveway and walks will be short and economical, snow shoveling will be minimized, and utility pipes and wires from street to house will be short and economical. When the house itself is oriented toward the rear, you can take full advantage of a larger portion of your land for private use. Also, check privacy in relation to the houses next door and the nearest ones in back.

The two main reasons often given in favor of setting the house well back from the street are privacy and less traffic

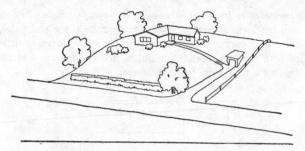

Fig. 7 *Good.* House on a high and large lot can be spread out. The garage can be located at a lower level to avoid a steep driveway. House entrance walk and driveway can be combined to get an unbroken front lawn.

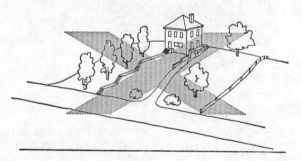

Fig. 8 *Bad.* Boxy, two-story house should not go on a high lot; this adds unnecessary height. Long flights of entrance steps plus a steep driveway with retaining walls are also required. Poor tree location divides the lot and exaggerates the steep approach.

noise. But if a house is properly planned, with few front windows and no front picture window, it can be close to the street and you'll have as much privacy as do the earliest town houses in colonial Boston and Philadelphia which are built practically on top of the street. Setting the house well back with a great lawn is a hang-over from Victorian days when the *nouveau riche* wanted to impress everybody, and besides they could have their lawns trimmed and driveways cleared of snow with 10¢-an-hour labor.

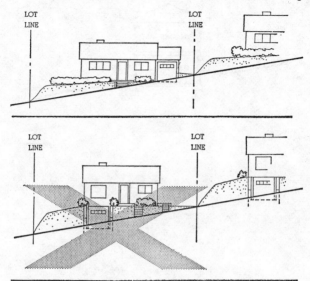

Fig. 9 *Good.* On a side-to-side slope, this house looks much larger than one below because garage on high side adds length to the house. Access to garage is nearly a level grade, which reduces excavation costs, and the driveway is also the service entrance.

Fig. 10 *Bad.* Small house looks downright tiny because it sits on a mound like a bump on a log. Expensive retaining walls are required on both sides of driveway, and a separate service entrance to the house is also needed.

Noise is nearly as bad a hundred feet back from the street as close to the street. A house set 700 feet back from a major highway would need a wall about ten feet thick and thirty feet high, or a fifty-foot-thick forest of trees, to reduce heavy traffic noise. So if you are noise-sensitive do not buy closer than a mile (yes, that far) from a major highway, and at least ten miles from a big airport (more if jet planes are roaring in and out every day). A cardinal rule for reasonable quiet indoors is that windows and doors be shut at almost all times, and this in turn calls for air conditioning.

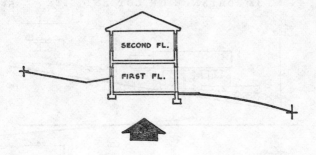

Fig. 11 *Good.* This two-story house (which could also be a split level) gets two floors for living (whereas its bad counterpart has all living space crowded into one floor). This house also has its first floor opening up on ground level, thus eliminating steps.

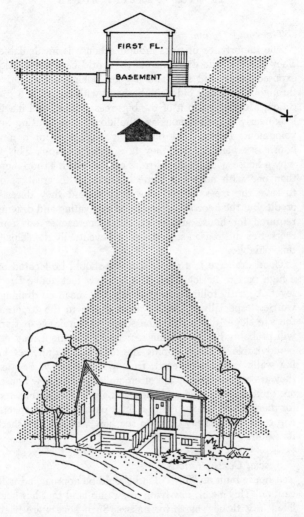

Fig. 12 *Bad*. The lower level is sacrificed for use only as a basement. Steep steps must be climbed to the entrance, and the high basement wall is decidedly unattractive.

Trees and Drainage

The importance of trees around a house is incalculable. They make all the difference in the world between a bald, exposed house and site, and a good-looking home. Drive through almost any old neighborhood with charm and tradition. Mentally strip it of the big trees around, and it will look nearly as monotonous as a bulldozed new housing development. Buying and planting young trees for a new house is expensive, and they take years to grow. This is why a house with plenty of trees can be worth $1000 more than one with no trees. Some builders go to great pains to save the trees around new houses, and they deserve credit. But the necessary foundation excavating and digging required for house and utility lines encroaches on some roots. For this reason some trees will eventually die. This is unavoidable.

Good drainage is a must. A house should be located on a high part of its lot, even if only a few feet above street level. A gently rolling site generally will mean no drainage worries, especially if the lot slopes down to the street. If the site slopes down from the street, the drainage pattern will probably be toward the rear and a basement may not be advisable. A steep sloping site may well require retaining walls to keep the earth from washing away. Because they are expensive they are often omitted when new houses are built on hilly land and then you are in for trouble. Ask for them. Drainage is so important it pays to make a special trip on a day of heavy rain to see how well the site sheds its water.

Special Considerations

A house built on "filled" land should be approached with caution. This means low-lying or swamp land that has been filled in with new earth for houses. Such houses are likely to settle, wrenching both the structure and the underground utility pipes out of joint. They are also vulnerable to wetness.

If there is a septic-tank system, it should be located in

front of the house or on the side. This will mean the least expensive hookup when a street sewer is put in later. Is the driveway short and efficient? A driveway sloping down from the street is a black mark. It means extra trouble during snowy weather or when your car battery goes dead and you must push.

If you buy a lot to build a house, *never* buy sight unseen. It may be three feet under water, on solid rock, on the side of a cliff, or so small and irregular that it is hopeless for building. Selling lots by mail is a racket that has cost many people dearly. A lot should be checked for drainage, for a good location near stores, and transportation. The neighborhood is important (as already mentioned). Some "neighborhoods" vary and change almost from block to block. A general idea about the area is never enough. If roads, water, and sewer lines are expected later, check with local officials about extra tax assessments that often follow such improvements. Get a copy of the local zoning rules to be sure they permit the kind of house you wish, as well as allowing for expansion later.

A common error is taking somebody's casual word that water, sewer, and electric lines will be forthcoming at little or no expense. Go direct to the appropriate officials for this information (water- and electric-company officials, municipal public-works chief). If a water well is needed, talk to city and state water people about your ground water conditions. Talk to several well diggers; let each know you are shopping around.

Avoid the need for major excavation, retaining walls, and earth-moving chores, because these can cause a major explosion in your building budget. A house should fit the natural contours of the land. Before building, have a topographical survey and site plan made showing property lines, trees worth saving, slope contours and such things as rock outcroppings. Before you even buy a lot, have an architect check its feasibility for building. He is also your best guide for site planning, often saving his fee many times over in reduced development and building costs.

CHAPTER 8

WHICH WAY SHOULD A HOUSE FACE?

Most houses are built so they face the street. This flies in the face of logic. When a house is properly oriented in relation to the sun, it will be warmer and easier to heat in winter, which can mean large fuel-bill savings, most rooms will be bright and full of sunshine, and there will be a minimum of condensation on windows. In summer, the same house can be 5 to 10 degrees cooler than an ordinary house, and you benefit from cooling breezes.

This is simply because the sun is in the south almost all day long in winter. It rises in the southeast and sets in the southwest. But in summer the sun rises in the northeast, travels in a much higher arc across the sky, being almost directly overhead at noon, and sets in the northwest. A few scientific facts emphasize what this means:

1) The south side of a house receives five times as much sun heat in winter as in summer. 2) The east and west sides, on the other hand, receive six times as much sun heat in summer as in winter. 3) Walls and windows facing north receive no sun heat in winter, but a certain amount in summer; the farther south you are, the more sun is shed on the north side in summer.

In general, therefore, a house should face broadside to the south to receive the most sunshine in winter, the least in summer. Actually, the house itself can face any direction. The important thing is that the big windows of your daytime living areas (kitchen, dining, and family rooms) should face south so that sunshine and natural light will flood in. A south orientation is not so important for the living room, unless you use it a good deal during the day; many people use it mostly at night.

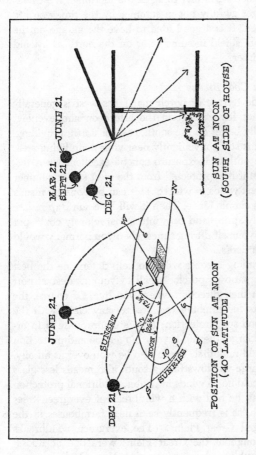

Fig. 13 Changing travel of the sun from summer to winter affects house exposure and how warm or cool you will be inside. In general, large window areas should face south. Then they can be well shaded in summer by wide-brim roof overhangs. But in winter (December 21 arc) sunshine will come in through the same windows under the overhangs since the sun is much lower in the sky. In fact, sunshine is available in winter only through windows with a southeast to southwest exposure.

The bedrooms obviously have less need for sun and are best on the north or east. On the east, you may appreciate bright sun flooding in first thing in the morning. West bedrooms can get awfully hot in summer by the time you are ready for bed. It is a good idea to have the garage on the west as a sun shield in summer or on the north as a wind shield in winter.

Sun vs. a Cool Breeze

An outside terrace or porch that faces west is generally much too hot for comfort in the afternoon and evening. It is generally better on the south, east, or north, providing, of course, it is still conveniently near your main living area. A south or southwest exposure can be excellent for a terrace or patio if it is protected from the west sun in summer and northwest winds in winter. This can be done by means of trees or a simple fence. Then it will be a sun trap in late fall and early spring and turn into a marvelously cozy spot for sunning yourself during times when you normally would never be outdoors.

The prevailing breezes will also help determine the best location for patio or porch. A call to your nearest airport will tell you their direction where you live. Of course, the requirements for catching the breeze may clash with the need for good sun protection; then a compromise is in order. By and large, the sun is your bigger foe and protection from it should rank first. It can also be won over as an ally.

Having large windows facing south also means less glass exposed to cold north winds in winter. Additional protection in winter can be had with a windbreak of evergreen trees on the north, as is frequently seen near farmhouses in the wind-scourged Great Plains. (The evergreen windbreaks planted throughout the Great Plains were one of Roosevelt's little-publicized but pioneering New Deal conservation projects that turned out far more successfully than even its most ardent advocates had expected.) If you live in the South, a south orientation may be less desirable. You may do better if your house faces north with patio on the north or northeast. And by all means, avoid a southwest or west orientation.

Window Shading Tips

Few houses have perfect orientation. Poor window exposure is distressingly common, with the result that the worst sun heat of the day pours inside in summer. But if you know a few facts about window shading, you can judge whether or not a bad window exposure can be compensated by shading.

Wide roof overhangs, like wide-brimmed hats, effectively shade windows facing south. But they happily let in winter sun which comes at a lower angle from the south. Overhangs are much less effective for shading east and west window glass, since the morning and afternoon sun come in at such a low angle all year round that all but the widest overhangs cannot shut it out. Deciduous shade trees on the south, west, and east sides will provide much-appreciated shading in summer, and since they lose their leaves in winter, sunshine is allowed in when you want it.

By the way, it is not generally realized that sun from the east in summer can pour just as much heat into houses in the morning as the west sun in the afternoon. It is hard fact, in other words, that the east sun is just as hot as the west sun. The outside *air* is hotter in the afternoon, so you feel the west sun more. But try to shade east windows as well as west ones. Then the house will stay cooler longer into the day to help combat the fierce heat of afternoon.

You can get a striking idea of orientation importance by observing the periods of sunshine in your present home or apartment. Are the kitchen, dining room, and living area light and cheerful most of the day? Or are they gloomy most of the time, or too hot on a summer afternoon? Are some rooms particularly chilly and cold in winter? The chances are that its orientation makes the difference.

Best Exposure for a Development House

When you choose a new house in a development look for the street side and location with the best orientation.

The same applies when you buy a lot to build on. In general, a lot on the south side of the street is best. The house can be oriented to the south for both sun and privacy, and the garage can be near the street on north or west. A lot on the north side of the street is one of the toughest to develop (except perhaps in the hot South). The house has to be set far back to take advantage of a south orientation, which means a long driveway and trees, shrubs, or fencing needed in the front for privacy. East and west lots should be fairly wide to give you elbow room on the north and south. Then the house can be turned toward the side and planned for south orientation and maximum outdoor living area where you want it.

And remember, every house need not face south. The principles of good orientation are what you keep in mind. Suppose there is a clash between a good view and good orientation. Naturally one or the other must give; you can't have both. But a good view need not be a distant scene. A nearby flower garden or lawn can be equally satisfying.

PART 3

THE FIVE BIGGEST CAUSES OF HIGH UPKEEP AND REPAIRS IN HOUSES AND HOW TO CONTROL THEM

Five basic house needs cry out today for special attention. Too often they are taken for granted or overlooked.

As a result, most homeowners are cursed with unsatisfactory, high-cost heating that is both expensive and inefficient; skimpy insulation that adds further to high fuel bills and low comfort; inadequate wiring that is both a fire hazard and a maddening inconvenience; termites and wood rot that commonly stem from similar causes and wreak the same kind of damage; and low-grade, undersized water heaters. Here is how to judge each for quality and long-term satisfaction.

CHAPTER 9

HEATING

Heating is one of the most expensive elements of a house. After taxes and mortgage payments it generally accounts for our biggest single annual household operating expense. A poor heating system will not only cause swollen fuel bills but also permits cold, drafty discomfort in winter. Yet for a typical seven- or eight-room house, a really good heating system is only about $50 to $75 more in first cost than the usual borderline system.

The two most common kinds of central heating are forced warm-air heat and hot-water heat (sometimes called wet heat). There are also various forms of electric heat, including the heat pump. Forced warm air, by far the most popular, is used in roughly three out of four new houses, chiefly because it costs less to install than hot-water heat, the second-runner. Forced warm air consists of a furnace, a blower for pushing the air under pressure to rooms, and ducts (usually of sheet metal) for channeling the air to the rooms. The presence of ducts and metal air outlets in the rooms, rather than radiators, indicates a warm-air system.

Some people, particularly in the Northeast and parts of the Midwest, distrust forced warm air. They do not believe it can heat well. They are used to radiators or have had unhappy experiences with old, obsolete gravity warm-air (no blower) systems, or with a poorly installed forced-air system. Actually, forced warm air can be perfectly satisfying in any house, provided it is properly installed.

The chief advantages of warm-air heat (a shorter term that we will use from now on) are: that central air conditioning can be easily added with it, using the same ducts used for heating; it gives quick response to calls for heat from the thermostat; a filter in the furnace cleans the air; and moisture can be added to prevent excessive dryness in winter. Its chief drawbacks: openings may have to be cut in rugs or carpets for warm-air outlets in the floor, and furniture placement may be limited to prevent interference with warm air discharge from the floor outlets.

Judging the Furnace

A heating system should be judged in two parts: the heating equipment, and the duct or pipe system used to distribute heat to the house. With warm air, the furnace should carry a ten-year guarantee. All good ones do. But it will last for twenty-five years or more. There are also lower-grade furnaces with a one-year guarantee made chiefly for the development-house market (where builders apparently rate low first cost more important than good quality).

The air blower within the furnace should be belt-driven with a pulley much like an automobile fan belt. A cheap furnace usually has what is called a direct-drive blower; it is directly connected to the same shaft as its electric motor. You can quickly check the blower merely by slipping off the front panel of a furnace. If a fan belt is absent, it is very likely a poor-quality unit. Operating cost for the blower alone can cost you $10 to $15 more a winter than with a belt-driven blower; the direct-drive requires that much more electricity. A few good furnaces, however, do come with a direct-drive blower and no pulley, but these will have a ten-year guarantee.

These key characteristics—ten-year guarantee and belt-driven blower mechanism—are two of the principal differences between a good furnace and the cheap kind. The good furnace can be guaranteed for ten years because it has a thicker, better-made heating chamber. You cannot go by brand name alone, since many manufacturers offer both kinds—a cheap unit chiefly to meet the fierce competition they encounter in the hotly competitive development-house market and a better-quality furnace, often only $20 to $25 more in price.

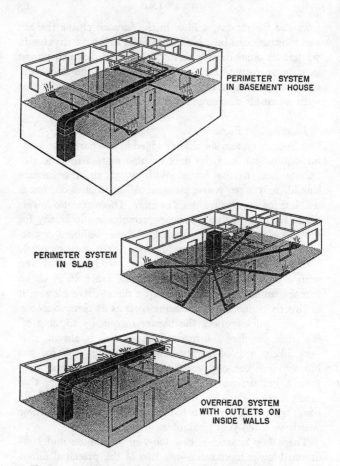

PERIMETER SYSTEM
IN BASEMENT HOUSE

PERIMETER SYSTEM
IN SLAB

OVERHEAD SYSTEM
WITH OUTLETS ON
INSIDE WALLS

Figs. 14, 15, 16   Good duct work is the key to efficient heating with warm-air heat. In the North, perimeter heating ducts with outlets under windows should be used, as shown for a basement and a non-basement house. In the South, overhead ducts can be used with outlets on interior walls. Same duct systems are also best for distributing air with year-round central air conditioning.

The Air-Distribution Ducts

Their design and installation are crucial. Poor ducts are the chief reason why many warm-air heating systems do not heat well. In general, the best duct system is called perimeter duct distribution. The warm-air discharge outlets are located around the exterior walls of your house (the house perimeter), mostly under windows. Warm air from the furnace is discharged into each room at the source of the greatest cold. This is good heating.

In general, there should be at least one warm-air outlet register for every exposed wall, except perhaps in the kitchen and bath where exterior outlet locations may be impossible. Two or three air outlets should be spread out below a long wall, as in a living room, particularly under large window areas. The warm-air discharge rising up helps counteract cold downdrafts from windows. You should also look for at least two warm-air outlets in bedrooms with two exposures, especially in children's rooms. A perimeter duct system is usually essential for a house in the North without a basement, especially to prevent cold floors.

Noisy Operation

Noisy ducts are often a problem. The ducts rattle and bang. Check this by having the furnace turned on and off a few times. Notice how the main trunk ducts are connected to the furnace itself. They should not be attached directly to the furnace. There should be a short piece of canvas between the furnace discharge and the beginning of the ducts. This puts a stop to the transmission of noise and vibration from furnace to house. It is a touch that distinguishes a good heating job from a poor one.

Can the air filter be removed easily for cleaning? This is important. Can you get it in and out easily? Clogged-up filters are a major cause of poor warm-air supply. Filters require periodic cleaning or replacement. But they should not require a $10 service call or a judo expert every time cleaning is necessary.

Insist that a warm-air system be adjusted for what engineers call "Continuous Air Circulation" (CAC), sometimes called Comfort Air Circulation. The blower is adjusted to operate much of the time in mild weather, most of the time in very cold weather. You get a continual supply of warm air in bucketful quantities rather than a truckload blast of warm air once an hour, and then no heat for the long intervals in between. The extra fan operating cost is very small, especially when balanced against the increase in heating comfort and satisfaction. Continuous Air Circulation alone often can turn a sluggish heating system into a top performer. It requires only a change in the furnace control and blower setting.

One assurance of getting first-class warm-air heat is to insist on a "Silver Shield" system. This is the name of a rating program sponsored by the National Warm Air Heating and Air-Conditioning Association to guarantee good home heating. You are protected by a $1000 bond to cover repairs if necessary. Ask if the heating is a Silver Shield job. The program is new, however, and so far available only in a few dozen cities, including Buffalo, Kalamazoo, Philadelphia, Tulsa, Memphis, and Nashville. Even if not formally available where you live, any good heating dealer can still conform to the same stiff Silver Shield requirements and give you a top-notch warm-air heating system.

What about central summer air conditioning? Do you think you will want it someday? Then a few simple provisions made for it in advance when the heating is installed can sharply reduce the future installation cost of cooling. Facts on this as well as other aspects of air conditioning are given in Chapter 17.

Hot-Water Heat

Water is heated in a boiler and flows through pipes to radiators in each room. A pump called a circulator (which should be located at the boiler) forces the water around under pressure.

Hot water is less susceptible to design and installation errors than warm air (a piece of pipe is a piece of pipe, but air ducts have to be sized and hand-fabricated for each house); hot-water boilers are generally smaller and more compact than furnaces; you get more basement headroom because pipes take less space than ducts; a separate water heater for faucet hot water may not be needed—it can come as part of the heating boiler; and some people simply prefer the kind of heat given off by radiators (though warm air can provide equal comfort).

On the other hand, hot water not only costs more than warm air in first cost but, unlike warm air, it can neither filter the house air nor add moisture in winter (humidification). The cost of central air conditioning runs from 10 to 25 per cent more in a house with hot water than one with warm-air heat. And a hot-water system must be drained if you leave the house for a winter vacation, since freezing can cause pipes to burst.

The Heating Boiler

The first question to ask about hot-water heat concerns the heating boiler. Is it made of cast iron or steel? Cast-iron boilers are normally guaranteed for twenty to twenty-five years and are especially recommended if you have hard water. Steel boilers are more susceptible to rust and corrosion from hard water, and are usually guaranteed only for a year. Don't use one if you have hard water unless you also have a water softener. (Steel, however, is perfectly acceptable for warm-air furnaces, since air and not corrosive water is being handled. Nearly all furnaces are made of steel today.)

A cast-iron boiler should carry the IBR seal of the Institute of Boiler & Radiator Manufacturers which indicates that its heating output has been confirmed by stiff tests. A steel boiler should carry the SBI seal of the Steel Boiler Institute which is assurance that a steel boiler will deliver its rated capacity. Both cast iron and steel should carry the small H insignia of the American Society of Mechanical Engineers (ASME). This indicates that design and construction conform to strict standards. Look for these seals on the name plate.

In addition, gas-burning heaters (hot-water or warm-air) should carry the American Gas Association (AGA) emblem on the burner, a must for safety. An oil-fired unit should carry the Underwriters' Laboratories (UL) approval emblem. (This applies to oil-fired warm-air furnaces, too. Oil warm-air furnaces also should meet U. S. Government Commercial Standard CS 195–57.)

Judging the Radiators

The best radiators are baseboard radiators—long, low, spread-out metal units seven to nine inches high. They are much better-looking than the old-fashioned stand-up radiators and give more uniform heat. There are two main kinds: the cast iron and the non-ferrous (aluminum or copper). The non-ferrous can be identified by the presence of metal fins along their length.

Like cast-iron boilers, cast-iron baseboard radiators cost more but last longer and provide better heat. A frequent complaint about aluminum and copper baseboard radiators is that they can be noisy. Regardless of type, every baseboard radiator should conform to the standards of the IBR. This may not be marked on the radiator; you have to refer to the manufacturer's literature which will mention it. If unmentioned, the radiators should be flatly rejected.

Radiant Heat

Radiant hot-water heat uses the same kind of heating boiler as a regular hot-water system. The house is heated by pipes embedded in the floor—usually a concrete floor in a house without a basement—through which heated water flows from the boiler. Radiant heat had a short spell of great popularity in the early 1950s but is less popular today. It can provide very comfortable warmth underfoot. But if a pipe leak occurs, the floor has to be dug up.

Radiant heat is also likely to overheat a house, or it will not provide heat fast after a sudden dip in outside temperatures. The entire concrete floor has to be heated up first, and this may take an hour or two. Then if the sun abruptly breaks through and you no longer need much heat, there is little you can do; the floor will continue to radiate heat even though the boiler has gone off.

For these reasons, a radiant-heating system requires a top-notch installation contractor and special indoor-outdoor controls for tipping-off the boiler in advance when rapid outdoor temperature changes occur. Radiant heat is theoretically a splendid idea, since it removes the radiators from our rooms, but unfortunately its idiosyncrasies can cause special problems.

Steam heat is rarely used any more for houses. It is encountered chiefly in old houses. The same check points given above for hot-water boilers apply to steam boilers, too. Other checks for steam heat are given in Chapter 18.

Which Is Better: Gas or Oil Fuel?

You can burn either, regardless of whether you have warm-air or hot-water heat. In general, gas has the edge over oil heat, provided low-cost natural gas is available. By and large, gas tends to be cleaner heat, is lower in first cost, requires less service, and gas burners last longer than oil burners (twenty-five to thirty years versus seventeen years' average oil-burner life). But beware of gas if your local gas rates are steep, for then fuel bills can climb painfully high.

With natural gas available, gas will generally, but not always, be cheaper. Oil costs today average about 15¢ a gallon, more or less. Gas heat is generally competitive with 15¢ oil when gas costs from 12¢ to 14¢ a therm. The therm is a standard measuring unit for gas. It is a quantity of gas equal to 100,000 B.T.U.s (British thermal units) of heat value. (A gallon of oil gives about 148,000 B.T.U.s, but don't use these figures for a straight comparison of each. For one thing, most gas burners operate at a higher efficiency level than oil burners—about 80 per cent to 70 to 75 per cent for oil. Other technical factors also intrude.)

If gas costs are more than 12¢ to 14¢ per therm, it will generally pay to use oil. Call the gas company to find out cost per therm. Gas rates are sometimes given in terms of cubic feet of gas. Natural gas has a heat content of roughly

1000 B.T.U.s per cubic foot. Thus 100 cubic feet of natural gas is the equivalent of one therm, or 100,000 B.T.U.s of heat. If your gas rates are given in terms of cubic feet, have the gas-company people tell you what it is equivalent to in price per therm, a better yardstick.

For Lowest-Cost Gas Heat

Gas heat is cheapest when you also have a gas range and a gas water heater. Gas is billed on a sliding scale; the more you use, the lower its unit price. A typical family will consume about 800 cubic feet of natural gas or eight therms a month for cooking, and another 2000 to 3000 cubic feet (twenty to thirty therms) a month for water heating. After this much consumption, approximately, the price you pay for additional gas falls to the cheaper heating bracket.

If, however, you use gas for heating only, you are charged for the first 2000 to 3000 cubic feet each month at the higher end of the scale and heating bills will be higher. A typical six- or seven-room house with insulation will use about 20,000 to 30,000 cubic feet of natural gas a month for heating in a climate like that of New York, Pittsburgh, or Indianapolis with approximately 5000 degree days per winter.

LP or bottled gas is by and large too expensive for central heating. It comes closest to being competitive with 15¢ oil in the Midwest where it costs from 14¢ to 16¢ per gallon. This is for propane with 96,000 B.T.U.s of heat value per gallon. LP prices are higher in the East and New England, where it is generally much too expensive for central heating.

If you're uncertain about the comparative cost of oil and gas, talk to the gas-company people and to oil dealers. If either beats around the bush, tries to sell you on all of the real and imagined advantages of his particular fuel, but will not flatly give you actual cost figures, then beware.

New High-Efficiency Oil Heat

If you get oil heat, insist on one of the new, high-efficiency oil-heating units. They are far cleaner and more efficient than conventional oil equipment, they cut conventional oil units' fuel bills by about 25 to 33 per cent, and for the first time, they make oil heat as clean and efficient as gas. They are called *forced-draft* oil burners; that is what to ask for. Some of the first brands introduced are made by Jet-Heet, Inc. (152 South Van Brunt Street, Englewood, New Jersey); and Iron Fireman (Cleveland 11, Ohio). Other new forced-draft oil burners, still in the laboratory as this is written, are expected from such oil-heat people as Shell, Gulf, and Esso.

Electric Heat

Electric heat generally is economical only if electric rates are very low. Its operating cost will be roughly the same as average oil or gas fuel bills if the electric rate is a low 1¢ per kilowatt hour (Kwh). The kilowatt is the standard measure of electricity. If your rate is more than 1¢ per Kwh, your electric-heat bills will be higher than they would be with gas at roughly 12¢ a therm, and oil at 15¢ a gallon.

Nevertheless, electric heat is being heavily promoted by electric companies whose rates are as high as 1.5¢ and higher. If you pin them down they will frankly concede that the homeowner pays more for electric heat than he would with gas or oil fuel. But other advantages, they say, offset the "somewhat" higher electric cost. They cite these advantages: clean, quiet heat; negligible maintenance (since there is no furnace or boiler to give trouble); lower first cost of installation than a comparable gas or oil heating system in a new house; you save the construction cost of a chimney (about $100 to $150 on the usual prefabricated chimney used nowadays); and you often can get individual room control by means of a thermostat in every room.

Even when local power rates are very low, electric heat demands that a house be insulated to the hilt. Storm doors, storm windows, and thorough weather stripping are mandatory, otherwise operating costs can skyrocket. Such tight construction, however, gives rise to complaints of stuffiness, lack of ventilation, and excess moisture built up inside of electrically heated houses. A good-size kitchen exhaust fan is therefore necessary for ventilation and moisture exhaust. Bathroom exhaust fans are also recommended, particularly if there are two or more baths. And if you live where lengthy, storm-induced electric failures are common in winter you would probably do well to pick another kind of heat.

If in doubt don't accept electric heat until you have talked with other families who have it. Get a line on their operating costs. Are they satisfied with its comfort and other characteristics? Talk to the electric company and get an operating-cost estimate from them. Electric heat is fine and inexpensive if not downright cheap in low cost power areas like the TVA region and the Pacific Northwest. Heating contractors in these areas are also familiar and experienced with it, so they make few mistakes. But it is still new and relatively untried in other areas where it has been introduced only recently. Here is where a thorough check is advised. You don't want to be a guinea pig.

Is the Heating System Large Enough?

Note the capacity of the heater on the name plate. It is given in B.T.U.s per hour. The usual house in the North with ordinary amounts of insulation requires from forty to fifty-five B.T.U.s of heating capacity per square foot of living area. A 40,000 to 55,000 B.T.U. heater is therefore required for a 1000-square-foot house, somewhat more in the extreme North, less in the more temperate areas.

A really well-insulated house, however, may require only about thirty B.T.U.s per square foot, or 30,000 B.T.U.s of capacity for 1000 square feet. An electrically heated house, the best insulated of all, should require no more than about 35,000 B.T.U.s of capacity per 1000 square feet of house area. (In fact, electric heat should not be used unless enough insulation, plus storm windows, has reduced the total heat requirements down to this figure. The same thick insulation with oil or gas heat will bring about a proportionate decrease in the amount of heat needed, and rock-bottom fuel bills.)

A rule of thumb for judging the heat capacity needed is impossible to give. It can vary greatly from house to house and from city to city. It is figured for each house by what an engineer calls a heat-loss computation. He takes into account the amount of wall, roof, and glass area, type of construction, air volume, and so on, to figure the heat-leakage rate of the structure, and then the heat capacity needed to offset the leakage loss. By and large, marginal heating capacity is more likely in a development house. Conversely, an oversized heating plant is often likely in a custom-built house. This is almost as bad as too small a heater. It happens when, for example, an old-timer in the heating business plays safe and throws in much more heating than needed. You pay more than you should and inefficient operation results. It's as bad as a Cadillac engine in a small car.

Other Heating Tips

If you intend to enlarge the house or finish off the basement or attic someday, ask for extra heating capacity to handle such space. When building, consider running heating lines up to the unfinished area, but seal them off. Check the heating controls. An automatic thermostat should be included. If you have a particularly large, spread-out one-story house, or much glass in some rooms, or a two-story house or split-level house, you will probably need zone controls—separate heating thermostats for each level or heating zone. This prevents overheating part of the house, while another part gets chilly. Also check the chimney. A masonry chimney should be lined on the inside with a special fireproof tile lining such as fire clay (not ordinary clay tile). The metal smoke pipe from furnace to chimney should be wrapped with fireproof asbestos when it passes within eight inches of any wood or other combustible material.

When you build or buy a new house, get the name of the heating dealer and call him. Is the system guaranteed? Does he provide free service for the first year? Ask him frankly how good the heating job is. It is surprising how candidly he may answer, saying, for instance, that the system was put in to meet a price and therefore lacks a few touches he would otherwise recommend. If he does, you can have him make the necessary changes before you move in for comparatively small extra expense and then you get a first-class job. Talking person to person, with those who build your house can help.

CHAPTER 10

INSULATION AND VAPOR
BARRIERS

Research shows that most houses today are underinsulated. Many a new house has only the ceilings insulated, not the walls. This is unforgivable penny pinching in a cold climate. A recent study shows that if a typical 1200-square-foot house is really well insulated, it can be completely heated *and* air-conditioned nearly anywhere in the United States for no more than $150 a year, less than $13 a month on the average. Don't skimp on insulation.

Besides cutting heating and cooling bills (and making a non-air-conditioned house cooler in summer), insulation is essential for indoor comfort in winter. This should be clearly understood.

With little or no insulation, floors, walls, and ceiling get quite cold. Cold drafts are set up inside of rooms much like the cold downdrafts you feel by a cold window. Equally important, cold surrounding surfaces in a room draw off excessive body heat, a key reason for goose pimples—i.e., excessive body heat is radiated from the skin to cold walls, causing discomfort for the same reason you feel chilly standing in front of an open refrigerator. Such conditions can prevail in a house despite the most expensive heating system. We tend to compensate by raising the thermostat setting up to 75 degrees or higher; not only do we remain uncomfortable, but things also get stuffy.

Thick insulation, on the other hand, keeps floors, walls, and ceilings warm. Then a house will be supremely comfortable at a lower 70 to 72 degrees temperature (another little-known reason why good insulation reduces fuel bills).

How Much Insulation?
Insulation is cheap. Plenty of it should be put in when

a house is built. Putting it in walls and floor after the house is finished can cost two to three times as much. If you must economize, save the attic insulation for later, since this normally can be added any time at no more cost than if it were done during construction. Here are good insulation standards for all cold-climate houses and also for air-conditioned houses in the South:

Walls should contain at least two to three inches of mineral-wool (rock wool, glass fiber) insulation thickness or the equivalent in another insulation type.

Ceilings should have at least three-inch-thick mineral wool, six inches if there is no attic or if you have air conditioning or electric heat.

Floors of a crawl-space house (first floor raised eighteen to thirty inches over the ground and no basement) should have at least two-inch-thick insulation directly under them, or around the inside surface of the foundation walls if the crawl space is closed off and heated. A concrete floor on the ground requires two to three inches of what is called perimeter, or edge, insulation around the entire perimeter of the concrete; this is essential for preventing cold floors.

The above recommendations are based on using mineral-wool insulation, the kind most recommended because it is bugproof, fire-resistant, and, compared with other types, generally superior in other characteristics. Mineral-wool insulation is now graded by manufacturers for its R value (resistance to heat flow). This is generally marked on the package. The higher the R value, the better. Makers of other kinds of insulation are adapting the R value of identification.

If a builder tells you about insulation's R value, here is how to judge if you are getting enough, or how to specify adequate insulation in terms of R value when you build a house. Another term, the U value, is also given here for technical readers; it indicates thermal heat transmission characteristics. Unlike R values, the lower the U number, the better.

For maximum year-round comfort and lowest heating and cooling bills

(*Houses with central air conditioning, electric heat, or heating only in a very cold climate*)

	U VALUE	R VALUE	
Ceilings	.05	19	Equivalent to 5 to 7 inches of mineral wool depending on brand
Walls	.07	11	Equivalent to 2½ to 3 inches of mineral wool depending on brand
Floors over vented crawl space	.07	13	Equivalent to 2 to 3 inches of mineral wool depending on brand

For reasonable comfort and economy

(*All other houses with heating only, except in a warm climate*)

	U VALUE	R VALUE	
Ceilings	.07	13	Equivalent to 3 to 4 inches of mineral wool
Walls	.09	8	1½ to 2½ inches
Floors over vented crawl space	.09	9	1½ to 2½ inches

Insulation for a concrete floor perimeter is not rated according to R value. Technically, such insulation should be sufficient to keep the heat loss from the floor at or under thirty B.T.U.s per lineal foot of floor perimeter. This normally requires two-inch-thick edge insulation, three inches in northern states such as Michigan and Minnesota. It is especially important that such insulation should be a rot- and bug-proof material such as mineral wool, not a wood-fiber material that will rot or be eaten.

Other Insulation

Besides mineral wool, there are wood-fiber, cotton, macerated-paper, mineral-aggregate (e.g., perlite and vermiculite), and aluminum-foil insulation. Wood fiber, cotton, and

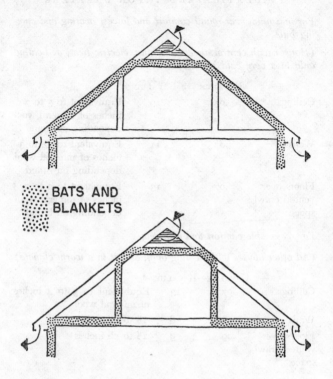

ATTIC INSULATION
SATISFACTORY METHODS

Figs. 17, 18 Attic insulation normally should be applied on the attic floor, directly over the ceiling. But if the attic has living space, insulation can be applied as shown here: under the roof on both sides or across attic floor of unoccupied space, up the vertical walls and across ceiling of finished space. Insulation does not go to very peak of the roof in order to leave area free for essential natural ventilation in summer *and* winter. *National Mineral Wool Association.*

macerated paper require chemical treatment to make them resistant to fire and bugs. Their quality varies greatly from brand to brand. The mineral-aggregate kind gives less insulating efficiency per inch of thickness than most of the others. Thus, as much as nine to ten inches of it is needed over a ceiling to give the same insulating protection you would get from a six-inch-thick blanket of mineral wool (R value of nineteen) over the ceiling.

Aluminum-Foil Insulation

Aluminum-foil insulation comes in layers of one or more parallel sheets of foil. Many houses only get one or two layers which is decidedly *not* enough. Each layer of foil gives you the equivalent insulating effect in winter of roughly ½ to ¾ inches of mineral wool. This calls for at least three-layer foil for walls and at least four layers for ceilings. In general, foil gives more protection per dollar for keeping summer heat out of a house than for keeping winter heat in.

Besides exterior walls, ceilings, and the floors of non-basement houses, insulation should be used for all walls next to unheated spaces such as the house-garage wall, under the floors of all rooms above an unheated garage (particularly important and often omitted), around dormers, and under any raised part of the house whose floor is exposed to outdoor cold. The first floor of a house with a basement normally does not require insulation. Experts advise, however, that some heat should be supplied to the basement to provide a protective cushion of warm air under the first floor.

Vapor Barriers

Regardless of the kind of insulation, ask if it comes with a vapor barrier, or insist that a separate barrier be installed. This is essential to prevent vapor infiltration of the internal structure of a house and help prevent moisture troubles such as paint peeling and wood rot. A vapor barrier is a layer of vapor-impermeable paper or foil on one side of the insulation, or a polyethylene plastic sheet independent of the insulation. Vapor barriers should be mandatory for almost all houses, except perhaps in a very warm climate. Special vapor-barrier material with no accompanying insulation is also mandatory under crawl-space and concrete-slab houses, as noted in Chapter 15.

Weather Stripping

A well insulated house also calls for weather stripping around all doors and windows. According to University of Minnesota tests, weather stripping can reduce total heat loss as much as 37 per cent. It is weather stripping, of course, that makes for snug-fitting windows and doors and prevents cold air from leaking in all around their frames. Good-quality windows come with integral weather stripping.

CHAPTER 11

ELECTRICAL WIRING

"In many large projects half the home buyers have to spend nearly $100 within six months for additional electric service that the builder could have provided during construction for less than $20." So says a leading professional building magazine.

Inadequate wiring is one of the most widespread flaws in houses, new or old, because we use so much more household electrical equipment today than we did only ten or fifteen years ago. What's more, an applicance like an electric clothes drier pulls by itself as much electricity as was formerly required for a whole house. When adequate wiring is installed, instead of the more common marginal wiring, you not only save money in the long run but there will be no danger of overloaded circuits and none of the inconvenience encountered as a result of too few outlets and switches.

There are three separate parts of the wiring system to check:

1. *The capacity of the main electric board:* How much input capacity is installed for the whole house? This is called your electric service entrance. The minimum recommended for most houses today is a three-wire, 240-volt, 100-ampere service. A larger 150- to 200-ampere service, also 240 volts, may be needed if you have an electric range coupled with electric heat or central air conditioning, or a house of more than 3000 square feet. The capacity is usually noted on the main electric board (where fuses or circuit breakers are located). The term "three-wire" means you sometimes can actually see three separate wires running overhead from the street to the house, not just two; sometimes, however, they are underground. The connec-

tions from the main electric board to these wires should be thick No. 2 wires in size, not No. 3 or 4 which carry less electricity.

Most people prefer an electric board with circuit breakers rather than fuses. When an overload or short circuit occurs and lights go out, a circuit breaker automatically snaps open, cutting off the electricity. When you have discovered the cause of the overload and corrected it, you merely push the circuit breaker back to "on" and electricity flows again. You do away with the fuss and bother associated with fuse changing. But you generally have to specify circuit breakers if you want them.

2. *The number of branch electric circuits (wires) from the main switch box to the house.* Most houses need at least eight or ten separate circuits, but get only six. If you have much electrical equipment, many appliances, or a large house, you need at least twelve to fifteen circuits. Each individual 120-volt circuit is represented by a separate fuse or circuit breaker. Each 240-volt circuit is protected by two fuses or a double circuit breaker.

A typical house requires three to four individual circuits just for lights and outlets, plus two to three heavier circuits for kitchen appliances, and one circuit each for such things as electric range, furnace, washer, water heater, freezer, and attic fan. In addition, it pays to have two or three spare circuits available for a future drier, air conditioner, or workshop. Count the number of fuses or circuit breakers at the main board. An electric board with twelve to twenty circuits costs only about $5 to $10 more than one with only six, *if installed when the house is built.* Increasing its size later can cost from $50 to over $100.

3. *Electric outlets and switches.* The rule for outlets is one for every twelve feet of wall, because lamps and appliances have six-foot cords; closer than twelve feet when a door comes between two outlets. Otherwise you end up spreading extension cords all around. The kitchen should have a series of outlets above the counter top to handle appliances safely. You may also want special appliance outlets in the dining room and outside on the patio for plugging

in a toaster, waffle iron, or coffee maker. These should be fed by heavier No. 12 wire, not the usual No. 14 wire for ordinary outlets. The lower the number, the heavier the wire.

There should be light switches at every entrance to every room and, for safety, at the top and bottom of stairs and at garage and basement doors. Adding switches and outlets cost about $3 to $4 each when a house is being built, twice that afterward.

If you build a house insist on "intermediate" or "specification" grade outlets and wiring quality. There are also "competitive" grade, the cheapest in quality though only pennies less in cost. "Specification" grade, the best of all, is usually recommended only for heavy-duty commercial use or ships, but is worth the extra cost if you want top quality, particularly in the kitchen and for all switches. Also specify no wiring smaller than No. 12. Because much wiring today is usually No. 14 grade, lights will flicker and appliances work sluggishly. (A common occurrence when more than one or two lamps and appliances are plugged into the same circuit). In all, total extra cost for good-quality wiring will raise total wiring cost in a $20,000 to $25,000 house by $50 to about $125, less than 1 per cent, compared with minimal wiring.

Special Wiring Features

Here are a number of recent wiring ideas. Some are decidedly luxury features. Not everyone will want them. Decide for yourself.

Noiseless (no-click) light switches which make no noise when you turn lights on or off. There are also silent, touch-button switches which require slight finger pressure. These also come in flat-plate models, set flush against the wall. Slight pressure on the top turns the lights on, pressure on the bottom turns them off.

No-shock outlets, a safety feature with small children. They are designed so a child cannot jab a hairpin or anything metallic into the outlet and get a shock.

Ivory or white outlets and switches, rather than the usual brown or tan which may clash with your decor.

Grounded outlets, particularly in the kitchen, bath, basement, garage workshop, and outdoors. They are required by some electrical codes and are added protection against shocks and a good way to reduce the possibility of electrocution in the bathroom.

Multiple switch control which allows you to turn the same light on or off from several different locations; i.e., at every entrance or exit to or from a room, and from the top or bottom of stairs.

Automatic closet lights which turn on the closet light when the closet door is opened and turn it off when the door is closed, the way a refrigerator light works.

Dimmer controls which enable you to adjust light brightness up or down according to your needs. Illumination in a room can be dimmed to candlelight glow for a dinner party, kept subdued for television, or turned up brightly for reading. Dimmers are chiefly for living and dining rooms.

Remote-control lighting which permits you to turn indoor and outdoor lights on or off from a central location such as the kitchen or master bedroom. A remote kitchen switch can control front-door or garage lights, for example, saving steps. A control panel next to your bed will eliminate that final tour of your house and grounds every night to make sure all lights are out.

Automatic garage-door opener which enables you to open the garage door from a button in your car. Cost runs about $75 to $150.

Electric snow-melting panels for the front walk, driveway or both which cost from $150 to $250 for a forty- to fifty-foot drive if done at the same time as the paving. They are turned on when snow begins to fall.

CHAPTER 12

TERMITES AND WOOD ROT

These two widespread causes of damage go hand in hand. They are often caused by the same construction flaws, and can be prevented by similar safeguards. Consider termites and what to do about them first.

Formerly encountered only in warm sections of the nation, termites have spread in recent years to nearly every state. Some built-in safeguards against them are therefore recommended today for almost all houses in the country. Invincible protection is needed in rampant termite areas like the South and southern California, and also in such areas as the Mississippi and Ohio River valleys, and New York's Long Island, where they are spreading fast.

Stopping Termites

The safeguards required are comparatively simple and inexpensive if done when a house is built; fortress construction is not necessary. There are five principal controls. You should insist on one or more for any house located in regions I and II, the two heaviest termite areas of the country, shown in the accompanying map. They are:

1. Soil "poisoning," the injection of a special chemical into the ground under and around a house. It is anathema to termites for at least five to ten years but harmless for trees and plants. After that time the chemical treatment is repeated. Examples of such chemicals are Aldrin, made by the Shell Chemical Corporation (50 West Fiftieth Street, New York 20, New York) and Chlordane, made by the Velsicol Chemical Corporation (330 East Grand Avenue, Chicago 11, Illinois). This is generally the best way to forestall termites.

2. The use of chemically treated lumber for the main

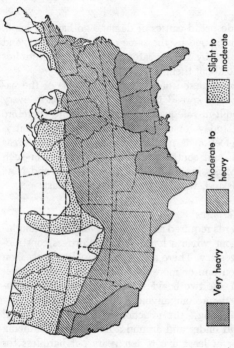

Fig. 19 Termite-incidence map indicates degree of protection against termites required where you live. Maximum protection is required in Region I, where termites are rampant; good protection is required in Region II, and some safeguards are recommended even in Region III. Point to remember: termites are spreading constantly and increasing in regions II and III, and are even showing up in the northernmost (white) areas where, up to now, they have almost been unknown.

Very heavy

Moderate to heavy

Slight to moderate

underpinnings of a house, preferably all wood around the base of walls and under the floor. Pressure-treated lumber should be used, which means a chemical preservative is injected into the lumber under pressure. The same treatment gives excellent protection against decay, the scientists' term for wood rot. Wood merely dipped in a chemical bath is not so good.

3. The use of reinforced concrete foundation walls, rather than walls of concrete block or cinder block. But they must be free of cracks and porous areas.

4. Metal termite shields properly placed all around the top of the foundation walls to prevent termite entry into the house.

5. A four-inch-thick capping of concrete laid around the top of concrete-block or cinder-block foundation walls.

Additional notes: Treated lumber is excellent permanent protection, but it can get a bit expensive. Reinforced concrete walls, termite shields, or foundation caps are generally not considered adequate by themselves, particularly in bad termite areas. Termites are resourceful little bugs that constantly infiltrate each of these defenses. For this reason, experts strongly recommend a termite inspection by an expert at least once a year. The few dollars it costs are well worth it. Some homeowners can learn to do it by themselves. But unless you truly know how and where to look, it is a pennywise, pound-foolish undertaking.

A house with a concrete-slab floor on the ground and no basement is commonly assumed to be termite-proof. This is folly. You cannot let down your guard in such a house. Much termite damage has been done to slab houses. Termites get up into the house wood through the inevitable cracks in the concrete or through the openings made for plumbing pipes. A slab house demands protection as much as other houses.

How Termites Work

Most termite damage is done by what is called the subterranean termite. It lives in the ground and is seldom seen except during swarming time in late winter or early spring,

VENTILATION AND BARRIER REQUIREMENTS TO PREVENT CONDENSATION*

Map: **CONDENSATION ZONES** — ZONE 1, ZONE 2, ZONE 3

Zone 1. roughly includes design temps. of −20°F. & lower
Zone 2. from 0°F. to −10°.
Zone 3. areas warmer than 0°F.

Attic	Type of Roof	Total Free Area of Ventilation	Vapor Barriers Zone 1	Zone 2	Zone 3
Unheated	FLAT ROOF Slope less than 3/12 (ctr.)	1/300 Uniformly distributed at eaves. Free circulation through all spaces required.	Required on warm side in top story ceiling.		
Unheated	GABLE ROOF Slope over 3/12 (ctr.) HIP ROOF	1/300 At least 2 louvers on opposite sides near ridge.	Required on warm side in top story ceil.	Considered unnecessary.	Considered unnecessary.
Heated	GABLE or HIP ROOF	1/600 uniformly distributed at eaves & 1/600 at ridge with all spaces interconnected. (ctr.)	Recommended on warm side in top story ceiling.	Considered unnecessary.	Considered unnecessary.
			Recommended on warm side in top full story ceiling, dwarf walls sloping part of roof & attic story ceiling.		Considered unnecessary if insulation is omitted.

*The figure given indicates that the clear opening of vents totaled should be 1/300 of the bldg. area at eave line. Only 10% of given figure necessary if bsmt. has slab, or crawl space earth covered with 55# felt lapped 2".

Fig. 20 Wood rot is a major problem in zones 1 and 2, where winter cold causes moisture condensation inside structure in winter. Some safeguards against it are also recommended in Zone 3. Chart at right gives minimum venting area required to prevent condensation, and also tells where vapor barriers should be used.

their mating season when clusters of them take to the air. In a day or two they will have found their mates, shed their wings, and disappeared back into the ground. They bore into a house from below and can thrive inside a wood beam, eating away for years, without being discovered until the piano falls through the floor.

They should not be mistaken for flying ants which have a narrow waist. The termite is identified by its large head, grayish-white color, and stubby, oblong body that does not narrow down at the waist like an hourglass. There are also dry-wood and damp-wood termites with similar appearance and habits. These are found chiefly in a narrow band across the southern part of the United States from the Carolina coast around to southern California. Additional precautions may be required for these species, according to local building practices.

Termites thrive on moisture, darkness, and dead wood. Good drainage is needed around a house. All wooden parts of the house should be at least four to eight inches above soil level. Dead tree stumps nearby should be pulled and removed because they attract termites and the next jump is into the house. The underside of porches, outdoor stairs, and inside crawl spaces are especially vulnerable. They should be kept dry and well ventilated.

Excellent sources of information about termites are: "Subterranean Termites, Their Prevention and Control in Buildings," U.S.D.A. Bulletin 64, 15¢; "Preventing Damage to Buildings by Subterranean Termites" at 15¢; and "Control of Non-subterranean Termites" (dry-wood kind) 10¢—all available from the U. S. Government Printing Office, Washington 25, D.C.

Wood Rot (Decay)

This is even more destructive than termites in many areas, particularly in wet and humid climates. The overriding principle to remember is that a house structure should be kept dry to prevent rot. Dry wood does not rot. (There is no such thing as "dry rot," a misnomer which came

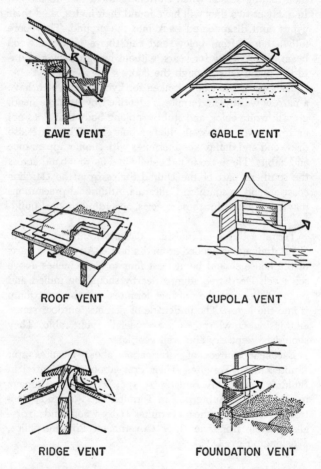

EAVE VENT

GABLE VENT

ROOF VENT

CUPOLA VENT

RIDGE VENT

FOUNDATION VENT

Fig. 21 Here are various kinds of vents that can be employed to safeguard structure condensation and wood rot. *National Mineral Wool Association.*

about because rotted wood in the final stage of decay often looks deceptively dry.)

Preventing rot therefore comes down to keeping the structure free of water and moisture. This puts additional emphasis on good drainage; adequate air vents for crawl spaces, under porches, stairs, and attic; on vapor barriers built in with your insulation; and on preventing condensation. These last three—minimum venting rules, vapor barriers, and condensation—are discussed in detail in the construction chapter.

All pressure-treated wood is rotproof, and certain kinds of wood are naturally rot-resistant. If practical, these can be used for such vulnerable parts of a house as windows, doors, exterior woodwork, and fences. They are California redwood, Tidewater red cypress, and western red cedar. Be sure that the proper grade of each species is used. Hundred-per-cent heartwood grade of each is required and the lumber is so marked.

CHAPTER 13

WATER HEATERS

Water heaters have been notorious for low quality in recent years. They are one of the first major parts to fail in houses, fifth biggest cause of high upkeep. Many go bad in two or three years, and you have to spend upward of $125 for a new one. They need such frequent repairs and replacement that they appear as one of the largest single housing-cost items in the government's Consumer Price Index. This is because most new houses get the cheapest kind, or undersized units that are pressed beyond their capacity.

Yet only about $20 more in first cost will get you a first-class water heater that will last two to three times as long. Brand name means little. Even the best manufacturers sell both good and not-so-good models. Besides, a poor choice for a particular family and area can cause even the best-quality kind to fail in little time. The trick is in choosing the right size and kind for your house and the kind of water you have.

What Size Heater?

The capacity of the water heater is crucial. It is marked on the name plate in gallons of storage capacity. Is it large enough? Water heaters range in size from twenty gallons to over ninety. With a gas water heater, the minimum size recommended is one with a thirty-gallon tank. The accompanying chart will give you an idea of the capacity you need. If in doubt, choose a slightly oversize unit which will give you spare capacity for emergency use, rather than a borderline unit that has to work overtime. Continually forcing a small unit to provide hot water at peak capacity is a major reason for early failure. Or get what is called a "quick recovery" unit. The chart also shows that if you expect to have an automatic clothes washer, a larger water heater will be needed than without one.

WHAT SIZE GAS HOT-WATER HEATER?

Minimal Capacity in Gallons

NUMBER IN FAMILY	WITH NO LAUNDERING	WITH NON-AUTOMATIC WASHER	AUTOMATIC WASHER
3	30	30	30–40
4	30	30–40	40–50
5	30–40	40–50	40–50
6	40–50	40–50	50–65
7	40–50	50–65	65

Electric vs. Gas Water Heaters

Electric hot-water heaters must be larger than gas ones. The minimum-size electric heater needed for most families is a sixty-six-gallon capacity tank. If you have an automatic washer, an eighty-gallon tank is usually essential, unless you get a "high speed" or "high watt" electric unit. These have greater heating capacity as a result of larger heating elements. Not all electric companies, however, permit them. With them a smaller tank capacity than normally required can be used.

Gas water heaters generally have the edge over electric ones. Gas units are lower in first cost, provide hot water faster than electricity, and generally are cheaper in operation. Electric units should be used only when you get a low, preferential power rate for water heating.

There are also oil-fired water heaters. Comparatively new, they are high in selling price but nevertheless can be cheaper per year in the long run if you live where gas is expensive or unavailable, because operating costs with oil are quite low. They are generally best in areas where oil fuel has the edge over gas for house heating.

Recovery Rate

Regardless of heater size, ask about its *recovery rate*. This indicates how fast the heater can bounce back and provide new hot water when you are using a lot at once. It depends on the size of the burners. The recovery rate normally should be such that the heater is capable of providing at least thirty gallons of hot water an hour, based on heating the water by 100 degrees.

In other words, it should be able to heat thirty gallons of 60-degree water to 160 degrees in an hour. Sometimes the recovery rate is deceptively based on a sixty-degree rise of temperature. Watch for this on the name plate and don't accept such a unit. A thirty-gallon unit with a high recovery rate can be better than a forty-gallon unit with a low recovery rate.

Getting Good Quality

Water-heater quality is judged largely by the kind of tank and its guarantee. The lowest quality is one with a galvanized steel tank and a one-year guarantee. This kind normally should not be accepted, since it is likely to rust out in a few years.

Then come glass-lined tanks, the most popular kind. But there are poorly made glass ones as well as good ones. The better ones are guaranteed for ten to fifteen years; one of these is your best bet if you decide on a glass unit. Make sure it has an unconditional guarantee—guarantee wording can be tricky. The usual guarantee for a ten-year model, for instance, promises a new unit free if the unit fails within five years (half the guarantee time); after that you get diminishing credit toward a new unit on a sliding scale according to how long afterward the original unit lasted.

Sometimes, however, the guarantee only offers a new tank, not a complete new tank and burner assembly. What's more, you may be charged for shipment and installation labor. Or nothing is said about how you are to get hot water while the old parts are being inspected at the factory. It depends on the particular brand and unit. You have to compare the small print of each guarantee against the others.

There are also water heaters with ceramic lined, aluminum, and copper tanks. These can be even better than glass but in general are recommended chiefly in areas with particularly corrosive water. There are more than 18,000 different kinds of water (in chemical make-up) in the United States, so it is difficult to generalize about when you may

need one of these special models. Ask local dealers or gas-
or electric-company officials where you live.

Why Soft Water Can Hurt

If you live in an area with soft water, such as New England and much of the South, it is particularly important
to get a top-quality, non-corrosive water heater. This is a
paradox with water heaters. Women find soft water fine
for their hair, but its high oxygen content makes it murder
on an ordinary water heater. A really good glass, aluminum,
ceramic, or copper unit is essential.

On the other hand, galvanized heaters can be a bargain
in areas with hard water, such as parts of the Midwest
and California. Lime in the water forms a protective film
inside the tank and inhibits corrosion. A galvanized heater
that will fail in three years in parts of Texas might last ten
years or more in Chicago. But even in a hard-water city
like Chicago get the best possible galvanized unit, one with
the longest unconditional guarantee; cost is a mere $10 to
$15 more than the usual cheap kind.

Galvanized steel water heaters sometimes come with
what is called a magnesium rod inserted in the middle of
the tank. The rod inhibits tank corrosion by giving itself up
as a sacrificial offering; it draws the corrosive acids away
from the tank and lets itself be eaten away. Much hoopla
has been written about these rods. The catch is that they
may be used up in a year or two and the tank goes next.
Being human, most of us forget to check them and replace
them in time. The conclusion here is not to be sweet-talked
into buying a galvanized tank instead of a better tank, say,
just because the galvanized tank comes with a magnesium
rod. However, in hard-water areas where a galvanized tank
may be used, one with a rod is preferred over one without.

"Domestic" Water Heaters

This refers to the special kind of water heater used in
houses with hot water or steam house heat. It is also called
an indirect or instantaneous water heater. It is integral with
the heating boiler, a pipe coil inserted in the boiler water.
The same heating mechanism used for heating the house

also heats your faucet water. Water heating costs may be somewhat higher in summer but lower in winter, compared with a separate water heater and tank.

The chief advantage of a domestic water heater is that you save the space normally required for a separate water-heater unit (as with warm-air heat). They are not recommended, however, if you have very hard, mineral-laden water, a hardness rating of about seven grains or higher. Then it is better to have a separate, conventional water-heater tank unit. Hard water tends to clog up domestic water coils with scale, reducing efficiency and requiring frequent cleaning. The hardness rating of your water can be determined by having a sample tested by a nearby water-conditioner dealer, at no charge, usually.

Two important facts about the domestic water heater should be checked. First, it should have an IWH seal. This is the seal of an approved Indirect Water Heater, a good-quality unit matched to work with the boiler. This should be noted on the water-heater coil itself, which can be seen sticking out of the main heating boiler. Insist on an IWH seal.

Second, adequate capacity is needed so you won't be chronically short of hot water. Minimum rating for a one-bathroom house today is 2.75 g.p.m. (gallons per minute) of water-heating capacity; at least 3.25 g.p.m. with two baths. If you have more than two baths, or a big family, or use hot water liberally, get a 3.75 g.p.m. coil or larger. Sometimes the indirect water heater comes with a supplementary water tank. Then less heating capacity is needed.

Summed up, the faucet hot-water heater commands far more attention than many people realize. It is often overlooked or taken for granted and has to be replaced in short time, or you never have enough hot water. It is human nature to downgrade your requirements at the very time of selecting such a unit or when buying a house just to save a few dollars. You end up paying twice as much in the long run. And figure on a unit large enough to satisfy future hot-water needs if, say, you have a growing family, or do not have an automatic clothes washer but expect to get one.

PART 4

THE STRUCTURE AND SPECIAL BUILDING FEATURES

This section deals with basic construction—how to judge the structure. It stresses the best-quality standards consistent with long-term economy, the kind of structural components that are worth a few dollars more in first cost but pay off by giving you the longest and most satisfactory service at the lowest upkeep and maintenance cost. In each case you must decide for yourself whether the extra quality is worth the extra first cost. To help you decide, practical facts about each part of the structure are given along with why special materials or construction may be needed.

Most of us, however, are not equipped to judge construction. Here also, therefore, is information on "Who can check a house for you?" and what you can expect from the FHA. Finally, air conditioning also rates your attention.

CHAPTER 14

WHAT IS GOOD CONSTRUCTION?

Much special knowledge is needed to judge a house structure. Without it, you must depend largely on the integrity of the builder and architect. A local building code helps but falls short of what many people expect. It lays down minimum rules for safety and health but that's all. The structure will meet certain strength requirements; wiring and heating will meet minimum fire-prevention standards; and water, plumbing, and sewer pipes meet minimum sanitary standards.

This does *not* mean that you will get the most durable structural materials, efficient heating, and the best wiring and plumbing for the money. It does not mean that you get good windows and doors or interior wall and flooring materials that will stay handsome and new-looking with little maintenance. The cellar may leak like a sieve, but the house will remain standing.

You can go a step further if a house conforms to the minimum construction standards of the Federal Housing Administration (FHA). Its rules apply to virtually everything in the house; but, like a building code, its standards are minimum rules consistent with accepted building practices. When you build a house, the FHA construction rules should be your starting point. A copy of "FHA's Minimum Property Standards" can be had for $1.50 from the U. S. Government Printing Office, Washington 25, D.C.

One aspect of the structure rates special mention: the prevention of damage due to water and moisture. These together are probably the biggest single cause of deterioration in American houses. They cause wood rot and decay, condensation, unsightly paint peeling, and troubles such as wet cellars. Preventing such damage calls for good waterproofing, proper drainage, vapor barriers, and good attic and crawl-space ventilation (which means that attic and crawl-space vents should not be shut in winter). Preventing wetness is therefore strongly emphasized in this chapter.

By necessity, the following is somewhat technical. It is mainly for those who want to know specific points of construction. Others can skip it and go on to the next chapter.

Foundation, Basement Walls, and "Footings"

The foundation should be built on solid earth. Placed on poorly filled or low-lying wet land, it is apt to settle. The footings underneath the foundation walls are the base on which the foundation walls rest. In general footings should be at least six inches below the frost line (which means two to three feet below ground level in the North). This dimension depends on your building code. Footings generally should be at least eight inches thick and sixteen inches wide for one-story and 1½-story houses, twelve inches thick and twenty-four inches wide for a two-story house. Larger footings are needed for unstable earth and on filled land. A rule of thumb for footings is that they be as deep as the foundation wall is thick and twice as wide.

Poured concrete is best for foundation walls. It puts less stress on footings and sometimes regular footings are not even needed. Poured solid-concrete walls are usually ten or twelve inches thick, though eight inches is sometimes satisfactory. Poured concrete is your best precaution against a wet basement and termites, but it is also the most expensive foundation.

Concrete and cinder blocks are more often used for foundations. Though not as strong or impenetrable as reinforced cement, they can serve well if thoroughly cured. Concrete blocks are better than cinder blocks. With both kinds, it is poorly mortared joints, lack of drainage, and absence of exterior waterproofing that cause leaky walls and wet basements. The top layer (course) of all hollow-block foundation walls should be filled with cement. At least two coats of cement plaster should be applied on the exterior surface of all concrete-block and cinder-block foundation walls. The cement should provide a protective outside skin about ½ inch thick. Good waterproofing also calls for at least two coats of bituminous waterproofing material troweled over the cement plaster.

In areas where wet earth and wet basements are common, water collects at the foundation footings and can cause the house to settle. The water accumulates in the ground just outside the walls and eventually pushes its way into the basements. This can be avoided by drain tile pipes laid around the house at the base of the foundation walls to lead the water away from the house (to a well or open drain). They are clay pipes, open at the joints to catch settled water and drain it away. The omission of drain tiles is a major reason for wet cellars. Putting them in after a house is built is expensive since a deep house-encircling trench has to be dug. Just plain basement dampness and mildew is a nagging problem even in dry areas. It stems largely from ground vapor rising inexorably up through the concrete floor, particularly in winter. It can be squelched simply by specifying a vapor-barrier membrane *under* the basement floor, installed during construction and obviously before the concrete floor is poured. This is an excellent idea, except that it is rarely provided in new houses; you must insist on it.

Concrete-Floor Houses (No Basement)

The concrete is laid over a bed of gravel. Before the concrete is poured, a vapor impermeable layer of polyethylene plastic sheet or fifty-five-pound roll roofing material at least should be applied over the gravel. This is a ground vapor barrier, an all-important necessity for nearly all houses everywhere. It prevents ground vapor from rising into the house to cause moisture troubles such as dankness and mildew. It is recommended even in the driest areas of the country, since ground vapor will rise into a house from all kinds of soil, wet or dry, and pass through concrete as smoke through cloth. Research in the Southwest, in fact, shows strong vapor rise from deep below the desert ground.

The footings of houses with concrete-slab floors normally

should extend below the frost line, twenty-four to thirty-six inches below ground. Shallow foundations are generally acceptable in areas such as the West Coast, where frost is no problem. Keeping a concrete floor warm and dry usually requires that the gravel base under the slab be higher than the surrounding ground. Then water will drain away from the house. The top of the slab normally should be about eight inches above the ground. Floor slabs normally should be at least four inches thick.

Crawl-Space Construction

This is a house without a basement but with a space eighteen to thirty-six inches high between the ground and the first floor—i.e., just enough space to crawl in. Such a house should not be built where the space is likely to be flooded. Above all, it must be kept dry. A wet crawl space can cause the sub-floor structure to rot and can send up damage-causing vapor into the house.

Two other requirements are also recommended—ventilation of the crawl space all year round and a ground vapor barrier as with concrete floor houses. At least four foundation-wall ventilators, one near each corner, should be provided. A total of one square foot of net vent area is needed for every 150 square feet of crawl-space area. Only two vents and one-tenth as much vent area are needed if the crawl-space earth is covered with a vapor-barrier material such as fifty-five-pound roll roofing. The vents should not be closed in winter. Insulation applied directly under the floor will prevent loss of house heat. If the crawl space is heated, it can be closed off entirely in winter. The inside sides of the foundation should then be insulated, and a vapor barrier over the ground is absolutely essential.

Floors

Cross bridging under floors, visible at the basement ceiling, will help prevent squeaky floors. This means 1 × 3 inch cross braces nailed up like X's between floor joists, or metal bridging, with no more than eight feet between each row of bridging. Floor joists are usually two inches thick and from six to twelve inches deep, depending on type of wood, spacing between joists, and span. The first layer of wood put over the floor joists is the sub-floor, which should be at least ½ to ¾ of an inch thick. When hardwood is used as your finished flooring, the sub-floor is covered with fifteen-pound asphalt-saturated felt, except over the heating plant; here thirty-pound asbestos felt or ½-inch insulating board is used. With a resilient finished floor (described below) a smooth ¾-inch plywood sub-floor is used with fifteen-pound saturated asbestos felt. If the plywood is not smooth, an underlayment of ¼-inch hardboard or ⅜-inch plywood is needed below the felt.

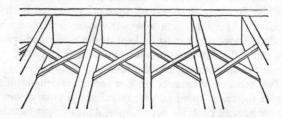

Fig. 22   Cross bridging under floor (at basement ceiling) helps prevent squeaky floors.

Flooring Surfaces

The principal kinds of finished flooring are hardwood, softwood, and resilient materials. Which to use depends largely on the room, personal taste, and budget.

A hardwood floor is usually preferred for living rooms, dining rooms, and bedrooms. Hardwood is handsome, has a warm look and rugged wearing qualities, and is an asset for resale purposes. Oak and maple are the king and queen of the hardwoods. The top grades of each are the best-looking, and most expensive. The lower grades are equally strong but lower in cost due to appearance flaws such as knots; they can be a bargain for a utility room, closets, attic floors, or kitchen sub-floor. Other hardwoods for floors are beech, pecan, and birch. They offer less variety and choice of grain than oak or maple. The softwoods include hemlock, pine, and fir. They give hard and long service but are not as handsome or durable as oak and maple.

Pure vinyl flooring, sometimes called solid vinyl, is considered the best all-round resilient flooring material. The most expensive, it is exceedingly tough, has a rich appearance, high resistance to oil, grease, water chemicals, and requires the least attention. Cork and rubber tile are usually ranked next to vinyl. Both are soft to walk on. Cork is noted for its warmth underfoot—it is a top insulator. It is ideal for a study, say, but not for a room or hall where it will get rough treatment; it soon shows scuff marks and scars from furniture feet, dents, and heavy foot traffic. Rubber is resistant to indentation marks and water but will show wear unless periodically finished, preferably with a self-polishing wax.

Vinyl-asbestos tile can be used in any room. Because of its durability and low cost it is becoming one of the most popular floor coverings. It is resistant to water, grease, and chemicals, but it is not so handsome or soft underfoot as the higher-priced materials noted above. It should be your minimum choice, especially when the alternative is asphalt tile, the cheapest of all, which is too often used. The step-up in quality from asphalt tile to vinyl asbestos is greater than the additional cost of vinyl asbestos. Asphalt tile is found in low-priced houses, particularly those with concrete floors. It is brittle, the least durable of all the resilients, and highly susceptible to stains, scuff marks, and dents; in short, it is the bane of many a woman's existence. Because of poor grease resistance it is decidedly not good in a kitchen. It has its uses; the best use is over a cement basement floor because of its good moisture resistance.

There are also ceramic tile, particularly handsome on bathroom walls but costly; and sheet, roll, and tile linoleum used widely in kitchens. Inlaid linoleum is good because its color and pattern go all the way through to the base. Inlaid provides a hard, durable surface, is greaseproof and easy to clean. But it should not be used on a concrete floor, or in a basement, because moisture from the concrete will cause it to rot.

Exterior Walls

Many people would like heavy masonry walls like brick or stone, but these materials are not only expensive in first cost, they are also less advantageous and require more up-keep than many people realize. On the other hand, various new kinds of durable non-masonry wall materials have been introduced in recent years which are giving masonry a run for its money. These include such long-lasting surfaces as aluminum siding and asbestos cement. And new long-life exterior paints have been developed which last 50 to 100 per cent longer than the old and still widely used oil-base paints on wood and reduce the frequency of repainting by that much. Here, first, are facts about the seven main kinds of non-masonry wall siding (the term used for the exterior wall skin):

Wood, including clapboard and plywood, is attractive on nearly all houses and can be painted any color. Redwood and cedar give a warm natural wood finish, are immune to termites and rot, and may be allowed to weather naturally, or be stained. New stains available for natural wood will last at least four or five years instead of the usual one-year lasting power of most stains (described in the exterior-paint section). Plywood panels are growing in popularity, are extremely strong and durable, and offer many design and texture possibilities. The new kinds are bonded with excellent waterproof adhesives and require no more refinishing than other exterior wood walls (with comparable paint). They are generally best, however, in a temperate climate, since freezing moisture in cold climate tends to open joints that are not well calked.

Hardboard (such as Masonite) is tough, durable, rot-resistant, and will not split or crack. Various kinds are available including smooth, striated surfaces, sheets, clapboard, and grooved or board-and-batten texture. It normally requires painting, and a vapor barrier within the wall is particularly important to prevent condensation and paint peeling.

Wood shingles and shakes are usually cedar, sometimes

redwood or cypress. Like wood roof shingles, they give a roughhewn traditional appearance with much texture. Mostly for traditional house styles such as the Cape Cod, they are durable and weather well naturally, or can be stained or painted. The best shingles are free from knots and pitch pockets. You can tell the difference between the best grade and lower grades by the grain; it should be regular and clear with few or no defects.

Asbestos cement sheets and shingles can give you a permanent wall because of its hard, stonelike surface. Both are exceedingly durable, fire-resistant, and rotproof, but somewhat brittle. Though painting is generally not necessary for durability alone, it may be required occasionally to renew exterior looks.

Insulating board siding comes in asphalt-surfaced panels with a coarse surface or large smooth surface panels. Although insulating value is greater than ordinary wood, it is not enough for comfort; additional inside wall insulation is required particularly in a cold climate. It weathers well, but some brands expand and contract with temperature changes, and knocks can damage them.

Prefabricated wall panels with porcelain enamel, plywood, aluminum, or a plastic surface are a new development. Such panels are made in factories and shops and merely assembled on the job. They represent one of the most significant new trends in home building. Made under shop-controlled conditions, they are usually better-made than walls put together piece by piece. A porcelain-enamel surface is virtually indestructible and rarely needs maintenance or upkeep. Being relatively new, some panels have had bugs in them but these flaws are being eliminated. By and large, prefabricated panels are quite good and are expected to be unbeatable as they become more and more available.

Aluminum is one of the newest and longest-lasting wall materials. Usually painted white, it is indistinguishable from conventional wood siding. More expensive in first cost than other materials, aluminum pays off in excellent service —it seldom requires repainting, is easy to clean, and helps keep a house cool in summer by bouncing back sun heat.

Masonry Walls

The biggest features of brick and stone are beauty, strength, and permanence (painting is seldom required). But a few facts on the other side of the ledger should be known. Insulation is absolutely essential with brick or stone walls, though it is often omitted. (It is recommended for all other masonry, too, not only in the North but also in the South with air conditioning, and even in northern Florida, say, where many people wish for a little insulation just for winter comfort.) Despite popular belief, even the thickest masonry has exceedingly poor insulating properties, which is why masonry houses are particularly cold and hard to heat. Insist on insulation regardless of the type of masonry.

Brick and stone walls are also quite vulnerable to water seepage through cracks and joints. Periodic painting will still be required for exterior windows and doors; this often accounts for more than half of total house-painting costs. And what you save on wall paint is sometimes offset by increased taxes, since tax assessors make a particular target of brick and stone houses. Nevertheless, some people are unswerving in their wish for masonry. If you are one, accept it with your eyes open. Masonry does give a house a solid, permanent appearance and increased value. But make sure that there is a space between the masonry and the interior wall surface and that this space contains both insulation and a vapor barrier. Letting your masonry serve as both the interior and exterior wall will not only mean cold walls; dampness coming through the masonry can leave ugly stains on interior surfaces.

Stucco is portland-cement veneer applied like plaster to either masonry or frame walls, with no seams or joints. A variety of textures and colors is used, but its appearance gets mixed reviews. You like it or you don't. The right mixture and proper application are required to prevent cracking and water seepage. Three coats with a total thickness of ¾ inch are generally recommended. Quality varies according to the ability and conscientiousness of the people who do the job; you are at their mercy.

There are also concrete block, cinder-block and plain re-inforced cement walls. The block walls, now available in colors or various designs etched into the blocks, can look quite handsome, particularly in a good design and when painted, or terribly dingy if raw blocks are left unpainted. Painting is equally important for cement. In fact, exterior paint or a surface sealer is mandatory to prevent cracking, chipping, and water seepage. And insulating them is just as important as with brick or stone. Block walls are often used because they are cheap and seem like a bargain. But when properly finished and insulated they may not be so cheap compared with other walls.

Exterior Paint

Probably the best all-round exterior paint today is an *acrylic* (latex) paint, a new water-emulsion paint that is blister-resistant, and will last about 50 per cent longer than conventional oil-base paints (from six to ten years' life versus four to five years for most conventional paint). It will also stand up well in areas where industrial fumes or mildew is a problem.

Like interior latex paints, the acrylics are flat (non-glossy) paints and therefore not recommended if a glossy finish is desirable. Like other paints, they require a thorough surface preparation, and a special primer coat, particularly before being put on bare wood; the maker's instructions should be followed to the letter. Somewhat more expensive than conventional paints (about $8 to $9 a gallon for top quality), an acrylic paint is easier and faster to apply, so it can save you money as a result of reduced over-all labor and painting time.

Special kinds are available for different exterior surfaces; i.e., for wood, masonry, etc., but generally not for redwood or cedar. Choose the absolute best grade you can get, which is generally the highest-cost can. It's cheaper in the long run. (Repainting an old house with an acrylic, however, can lead to trouble, depending on the condition of the walls and the old paint. A primer may be mandatory. Get an expert's opinion beforehand. If usable, it can serve as well as on virginal, new house walls.)

There are also alkyd and linseed-oil exterior paints, which together are still used in the majority of houses. Alkyds come in flat or gloss finishes and by and large are better than the linseed-oil kind, because of their tougher, longer-lasting finish, but not as lasting as the acrylic kind.

New Exterior Stain

One of the best outside natural finishes for most wood walls, particularly redwood and cedar, is a new stain developed by the Department of Agriculture's Forest Products Laboratory (Madison 5, Wisconsin). It should last about five years, sometimes more, whereas the best stain formerly available was generally good for only a year or two. The new stain is so cheap and easy to make you can make your own. Here are the ingredients for a five-gallon batch (all available at either a drugstore or hardware store):

Raw linseed oil	3 gal.
Mineral spirits of turpentine	1 gal.
Burnt sienna (oil color)	1 pt.
Raw umber (oil color)	1 pt.
Paraffin wax	1 lb.
Penta concentrate preservative	½ gal.
Zinc stearate	2 oz.

Mix in this way: Pour the gallon of the mineral spirits into a five-gallon can. Put the paraffin and zinc stearate into another pan and heat over a flame, stirring until uniform. Pour this mixture into the mineral spirits, stirring vigorously. Keep the flame away from the mineral spirits. When the solution has cooled to room temperature, add penta and linseed oil. Stir in the colors until the mixture is uniform. Then it's ready for use. The surface should be washed and brushed before application. A gallon will cover about 400 square feet of wall, more or less, the smoother the wood, the greater the coverage.

Information about commercial finishes for natural wood and special literature on redwood can be had from the California Redwood Assn., 576 Sacramento Street, San Francisco 11, California.

Exterior finishes can be crucial. You must be absolutely sure not only to use the right over-all kind of paint for your house, but also the particular special type for your kind of walls. Wall preparation is also crucial, and may require more time and effort than the actual painting. This is often ignored. Yet improper preparation is said to cause more paint troubles than almost anything else. Thus again, a word to the wise: Follow the instructions on the can. And insist on the best grade. Buying a cheap, low-cost kind will at best only save you about $10 to $20, all told, on the whole house, a penny-wise, pound-foolish saving when you realize that you probably will have to repaint in a few years; the best kind will often last twice as long.

Interior Walls

Dry wall (plasterboard) is gradually winning out over plaster because it is lower in cost and can be just as good. Often the joints show between adjacent sheets of plasterboard, but this should not be; it is the result of shoddy workmanship, an inexcusable flaw. The other big complaint about dry wall is that it is thin and weak. This is distressingly true for the thin ⅜-inch grade that is most often used. Defects also show up due to nail popping (unsightly pockmarks where the nails back out of the wall, caused by the use of green lumber). Dry wall can be perfectly strong and stiff if a thicker ⅝-inch or ½-inch board is used; a double wall of two ⅜-inch sheets is even better. Nail-popping pockmarks will not occur when a builder uses dried No. 1 framing lumber. Before you build or buy a new house with plasterboard, ask the builder what precautions he has taken.

The best plaster walls are solid-looking and handsome, but this generally requires three coats of plaster over lath and is not done everywhere. Two coats over gypsum-board lath is quite good. The lath should be reinforced at the joints between walls and ceilings, at corners, and around doors and windows. Even the best plaster ultimately may show cracks due to expansion and contraction, and there is little you can do about it. By the way, neither ordinary plaster nor dry wall by themselves is strong enough to support shelving or bookcases; the vertical 2 × 4 supports inside the walls must be located and used to anchor nails and screws.

Other interior wall products have special advantages. They are used for decorative reasons or in rooms like the kitchen or bath where rugged duty is required. Some are for ceilings, too. Quality varies according to type.

Hardboard walls (available in embossed, colored, and wood-grain finishes) are strong, durable, and water-resistant if you get the tempered grade. Asbestos board should be the premium grade which is strong, more flexible, and longer-lasting than the lighter-weight standard grade. Plastic panels and tiles are commonly used for kitchen and bath walls, offer good looks and long wear, and are easy to keep clean if waxed regularly. A good application is essential. Ceramic tile, also for kitchens and baths, give excellent long-term service but should be installed by experts. The glazed kind should not be cleaned with steel wool or gritty scouring powder. Plywood paneling's durability and looks vary according to type of wood, thickness, and finish it comes with. It should be protected by a good sealer. Composition board in particular varies greatly in quality according to brand and thickness. Some brands offer a little insulating value, others none. Soft kinds mar easily; those with a tough, hard surface are preferred. All are vulnerable to moisture and should not be used where wetness is likely. Unfortunately, more comprehensive advice on these materials is difficult to give because individual properties differ greatly from one grade to another.

Windows

There is a great variety in type and brand, much competition for the builder's business, and much cheap window stock on the market. This is one category where it pays to get a brand name (such as Anderson, Biltwell, Curtis, and Malta, big companies whose products cost a few dollars more than the cheapest windows but where the difference in quality is immense). The principal kinds of windows are aluminum, steel, and wood. Aluminum frames get cold in winter, and moisture condensation can be troublesome. The window panes fog up with moisture, and even the frames will drip water. This can be minimized if you insist on aluminum windows that are made so that the inside movable section containing the glass does not touch the cold outside frame. Special nylon fittings, for example, prevent actual metal-to-metal contact between the window section and its frame and the window glass does not get so cold.

Aluminum, on the other hand, requires less maintenance than wood and little or no painting. But double-check the manufacturer's reputation, for cheap quality aluminum windows (and storm windows) are common. A brand name should be used. Steel windows require periodic painting and are susceptible to rust and corrosion. Wood windows, in general, look best in most houses and are often preferred for this reason. Condensation is much less of a problem with them than with aluminum or steel.

All windows should come with integral weather stripping. There should be no air leaks around the frame. You can check this on a cold or windy day by moving the palm of your hand around the frame. Can you feel drafts coming in? Windows should be easy to clean and wash from the inside. You should be able to remove double-hung and sliding windows from their frames.

In the North storm windows or insulating glass such as Thermopane or Twindow will almost always pay off in increased winter comfort. Insulating glass has two parallel sheets of glass with a sealed air space in between. In a new house it will cost about 10 to 20 per cent more than the cost of combination windows and storm sash. But double glass offers better appearance, easier cleaning, and permanent installation. It is a good buy.

When you build a house or remodel, you can save considerable expense by using stock-size Thermopane units;

avoid special sizes. Savings can also be made by using fixed window glass where practical. Not all windows have to be opened, particularly if you have air conditioning. If you get ordinary single-glass windows in a new house, ask the builder about screens and storm windows to fit. Often he can provide them at lower cost than a regular dealer. Jalousie windows deserve special note. They have become a fad in spite of built-in deficiencies. They are quite leaky and generally ill advised in a northern climate even for a porch, and often become a nuisance to put up with.

Attic and Roof

Get strong enough attic floor joists if you plan to turn the attic into finished rooms. In general, floor joists should be at least 2 × 6 inches or larger. The requirements for attic construction should be obtained from an architect or building inspector.

Adequate attic or under-the-roof ventilation is important. Large vents are needed not only for summer cooling but also for ventilation to prevent attic condensation in winter. Attic vents should never be shut in winter, not even in the coldest parts of the North. If your attic floor is well insulated, the heat leakage from the house below will be inconsequential.

Roof "flashing" should be a non-ferrous material such as aluminum, copper, or plastic. Flashing is the covering used to seal roof joints and make them watertight. (It is also used to seal the cracks around window and door frames.) Gutters and downspouts should be used. Omitting them is false economy, since their absence increases the likelihood of paint blistering, rot, and wet cellars as a result of uncontrolled water runoff. Aluminum gutters are considered better than galvanized steel or wood, and the new plastic gutters, though the highest in cost, are said to excel all the others, including aluminum. Nearly every house should have roof gutters.

Roof Cover and Shingles

There are basically two kinds of roof-covering materials

—the temporary kind which has to be renewed or replaced periodically and the permanent material which lasts at least forty to fifty years and sometimes for centuries. The copper roof of Philadelphia's famed Christ Church is over 200 years old and still going strong.

Asphalt shingles are the most common roof material. They are sometimes called composition shingles. There are three main kinds. The minimum grade weighs 210 to 215 pounds per "square." (The number of shingles over 100 square feet of roof will weigh approximately that much. Roofers say 210 or 215 pounds per square.) Shingles of this weight will last about ten to fifteen years, more or less —closer to ten years in the South, fifteen years in the North where there is less hot sun. The 210- to 215-pound asphalt shingle is the minimum grade permitted by FHA and is the kind of roof most commonly found on new houses. There are also thinner, lighter-weight grades down to 150 pounds per square sometimes used in cheap construction. Such roofing is inferior. It should not be accepted.

In fact, the ordinary 210- to 215-pound asphalt shingle roof is giving way to special kinds that will stay put during high winds or storms. Wind can do great damage to roof shingles. To prevent such damage, 210- to 215-pound asphalt shingles should be either the: 1) seal-down kind, which have a factory-applied adhesive on their tabs to keep them down at all times; or 2) interlocking, which come with tabs and slots for hooking each shingle together with adjacent ones. Either of these two special features will cost about $1 per 100 square feet of roof more than regular 210- to 215-pound shingles—thus about $15 more on the average house. One or the other kind should be mandatory in hurricane areas such as along the Atlantic Seaboard and in areas like the Midwest where windstorms may come up at any time. The seal-down kind is generally preferred, since interlocking shingles give a roof an over-all sawtooth appearance which not everybody likes. If neither is used and you get ordinary non-stick-down shingles, it will then pay to have their tabs cemented down during application. A glob of roofing cement is squirted by hand under each shingle tab, one by one.

For a better asphalt roof, specify 250-pound or 300-pound-per-square shingles, the next steps up. The 250-pound asphalt shingle roof is something of a medium grade, while the 300-pound or heavier shingle is the grade recommended for the longest-lasting asphalt shingle roof. A 300-pound or heavier asphalt shingle roof should last from twenty to thirty years, sometimes more. It is the premium grade. Besides being more durable, it generally offers better colors which do not fade quickly as often occurs with ordinary, lighter-weight shingles. The 250- and 300-pound shingles are less susceptible to wind damage than 210- to 215-pound shingles because of heavier and stiffer construction. But if you live in a severe windstorm or hurricane area and use one of the heavier shingles, having their tabs cemented down still may be advisable.

If the roof is flat or low in slope, you will often get what is called built-up roofing, alternate layers of roofing felt and asphalt covered with a top surface of gravel or white marble chips. It may last five years or twenty to twenty-five years, depending on the number of layers or plies. Five plies are recommended; fewer mean shorter life and expensive upkeep. Cheap quality two- or three-ply roofing is too often used, which is why flat and low-slope roofs frequently deteriorate and leak in a maddeningly short time. Ask about the number of plies, or if it is a ten-, fifteen-, or twenty-year roof. This is a key question.

There is also what is called roll roofing, generally a second-grade material. It comes in rolls of asphalt sheet material, cemented down and overlapped on the roof, one layer after the other up to the top of the roof. By and large, roll roofing can be as good or better than the cheapest built-up roof but not as good as a four- or five-ply built-up roof. Use the heaviest roll roofing you can get.

Wood Roofing

Wood shingles and shakes are generally considered the next steps up in quality and price over asphalt. They may cost from 25 to 100 per cent more than asphalt shingles, and are lowest in price in the West near the great lumber forests. Shipping costs make them more expensive in the East.

The increased quality over asphalt depends on the kind of wood shingle; the thicker the wood, the better the quality. The cheapest are wood shingles approximately ⅜ inch thick which will last fifteen to twenty-five years, more or less. Then comes what are called wood shakes which vary from ⅜ up to about 1½ inches thick. The best shakes are the heaviest and thickest ones, usually ¾ to 1½ inches thick; they are normally good for fifty years or more.

It is often charged that wood shingles are a fire hazard. Its competitors make a big thing of this, but in the heat of a sales battle their charges may go too far. It is true that the codes in some localities prohibit wood shingles. But they are today less of a fire hazard than they formerly were. The thinnest wood shingles pose the greatest fire hazard, especially in a heavily populated area. Fire is less of a hazard with the better, thicker kinds. Besides, most household fires start within the house. Even a thick lead roof can't help you much then.

Permanent Roof Materials

These include asbestos cement shingles, tile, slate, copper, Terne and aluminum. Asbestos cement shingles are made of hard-wearing asbestos fiber and portland cement. They are somewhat higher in first cost than asphalt shingles but are the lowest in cost of the permanent roof covers. They come in various colors, give a pleasing striated appearance, are often indistinguishable from wood or asphalt, and are growing in popularity because of the much longer service they provide for comparatively small extra cost. They are somewhat brittle, however, and may crack if walked on. Use sneakers or soft shoes and insist that the TV repairman do the same, or lay down walk boards if he must go on the roof.

Ceramic tile, slate, and, Terne (tin-lead alloy) are the Cadillacs of roofing in quality and price. Most people associate tile with the oval-shaped, orange tiles seen on Spanish-style and California mission houses. Thick, flat tiles are more common today. They give a rich, substantial appearance. Both kinds will last for generations. But insist on "hard-burned" tile. When tapped with a coin it will ring with a clear tone. The cheaper, soft-burned kind is of uncertain quality and may not last long. Hit with a coin, it gives off a dull sound.

Like tile, slate also gives a handsome, durable roof. But because of cost plus heavy weight it is usually practical only within convenient shipping distances of slate quarries in Virginia, Pennsylvania, and Vermont. Like asbestos, both tile and slate are brittle. A misstep or stray home-run ball can crack them. Freezing rain and snow in winter also can mean occasional cracked shingles to be replaced.

Terne was quite popular during the late nineteenth century, was not used for a long while afterward, and is now said to be making a comeback. It is a good choice for a custom house that you expect to live in for a long time.

Aluminum shingles, recently introduced, are catching on because of long life, low upkeep, and high-sun heat reflectivity. They have a specially designed, striated surface texture, and come in various colors so that they resemble a wide conventional shingle. In bright sun, however, they glare. They are lightweight, easy to install, and will not rot, curl, or split. Cost in a typical house will range from about $200 to $400 more than conventional asphalt shingles. Though the metal itself should last indefinitely, the life expectancy of the bonded enamel surface finish has not been precisely determined; it is known to be good for about ten years at least. An aluminum roof generally requires that a house be well grounded to the earth for lightning protection. There is also aluminum-sheet roofing that is equally permanent but much less desirable for houses because of its industrial appearance. It is used primarily for farm buildings, barns and industrial structures.

Roof Color
Light colors are spreading in popularity since much pub-

licity has been given to their heat reflectivity which supposedly makes a house cooler in summer. This is not always true. Good heat reflectivity requires a smooth surface, as well as a light color. That is why smooth aluminum is even better at bouncing back the sun's heat than pure white (coarse surface) asphalt shingles. A light-colored roof, any kind, also can get dirty fast and reflectivity drops off sharply. By and large, a white or light-colored roof is good, but don't let it be the tail that wags the dog. Choose a medium or even dark color if it is better for over-all house appearance; the house can be kept just as cool in summer by good attic insulation and ventilation (as spelled out in the chapter on air conditioning).

CHAPTER 15

WHO CAN CHECK A HOUSE
FOR YOU?

Few people, unfortunately, make a full-time business of checking the *construction* of houses for buyers. For that matter, there are also certain "experts" not to use; they can do more harm than good.

A professional appraiser, for example, may be splendid for judging the market value of a house, what it is worth for financing purposes. But few of them really know much about construction. They do not probe the soundness of a structure, nor do they evaluate the condition and quality of various products and equipment in a house. Thus, you cannot ordinarily rely on an appraiser for a thorough structural check even if he is an FHA or VA appraiser.

A good choice, by and large, is an experienced architect or builder. He is familiar with construction, per se, the materials used, and the workmanship. But even the best architect or builder will usually tell you that you need a separate technical expert to judge such things as heating, plumbing, and wiring. (Houses are becoming so highly technical and complex that few people nowadays know everything there is to know about them.) If in doubt about these things, you should call in a reputable heating dealer, plumber, or electrician.

It is even more important, particularly when buying an existing house, to have checks by a termite expert and, if appropriate, a septic-tank expert. These two checks are just about mandatory in many parts of the United States. Both the VA and the FHA often require one or both, depending on geographical location. You can therefore call the nearest FHA or VA office for the names of the people *they* use for termite and septic-tank inspections.

Professional Experts

If you live in or near Chicago, Detroit, Indianapolis, Hackensack, New Jersey, or New York City, you can call on Home Inspection Consultants, Inc., one of the first engineering firms in the country established for checking new and old houses for prospective buyers. It expects to open up franchised branches in other cities, so check your phone book. Another similar firm in the New York area only, so far, is Home Inspection Service.

Both use professional engineers who will give you an exhaustive report of their inspection. Cost of an inspection ranges from about $35 to $50 for houses priced up to $50,-000, one tenth of 1 per cent of house price for houses priced over $50,000. HIC's phone number in New York City is WIsconsin 7-8184; HIS is in Great Neck, New York, HU7-6280. Firms like these are best for judging house construction.

If you live in a city with a home service club like Allied Home Owners Association (branches in some seventy cities), you could call them for recommendations. Some of their branches can recommend experts, others cannot, depending on your city. Other such firms to look for in the telephone book are National Home Owners Club and Mr. Service Club.

"Experts" to Avoid

The man who may do more harm than good is your brother-in-law, a friend of a friend, or a carpenter acquaintance who will as a favor "be glad to look at that house for you." This can be risky, experience shows, because such people often feel compelled to find something wrong in order to justify their status as experts.

This puts you on the spot. The house may be perfectly good except, like most houses, for a minor flaw or two which the "expert" proceeds to blow up way out of proportion. If you go ahead and buy the house, you fly in the face of a personal relationship. It's therefore best to steer clear of friends or relatives and pick an objective person who is neither a friend nor relative.

One other thing about construction experts: They should stick to construction. Many a so-called expert has spoiled a good house deal by offering gratuitous advice about the architectural design or the neighborhood which *he* does not like. Or he says the house is overpriced. Well, most houses are overpriced, according to many people, except their own. The value of a house is something *you* should decide.

Again we stress that there is no perfect house. Most of us have to settle for something less than the ideal. What's more, we may like a particular house for personal or emotional reasons. We want an expert to tell us only that it is or is not in reasonably good structural condition and if not, what is wrong. And that's all.

CHAPTER 16

THE FEDERAL HOUSING
ADMINISTRATION (FHA)

Do you get a really well-built house if it is "approved" by the FHA? Not necessarily. The FHA insures mortgages made by private lenders. It insures a mortgage only if a house conforms with its minimum standards. These are spelled out in its Minimum Property Standards book. The operating word is *minimum*. House quality must be up to a certain minimum construction level so that it will be reasonably strong and safe.

Therefore a house that conforms with FHA's minimum rules is not necessarily the strongest, best-designed house you could get. The equipment in it is not necessarily of top quality. In fact, much borderline equipment will pass FHA's standards. In certain things like insulation, the FHA rules are lax, if not downright inadequate. (Don't blame the government, though. The FHA people have tried to stiffen their rules, but each time they have run into a wall of opposition from certain segments of the building industry —manufacturers whose products would not pass tougher standards—and from many builders who scream that raising the standards would raise their costs.)

New Emphasis on Quality

In recent years, however, the FHA people have hit on a new way of improving house quality without changing their basic rules. They place greater value on high-quality materials, such as extra-thick insulation, longer-lasting exterior wall surfaces, maintenance-free windows, heavyweight roofing, and so on. They figure that they can give higher mortgage value and better mortgage terms for houses built with top-quality materials because this in turn brings about lower year-to-year upkeep expense for the buyers—i.e., the buyer is a better mortgage risk. This increases the builder's incentive to use better-quality construction materials and is a big step in the right direction. However, this emphasis on quality construction, over and above the minimum accepted quality, is still a new thing. It has not caught on among many builders so far. In other words, most builders still go only as far as they have to in order to meet FHA's minimum standards. In time, it is hoped that more and more builders will discover the benefits of lifting their standards above minimum quality.

You will do well to build or buy a house that conforms to FHA's standards. You can be sure that it will be reasonably well built and by and large of higher quality than the usual house built according to no standards at all or only those of a local building code. But for a really good house you must go beyond FHA's minimum rules, particularly for such important things as heating, wiring, insulation, interior and exterior wall surfaces, flooring and roofing.

Why doesn't FHA take the bull by the horns and really raise construction quality? The reasons are complex and varied and go back to 1934 when the FHA, one of Franklin Roosevelt's most glittering New Deal creations, was established. Its prime purpose was to stir up building activity at a black period when practically no new houses were being built. The problem then was not so much to lift housing quality (which FHA incidentally did) but, more important, to get home building rolling again. To prevent jerry-built construction and insure reasonably good construction, it set up its minimum standards, a floor under quality.

These standards were a major innovation in U.S. housing. They have been periodically brought up to date and still are your best available safeguard. The ultimate tribute to them is that most banks and savings-and-loan associations lean heavily on them for houses financed with conventional mortgages.

Defects in FHA-Insured Houses

Suppose you buy a house with an FHA-insured mortgage and it turns out later to have a major structural flaw.

What can you do? Not too much, unfortunately. FHA is neither a police enforcement agency nor a service organization. You should notify the FHA of such a flaw, giving them your case number and telling what you think is wrong. An FHA representative will inspect the trouble. If the builder is at fault, FHA will try to persuade him to correct the trouble, but legally they cannot force him. If the builder refuses, FHA's only weapon is to cut him out of the FHA-mortgage business by blackballing him. This power alone is usually enough to keep recalcitrant builders in line, particularly large builders who depend much on FHA financing. But if you bought your house from an indifferent builder who doesn't need FHA, or a used house from a seller who does not give one rap for FHA, there is little either you or the FHA can do about it. It's a bitter pill to swallow, but that's the way things are.

New vs. Old-House Defects

Defects are more likely to show up in an old house than in a new house bought with an FHA mortgage. FHA men make regular inspections of new houses during construction and can catch many mistakes, but since they are human an occasional defect will get by.

A stringent structural inspection, however, is not the rule for existing houses financed with FHA-insured mortgages—or with any other kind of mortgage financing, for that matter. Like other appraisers, FHA appraisers are not construction experts, and they make relatively little attempt to evaluate structural soundness thoroughly. This is not their business, both FHA and they claim. They are concerned chiefly with such things as the size of the house and its rooms, neighborhood characteristics, number of bathrooms, and other overt features that influence the market value of the house. Of course, an obvious flaw such as run-down exterior paint will cause them to downgrade the house value. But that's about as deep as they probe.

FHA has come under attack for these reasons. Home-owners charge that they thought they were getting good houses because the houses had been checked out by FHA appraisers, but later serious structural flaws turned up. This is FHA's fault, they charge. But unfortunately, FHA cannot be held responsible, according to a 1961 U. S. Supreme Court ruling, and the buyer is left holding the bag. The court ruled that Congress did not write in such protection for buyers when it passed the original housing law setting up FHA.

In short, you generally cannot rely much on an FHA appraisal or, for that matter, any other appraisal when you buy a house, particularly an existing house. A house may be appraised at a fairly high figure, but this is little assurance that the structure is in sound condition. You will still need an inspection by an unbiased construction expert.

Incidentally, there is no such thing as an FHA-approved house. FHA will neither approve nor disapprove a house in the sense that the design and construction get a stamp of approval. FHA requires only that a house meet its minimum standards to be eligible for an FHA-insured mortgage. Some builders advertise "FHA-approved" houses to sneak across the idea that their houses are superior. This is tricky.

CHAPTER 17

CENTRAL AIR CONDITIONING

There are four good reasons why you should seriously consider installing central air conditioning when you build or buy a new house today or else provide a few inexpensive provisions that will enable you to install it later at minimum cost.

First, central air conditioning for houses is rapidly growing in popularity. Within a few years a house without it may well suffer in resale value. Second, it costs considerably less to install central air conditioning in a new house than to install it after the house is finished. Third, air conditioning brings about marvelous health and other benefits in addition to sheer cool comfort, not only in the South but in the North, too. And fourth, both the initial cost and the operating cost have been brought down; they are, in fact, much less than many people believe.

Central air conditioning began making headway in American houses in the early 1950s. By the end of 1960 more than one million U.S. houses were equipped with central cooling systems, and new installations were being made at a rate of over 200,000 a year. It is already considered essential for new houses priced as low as $20,000 in parts of the South; without it many people would not buy them. This trend is picking up speed and spreading northward. Here is what to know about air-conditioning a house and how you can enjoy it at minimum cost.

Air-Conditioning Cost

Cost is lowest when central air conditioning is combined with forced warm-air heat. Then the total installation cost for central cooling in a new house, over the cost of heating, ranges from about $650 to $1000 in houses of up to about

	CENTRAL AIR CONDITIONING		OPERATING COST	
	Approx. elec. rate for cooling ¢ per kw-hr	Approx. hours of operation per summer	Cost per ton of cooling capacity, per summer	Average total cost for typical 1200 sq. ft. houses (2 tons)
Akron, Ohio	.0185 cents	600	$18 per ton per summer	$36
Charlotte, N. C.	.02	1000	31.40	62
Chicago, Ill.	.025	500	18	36
Corpus Christi, Texas	.02	3500	53	100
Denver, Colo.	.02	1000	25	50
Detroit, Mich.	.02	500	12	24
Ft. Worth, Tex.	.02	1400	50	100
Kansas City, Mo.	.025	900	33	66
Madison, Wis.	.023	300	21	42
New York, N.Y.	.021	500	21	42
Okla. City, Okla.	.021	1000	32	64
Salt Lake City, Utah	.0155	750	11.50	23
Phila., Pa.	.018	800	20	40
San Francisco, Calif.	.0128	1000	30	60
St. Louis, Mo.	.02	1000	28	56
Tampa, Fla.	.015	1750	30	60
Tucson, Ariz.	.0165	2200	65	125
Long Island, N.Y.	.02	750	25	50

Fig. 23 How much does air conditioning cost where you live? *The American Home.*

1400 square feet; from $1000 to $1350 for houses of up to about 2000 square feet; from $1400 to about $2000 for houses up to 3000 square feet. The exact cost you pay will vary according to the size of your house, the construction, climate zone, and equipment quality.

Operating costs range from about $50 a summer for a typical 1500-square-foot house in the North, up to about $100 a summer for the same size house in the Deep South. These are average figures based on actual bills for three and a half months of central cooling in the North up to five and a half months of cooling in the hot South. They are also based on an average national electric rate of 2¢ per kilowatt hour. Your cost will be slightly higher or lower therefore, according to whether electricity costs you more or less than 2¢ per Kwh.

Operating costs are even lower than the average for houses carefully designed for air conditioning. In South Bend, Indiana, for example, a builder named Andy Place guarantees that total annual heating and cooling operating bills in his 1150- to 1600-square-foot houses (selling for up to $21,000) will not exceed $150 a year. The bills received by families who have bought his houses actually run from $110 to $125 a year, which is not bad. Summer cooling accounts for about 30 per cent of the total annual bills.

And in Dallas, Texas, one of the hottest cities in the country, 1500- to 1600-square-foot houses (selling for up to $19,000) are heated and cooled the year around for an average of $9.30 a month, less than $120 a year. These are average figures for houses built and sold by Dallas builders, Fox & Jacobs.

Design for Lowest-Cost Air Conditioning

Cooling costs are held low in the South Bend and Dallas houses chiefly because the houses themselves pass three key tests for low-cost air conditioning. The over-all aim is to put a lid on outdoor heat entry in summer. (At the same time, heat leakage from the house is slowed down sharply in winter and you benefit a second time by reduced heating fuel bills.) Here is what the tests are:

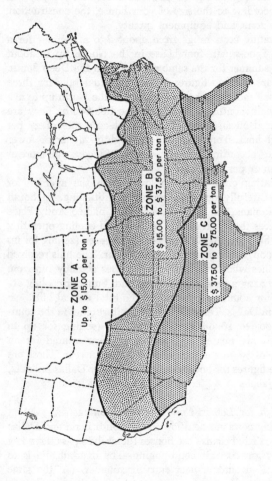

Fig. 24 Map shows estimated operating cost range for central air conditioning over a complete summer, based on an electric rate of 1½¢ per kilowatt hour. Exact cost for a particular house will vary according to house design, equipment quality, and family habits. Carrier Corp.

ZONE A. Up to $15.00 per ton

ZONE B $15.00 to $37.50 per ton

ZONE C $37.50 to $75.00 per ton

1. Is there plenty of thermal insulation? Follow the "R" formula given in the insulation chapter: in general, a minimum of six inches of insulation over ceilings, three inches in walls, and two inches for the floor of a non-basement house.

2. Are large window areas shaded from direct sunshine in summer? A staggering amount of sun heat will enter a house through glass. Windows on the east, west, and south require shading. Windows on the south often can be adequately shaded by roof overhangs, but not always. Windows on the east and west require other shading devices. Shade trees are excellent; other ideas are sun "fences" and outside awnings. Even better is good orientation—a house built with a minimum of exposed glass on the vulnerable east and west sides. A shading device on the outside of the window, by the way, is about twice as effective as a shade on the inside.

3. Is there plenty of attic ventilation? The roof is the biggest single source of summer-heat entry in houses. In addition to thick ceiling insulation, the attic should be thoroughly ventilated to prevent intense heat build-up. Attic vents should be made large. A light-colored or white roof also can help reduce air-conditioning costs (by bouncing back sunrays). But don't count too much on a white roof, because, as noted earlier, it inevitably gets dirty; the dirtier it gets, the lower its heat reflectivity.

Naturally, extra insulation, shading devices, and large attic vents cost money. They may increase the construction cost of the average house by perhaps $150 to $250, depending on how well the house was initially designed. But you get this money back in two ways. First, a smaller heating and air-conditioning system than otherwise required often can be used. This reduces the first cost of the heating and cooling systems. Half the time this saving alone more than pays for the extra construction cost for air-conditioning design. Second, operating costs for heating and cooling are cut by as much as 25 to 50 per cent a year.

The Air-Conditioning System

Check on the air-conditioning dealer above all. He should

be experienced in home cooling and be able to show you successful systems he has installed in other houses. Sometimes you will do well to handle the air-conditioning contract yourself when you build or buy a new house. You don't have to deal through the builder. Get an allowance for the heating and air conditioning and arrange it yourself. Get bids from two or three dealers. Don't fall for the lowest bid price or for a flat installation charge. Make sure that the dealer you pick is providing all the equipment, accessories and ductwork that the others specified.

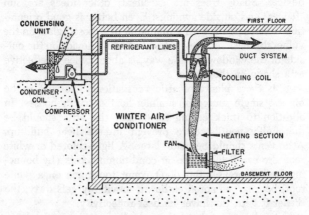

Fig. 25 The most common kind of central air conditioning is called a split system. The furnace and cooling-coil assembly are located inside the house and connected by refrigerant tubes to compressor-condenser section located outside (for access to outdoor air). It is an air-cooled system; no water is needed for operation. The same system can be used in non-basement houses with interior section located in utility room or garage.

It is also best to stick with the equipment of a top national manufacturer, such as Carrier, G.E., Lennox, Westinghouse, or York. Dealers who handle brands like these tend to be the most competent dealers. In any case, the equipment you get should carry the certification seal of the Air Conditioning & Refrigeration Institute (ARI). Equipment without this certification should be turned down.

How Much Cooling Capacity?

This should be given in B.T.U.s per hour. (One ton of cooling is equivalent to 12,000 B.T.U.s per hour. A ton is an amount of cooling equivalent to the cooling effect given off by a ton of ice melting over a twenty-four-hour period.) In general, houses require one ton of cooling capacity for every 500 to 600 square feet of air-conditioned area. A 1000- to 1200-square-foot house, therefore, would require a two-ton system. If, however, your house is very well insulated and designed for low-cost cooling, only one ton of capacity may be needed for every 700 to 800 square feet of floor area.

How Cool Inside?

The cooling system should be guaranteed to maintain the house interior at 75 degrees and 50 per cent relative humidity during the hottest summer weather where you live. Thus, the equipment should be capable of lowering the house temperature by 20 degrees in cities like New York and Chicago where the highest summer temperature (called outside-design temperature) is 95 degrees; and 30 degrees if you live in Phoenix or in Bakersfield, California, say, where the highest outside temperature averages 105 degrees.

An air-conditioning dealer may casually tell you that 80 degrees inside is all you need, and that is all he will guarantee. Or that an air-conditioning system should be designed to reduce the indoor temperatures by 10 to 15 degrees below outdoors and that's all. This is nonsense, even though mistakenly believed by some air-conditioning people and some doctors, too.

The fact is that nearly all humans require about 75 degrees and 50 per cent relative humidity indoors for comfort in summer. This is the temperature and humidity people require for comfort in offices, factories, and homes. It is borne out by exhaustive research sponsored by the American Society of Heating, Refrigerating & Air-Conditioning Engineers. And it is required indoors for comfort regardless of what the outdoor temperature may be. The body has no built-in radar telling it what is going on outdoors when you are indoors.

The Heat Pump

Most year-round central air-conditioning equipment is electrically powered for cooling. The heating side is designed to burn either gas or oil fuel. There is also what is called the heat pump, a device that provides both heating in winter and cooling in summer by means of electricity only. Gas or oil fuel is not required. The mechanism used is actually a standard refrigerating compressor unit, much the same as a conventional air conditioner. In summer, heat is wrung out of the house air and discharged outdoors. In winter, the cycle is reversed and heat is extracted from outdoor air (or water) and pumped indoors.

A heat pump therefore does away with the need for oil or gas fuel, its biggest feature. But it is also somewhat the same as using electric heat in winter. Thus, the heat pump is not recommended in a cold climate *unless* your electric-power rate is as low as it should be for conventional electric heat—i.e., no higher than 1¢ to 1.5¢ per kilowatt hour. Electricity cost is less important in the South. With a heat pump, a house also should be insulated and weather-stripped to the hilt, as recommended earlier for straight electric heat. Summer operating costs for cooling with a heat pump are about the same as they are for conventional electric air conditioning.

Summed up, the heat pump is a better bet in the South than in the North. And because it is an intricate mechanism and comparatively new, only a top-grade national brand should be used. Don't accept an unknown brand. And deal only with a reputable, well-established dealer.

Air-Cooled vs. Water-Cooled Units

Nearly all air-conditioning units, including the heat pump, require outdoor air (like a window cooler) or running water for operation; i.e., they are either air- or water-cooled. The air-cooled kind is generally better, particularly if you live where water is scarce or expensive. It not only eliminates the extra operating cost for water consumption, but it also requires less service and upkeep. A water-cooled model is good only if you have a limitless supply of low-cost water, an inexhaustible well, or your own private mountain lake.

Central Cooling vs. Individual Room Conditioners

For air-conditioning a whole house, a central system will almost always get the nod over individual room units. A central system gives you more cooling capacity per dollar, since one large unit is more efficient than a series of small ones. Operating costs are lower, service and maintenance are less expensive, and a central unit also will last considerably longer than individual room coolers. But in older houses, individual units are frequently the answer.

Provisions for Future Air Conditioning

If you build or buy a new house without air conditioning but plan on installing it sometime in the future, much money can be saved if a few provisions for the future air conditioning are made when the house is built. There are five simple things to do:

1) Warm-air heating should be used with the air ducts sized for cooling as well as heating, since ducts must be larger for cool-air flow than for warm air only. 2) The supply air outlets (registers) should be of the kind approved for cooling as well as heating. This calls for registers with adjustable louvers, not the fixed (non-adjustable) louvers often used for heating only. 3) The furnace blower should be large enough for cooling as well as heating. Many blowers are not. 4) The house electric supply should be large enough to take on the additional cooling load, with a spare 240-volt electric circuit set aside and earmarked for cooling. 5) The supply air ducts from the furnace to the house should be insulated if they travel through a space that will not be air-conditioned, such as the attic, garage, utility room. Ducts in the basement, however, normally do not need insulation.

You should also request that a cooling "plenum" be installed with the furnace in advance. This is an empty sheet-metal enclosure usually located atop the furnace. It remains empty until the air conditioning is installed. Then the cooling coil later can be easily slipped into it with a minimum of fuss and expense. In all, these initial provisions for central air conditioning may cost as much as $30 to $50 when a house is built. But they can reduce the cost of installing central air conditioning later by $250 to $500. In effect, they enable the installation of central cooling in a finished house almost as cheaply as it is done in a new house.

The Benefits: What Air Conditioning Does for You

Many people think of air conditioning as merely air cooling when it is uncomfortably hot outdoors. This is only part of the story. Air conditioning also brings a variety of other delightful benefits. It dehumidifies the air, giving freedom from wringing-wet humidity—a major benefit in northern cities where the summer humidity is as insufferable as the heat; the house is kept dry and mildew is banished.

Air conditioning also means a quieter and cleaner house, since closed windows shut out outside noise and dirt. It brings relief to people suffering from asthma, hay fever, and other allergies, since the average air-conditioning filter removes 99 per cent of the pollen in summer air. It is a boon for people with ailments such as heart trouble, since merely moving around in 95-degree heat puts about as much strain on the body as heavy manual labor in cool weather.

Other benefits cited by families in air-conditioned homes are: sharply reduced house-cleaning chores, reduced hot-weather mental fatigue, better sleep at night, fewer summer colds, savings on the cost of screens, less money spent on eating out in summer just to beat the heat, no more heat rash (particularly with infants), a better-working refrigerator, less frequent tuning for the piano, more hot meals cooked in summer.

Misconceptions about Air Conditioning

A few air-conditioning misconceptions should be cleared

up. Many people associate air conditioning with cold, clammy conditions encountered in overchilled restaurants and theaters which were generally the first public places to get old forms of air conditioning. Present-day equipment has come a long way since these systems were installed. In addition, movies and restaurants often are deliberately over-cooled, whereas an air-conditioning system in a house can be set to the exact temperature and humidity a family desires.

It is not true that air conditioning is unhealthy. Some people, to be sure, catch colds when abruptly exposed to air conditioning. Experience shows, however, that families with air conditioning have fewer colds than families without. One reason, perhaps, is that people with air conditioning sleep better and eat better in summer and therefore maintain better body resistance to stray cold germs. And with air conditioning there is much less likelihood of getting overheated and soaked with sweat on a hot day.

What about "thermal shock," the strain on the body experienced when you go from 95-degree heat into an air-conditioned house (at 75 degrees)? This is not damaging to people in good health, according to exhaustive research at the University of Illinois College of Medicine. It is no more damaging than stepping out of your 70-degree house in winter into the cold 30-degree outdoors—a 40-degree drop.

A sudden, sharp change in temperature and humidity may, however, be distressing to, or cause unwanted strain on, people with a weak heart. Such people should avoid abrupt temperature changes. In an air-conditioned house they could have the entrance foyer set at a temperature about halfway between indoors and out as a sort of decompression chamber. Better still, they should avoid excessive heat and humidity and during heat waves stay indoors with air conditioning, not expose themselves to the harshly debilitating effects of the hot humid outdoors.

Air-Conditioning Check List
1. Is the cooling system properly sized for your house?

Too small a unit obviously will not provide adequate cooling and dehumidification during a heat wave. An oversized unit can be just as bad, since too much capacity causes erratic operation and poor humidity control. The amount of cooling required must be individually computed for each house. This is called a heat-gain computation.

As a rule of thumb, a house with ordinary amounts of insulation will require one ton (12,000 B.T.U.s per hour) of air conditioning for every 500 to 600 square feet of floor area. A three-ton unit will take a house of from 1500 to 1800 square feet. A house with thick insulation all around coupled with good over-all air-conditioning design will require only about one ton of cooling capacity for every 700 to 800 square feet.

2. Does the cooling unit carry the certification seal of the Air Conditioning & Refrigeration Institute? It should.

3. Is the system being installed by a reputable dealer? How long has he been in business? Does he sell a top-grade, nationally known brand? What is his reputation for service? Get names of people whose houses he has air-conditioned and ask them about the quality of his work.

4. Is the equipment air-cooled, or is water required for operation? Insist on an air-cooled unit unless plenty of cheap water is available.

5. Is the duct work properly installed? This may be difficult to judge unless you are an engineer, but it is nevertheless highly important. Like heating, the most expensive cooling equipment will not work well unless the duct work is right. Does the duct work look well put together? Or is it sloppy and poorly made? Notice how the duct work is connected to the equipment. Is there a short piece of canvas connecting the equipment to the beginning of the ducts? As it does with heating, this will prevent noise and vibration transmission through the house, and its presence is also an indication of good workmanship throughout. If there is no canvas connection, the whole job may be of low quality. Do any of the ducts travel through un-air-conditioned spaces like the attic or garage? If so, they must be insulated.

6. What about the controls? There should be automatic

thermostatic control for both heating and cooling. Two or more individual thermostats—zone control—are recommended for most two-story and split-level houses.

7. Is the system guaranteed for at least one year? The builder and dealer should provide a written guarantee that the air conditioning will provide satisfactory operation that long or the necessary repairs will be made at no charge.

8. If central air conditioning is not furnished but you plan on getting it at a future time, are the five essential needs for future air conditioning included?

PART 5

SHOULD YOU BUY OR BUILD?

Two out of every three home buyers choose a used house.
The one out of three who buys a new house is most likely,
by far, to buy a ready-built house from a builder; fewer
and fewer people tackle the job of building their own
homes or having a house built for them. This division of
choices would indicate that used houses have more appeal
than new houses and, on the other hand, that building a
custom house apparently is the most expensive and troublesome proposition of all nowadays.

Which should *you* do? This section presents the case for
and against each choice, starting with buying an old house,
the most common choice. It tells why an old house is often
your best buy and how to spot the most common defects
encountered in old houses; the pitfalls to avoid when you
buy a ready-built house from a builder, or have a house
built for you; and important facts about prefabricated
houses, which are growing steadily in volume and popularity (for good reasons).

CHAPTER 18

BUYING AN OLD HOUSE
(One to 250 years old)

A man and his wife were on the verge of buying an elegant, thirty-five-year-old house with a huge thirty-foot living room, French doors, and other appealing features. It seemed a bargain at $28,000. But before closing the deal they had the house checked by an expert. Probing behind the expensive wood paneling in the downstairs game room, he discovered that the house was riddled with termites. Repairs would have cost an estimated $6000. The couple pulled out of the deal just in time.

Another couple found a sixty-six-year-old Victorian house with five bedrooms and a sweeping hillside view of a scenic river. Its price was a low $17,000, but it was in obvious need of repairs. An inspection showed that needed improvements would cost about $3000. They bought it. The same amount of space in a new house would have cost about $30,000. Today they are more delighted than ever with their buy.

Biggest Old-House Feature

These true incidents point up fundamental guides for buying an old house—any house one year to 250 years old. The biggest single feature of old houses is space, up to 50 per cent more space, sometimes more, than in new houses for the same money. But the cost of repairs and improvements could get out of hand. What may seem a bargain at first glance may be a Trojan horse loaded with troubles. This puts emphasis on checking for hidden defects, as well as obvious remodeling needs. A construction expert should be called in, especially for any house more than five or ten years old. (Experts to call on are discussed in Chapter 15.)

Age of the house should not limit your choice. To be

sure, the older a house, the more likely repairs are needed. On the other hand, some old houses have been the object of loving care from previous owners. The exact age, however, can indicate certain common flaws for reasons given in a moment. So find out when the house was built. This can tell more than the seller realizes.

Get estimates on the cost of repairs and improvements needed. The cost of such work plus the sales price will be your true total cost. Determine the house size in total square feet of living area. Compare this with the going price per square foot for new houses nearby (anywhere from $12 to $20 a square foot for a development house, more for a custom house). It will help you decide if it is a bargain.

Other Advantages of a Used House

You move into an established neighborhood and avoid the usual growing pains of a new development. Trees and grass are already there. Taxes are somewhat more stable. There is less likelihood of extra assessments for new roads and sewers. Schools, stores, and churches are usually nearby. Commuting to work may be quicker, less expensive. You can move in at once. And more and more used houses are being put on the market at reduced prices. Or after putting their houses up for sale at unrealistically high prices, owners will come down in price considerably.

Is the house well designed? The basic rules for a good floor plan, room arrangement, and so on have been noted earlier. Two highly common flaws in older houses are old-fashioned kitchens and inadequate bathrooms. Remodeling a kitchen can cost anywhere from $2500 to $5000 depending on the house and personal requirements. But be sure there is enough space to start with (noted in kitchen section), unless you don't mind tearing down walls and rebuilding from scratch.

Installing a new half-bath will generally cost from $750 to $1200. This is needed on the first floor of old two-story houses. Is there a place for one? A half-bath or powder room, fortunately, can be shoe-horned into a cubbyhole as small as 28 × 42 inches, no bigger than a closet. A full bath requires at least 5×7 feet and will cost from about $1200 to as much as $2500.

Here it is strongly emphasized that the estimated cost figures given above and below for repairs and remodeling are *approximations* based on average costs for typical houses. Their purpose is to give you a general idea of what to figure. To play safe, figure on the high side. Even better, get several firm estimates before you buy.

The Importance of Location

The location of a house, the climate zone, or a special condition peculiar to the area is important. Wet basements are widespread in areas with damp soil such as Long Island and much of New Jersey. Cracked or settled foundations are a special problem in marshy places, as around New Orleans and particularly in houses close to the levees. They are also a problem in houses built on filled or reclaimed land that was once marshy.

Septic-tank and cesspool troubles are prevalent with damp, low-lying ground or sandy soil, such as along the Atlantic Seaboard from Long Island south and including almost all of Florida. Rusty water pipes are troublesome in cities like Philadelphia with highly corrosive or hard water. On the other hand, run-down water heaters are most likely, as noted before, in areas with soft water that is nevertheless murder on water heaters.

Roofs are more likely to need repair or replacement in the hot South, due to the intense heat; the sun is savagely hard on a roof in hot, dry, west Texas, New Mexico, and Arizona. Deficient air-conditioning systems are more probable in the South, where the first ones were installed and where they labor hardest. Conversely, heating systems are more likely to be run-down in the coldest parts of the North.

Before starting out to judge an old house, arm yourself with a few tools: a clip board, paper, and pencil for taking notes; a fifty-foot tape; a flashlight to look into dark corners; knife or ice pick to detect termites and wood rot; a magnet to determine if pipes are iron or non-ferrous (copper, brass, or bronze); a level to check structural trueness;

a screwdriver; pliers; four-foot ladder; and coveralls for crawling under porches and into crawl spaces.

Seem elaborate? Not for the largest single purchase you've ever made—and one you will have to live with . . . and in.

The Most Widespread Flaws

Home Inspection Consultants, Inc., found that in a random sampling of 1000 houses over ten years old it had inspected for prospective buyers, the two main flaws were inadequate wiring in 84 per cent of the houses, and termites or wood rot in 58 per cent. In all, there are nine parts of an old house that deserve special attention before you buy. The older the house, the more the likelihood of these flaws.

This is not to say that all old houses are rife with defects. By and large, only two or three of the most common flaws may be present in a typical older house, and such flaws are not likely to be severe in a house less than ten years old. Since each of the following also is discussed in detail elsewhere in this book, some repetition is unavoidable. Conversely, reference to the other sections on the same subjects will provide helpful additional knowledge about each.

1. *Inadequate wiring* (the most widespread flaw of all). *The older the house, the poorer the wiring is likely to be unless a previous owner has rewired. Look for a three-wire, 240-volt, 100-ampere capacity main electric board, more for large houses or if there is an electric range or electric heat. You can sometimes see three wires from the electric pole to the house. Two wires mean an obsolete 120-volt service. Be sure you're looking at the overhead electric wires to the meter, not the telephone wires. The amperage capacity is normally noted on the main electric board. (There is also an amperage figure on the meter, but this is something else again.)*

The main electric board is usually located near or next to the electric meter. Open up its front panel; this generally requires turning the main switch at its side to the "off" position. Count the number of fuses or circuit breakers. If there are fewer than six or eight, electric modernization will probably be needed, particularly if your family comes loaded with major appliances.

In general, most houses built prior to World War II were equipped with a small 120-volt, thirty-ampere electric service. A sixty-ampere service became more common in houses built in the late 1940s and early 1950s. An adequate 240-volt, 100-ampere service did not become accepted practice in new houses until around the middle 1950s. Extra wiring capacity may have been added to many an older house in helter-skelter fashion as the family added appliances but often it is then necessary to replace the accumulated mess with one new large wiring center.

Also look for an adequate number of electric outlets, switches, and lighting fixtures throughout the house. In general, there should be at least one electric outlet in each wall of every room, two or more in long walls, at least two or three outlets concentrated above the kitchen counter-top work space for appliances, a wall switch for every ceiling light fixture and a light-control switch at each door in rooms with two or more doors (ideal wiring but seldom found).

New wiring will cost from about $250 up to $750 for a typical old house. Figure $150 to about $250 for a new 100-ampere electric service and main board; plus $7 to $9 for each new outlet and light switch needed; plus $25 to $50 for each special circuit for such things as a clothes drier or air conditioner.

2. *Termite damage and wood rot. These occur mostly in houses more than five to ten years old and are hard to detect unless you are an expert. So hire a termite expert to check the house. Many FHA and VA offices require this before they will approve a mortgage on an old house. The importance of a termite check cannot be overemphasized. Wood rot can be determined at the same time.*

A termite check calls for careful probing of the foundation and base wood structure of a house inside and out. A probing tool such as an ice pick can be used if you try it yourself. Dig your knife or a pick into all wood at or near ground level at two to three foot intervals around the inside and the outside of the house. The wood should be hard and tough. But if a beam is eaten away on the inside, the pick will sink into it and tell you so. Look also for termites' flattened mud tunnels leading up a foundation wall into the house, another telltale sign. Termites can be present without visible signs to the untutored eye; don't feel safe just because there is no obvious evidence of their presence.

On the other hand, don't give up a house and flee just because there are termites. The damage is not always extensive. Cost of repairing termite damage can range from about $150 to $5000 or more. That is why a thorough check should be made in advance. If extensive damage is discovered, get accurate estimates of repairs needed from two or more firms.

In recent years termite damage has been discovered for the first time in many northern communities, in New York, Connecticut, and New Jersey, for example. Because termites spend as long as five to ten years getting a foothold in a house before they are discovered, they are believed to be present even farther north, in areas where they never have been before. Wood rot on the other hand, is as common in the coldest northern states as in the South.

3. *Run-down heating. Many houses over twenty-five years old were built with a coal heating plant which may have been converted to oil or gas. If the original hot water or steam heat is still in a house twenty-five years or older, how much longer it will last is questionable. Look on the boiler name plate to see if it is cast iron or steel. The cast-iron kind is likely to last longer. If the heater is a large, old hot-air gravity furnace with no fan, it too is likely to expire at any time. In fact, an old gravity furnace still in a house today will almost always call for a new furnace within a few years. It is a serious drawback.*

What about the general condition of the heater? Does it look patched and bandaged, or fairly rugged and sturdy? A heater wrapped in white asbestos can well mean a sick unit that would collapse except for the wrapping. Look inside the heater for cracks and corrosion, outside and particularly around the base for rust and deterioration.

Is the heater large enough for the house? This can be

difficult if not impossible to ascertain except by a visit on a cold day. In any case, have the heating system turned on. Set the thermostat up to 80 degrees and listen for operating noise. How long does it take for heat to reach each room after starting? A warm-air system should provide heat within ten or fifteen minutes, a hot-water or steam system within a half hour.

A warm-air system should operate without bothersome noise. A good steady flow of air, though not a great blast, should come from the air outlets in each room. If the warm-air discharge is slow and seemingly inadequate, this is sometimes caused by a dirty filter at the furnace and is easily corrected. But if the filter is clean and the heat is still slow, the trouble can be serious.

If heating is by means of a hot-water or steam system, the radiators in each room should be hot. A cold, laggard radiator can mean either a bad air-vent valve which can be corrected easily or a basic defect that is expensive to correct. An expert can tell you which. The radiators on the top floor should be compared with those on the first floor. If heat output from each is not roughly equal, there may be a basic distribution problem.

Look at the water-pressure level in the glass gauge on top of the boiler as the steam builds up. It should not fluctuate more than half an inch. If it bounces wildly up and down something is radically wrong, a dirt-clogged boiler, for instance. With the steam full up, the water level should not read higher than two pounds per square inch (p.s.i.) of pressure on a mild day, no higher than five p.s.i. on a really cold day. All radiators should be hot within forty-five minutes to an hour at most. Slower response is generally the result of a boiler that is either undersized, dirty, crippled, or senile. If the radiators hiss, this generally means worn vent valves, but they are easy to replace.

Does the heater burn gas, oil, or coal? Gas burners last the longest and are generally best of all, provided gas rates are not high where you live, as mentioned earlier. If in doubt about an oil burner, a serviceman should give it a combustion test. (He checks the temperature of the exhaust gases leaving the heater. They should not exceed 600 degrees F. after twenty to thirty minutes; the CO_2 content of the flue gas which should be between $8\frac{1}{2}$ and 14 per cent; and among other things, the burner flame which should be bright yellow with orange tips and *no smoke*.) Look and sniff around the bottom of the oil tank and on the floor below the tank for signs of oil. If there are, the tank probably leaks and you will need a new one.

As for coal heat, experts say that it is risky to convert a coal unit to automatic gas or oil if the equipment is more than fifteen to twenty years old. So if it is older, you might want to figure on replacing the entire heating plant, not merely adapting it to gas or oil.

Radiant heat should be approached warily. Defects are difficult to correct. Though a good system when properly installed, radiant heat often is just not installed as well as it should be, particularly in development houses. It is less likely to be troublesome if encountered in a custom-built house. It should have indoor-outdoor temperature controls (a small temperature-sensing device on an outside wall wired to the inside controls).

Take the name and phone number of the heating dealer who services the system. This is usually noted on or near the heating unit. Ask him about the system. What kind of repairs are needed? How long will the system last? He may or may not come clean with you, but what you could learn is worth the effort.

Installed cost of a new warm-air furnace starts at about $500 to $750, a new hot-water boiler from $750 to $1500. The cost of a complete new heating system can run from $1500 to $4000, depending on house size.

4. *Sagging structure. The foundation may have settled and wrenched the house out of joint, or beams may have sagged as a result of wood rot. Look carefully at the squareness of the exterior walls, for level windows and doors, and for a level first floor. At each corner of the house, stand about two feet back and sight laterally straight down the wall for trueness. A major bulge or protruberance with bent or broken wall siding spells trouble. A few inches out*

of plumb, however, is usually of small importance. Inside the house, the condition of basement beams and supporting columns is particularly important. Notice also if doors line up evenly with their frames.

Nearly all houses settle somewhat after a few years, so do not panic if the structure is not straight as an arrow. On the other hand, severely cracked walls, windows and doors out of joint, and sloping floors should be thoroughly looked into. Sometimes an old house may only need one or two new supporting posts and beams underneath at a cost of a few hundred dollars. But a major structural flaw can require extensive rebuilding at a cost of $2000 to $5000, perhaps more. Get accurate estimates beforehand on the cost of shoring up the house.

5. *Poor plumbing. Common troubles are inadequate water pressure due to clogged or corroded pipes, and a bad septic-tank system. Bad plumbing is mostly a problem in houses with iron or steel pipes that are twenty-five years old or older. Copper tubing, brass, and bronze pipes will last much longer (though copper was not introduced until about 1940). With a magnet you can tell if the pipes are iron or steel. They will attract the magnet, but copper, brass, or bronze will not. Test for water pressure by turning on the faucets in the top-floor bathroom. Turn on the bathtub and sink faucets and flush the toilet at the same time. If the water slows down to a bare trickle you can expect plumbing woes. The pressure in the street mains, however, may be low, and then a booster pump will be needed. A call to the water company should tell you if street pressure is adequate.*

Is there a septic tank, a cesspool, or a city sewer? If no public sewer, be particularly cautious even if the house is comparatively new. Overloaded septic tanks and cesspools are major problems in many areas. Septic-tank problems are also more likely in a house with an automatic washing machine and several children. When was the septic tank or cesspool last cleaned? Cleaning is normally needed every three or four years. Who did the cleaning? Call him and ask about the condition of the tank. Another source of information about septic-tank problems is the public health department. They can often tell you if such problems are prevalent locally. New plumbing costs can vary greatly. Figure at least $750 to $1500, but get a plumber's estimate. Septic-tank repairs may run from $200 to $800.

6. *Roof and gutters. What kind of roof and how old is it? An asphalt shingle or built-up roof on a flat or low slope will often need repairs or replacement if it is more than ten to fifteen years old. Walk around the house, standing back, to inspect roof and gutters. A good roof will be even and uniform. A worn roof will contain broken, warped, or bent shingles, giving a ragged over-all appearance.*

To inspect a flat or nearly flat asphalt roof, go on the roof. Look for bare spots in the mineral surfacing, separations, breaks in the felt, and rusty flashing around the roof edges and around the chimney. Note the condition of the horizontal gutters, especially if they are wood. Are they clogged with leaves, or clean and well maintained? The best time to check for roof leaks and bad gutters is during a heavy rain. Check inside of the attic for water stains and discolorations, the ceiling below for stains and cracks.

Cost of patching a roof may run from $50 to $250. Cost of a good new asphalt roof will run from $20 to $30 per 100 square feet of roof surface, more if new flashing is needed or if there are many dormers and roof breaks. This means from $300 for a new roof for a small house or compact two-story house, up to about $750 for a roof of 2500 square feet of surface, more for better roofing or larger houses.

7. *Inadequate insulation. Almost all houses built before 1945 were built without insulation. Many houses built from World War II up to around 1955 were built with attic insulation but little or no wall insulation. Most houses built since 1955 got both wall and ceiling insulation, though not necessarily enough. Regardless of age, most houses with brick or stone walls do not have wall insulation.*

Nonetheless, insulation has been added to many houses. Attic insulation normally can be seen at the attic floor. Ask if wall insulation has been blown into the walls. During cold weather you can get an indication of insulation inside by holding your hand against the inside surface of an exterior wall. Then hold your hand against an interior partition. The exterior wall should not feel much colder than the inside wall. If it does, much heat is leaking out; there is little or no insulation.

Average cost of insulating an existing house runs about 20¢ to 30¢ per square foot of gross exterior wall surface, plus about 10¢ per square foot for the attic floor. Total cost: from $250 to $500 for a typical existing house (less for new houses).

8. *The faucet hot-water heater. Is it a separate water heater and tank? Or an indirect domestic water heater that is part of the regular boiler? If it is a separate tank heater, check the name plate for capacity and type, and judge it according to the standards in Chapter 13. Open the little door at the base of the tank where the pilot light and burner mechanism are; use a flashlight and look for signs of rust or leaks in here. These are the first indications of trouble brewing.*

The condition of a domestic water heater (integral with a regular hot-water house-heating boiler) is hard to ascertain unless you are an expert. The most common complaint about them is insufficient hot water. If possible, see if its heating capacity is given in gallons of hot water supplied per minute (g.p.m.), and then you can rate it also according to standards in Chapter 13. Installed cost of a new hot-water tank heater ranges from about $135 to $185 for a forty- to fifty-gallon gas-fired model, more for electric units. Failing water heaters are nearly as common in houses only four or five years old as in older ones.

9. *Wet basements. The basement floor and walls should look good and dry. But a basement that looks dry in August may be three inches under water in April. Stains on the walls and floor and flaky cement on the walls are the usual signs of wetness. So look carefully for signs of rot in the wood ceiling beams and the framing around the foundation walls. If they are mottled-looking, or pock-marked with stains like white measles, for example, wetness is prob-*

*ably a problem. The exterior of the foundation walls should
also look healthy. Or are they broken with bad cracks and
other signs of water penetration? Correcting a wet-basement
condition can be expensive and sometimes impossible if the
house was not properly built. It can cost from $500 to
$5000 or more, depending on the house.*

Other Checks for an Old House

Outside. Is the exterior paint in good condition? Most
houses require fresh paint every three to five years. If the
paint is failing, the kind of failure is highly important. Paint
normally should chalk as it ages, leaving a dull powdery
surface. It should not blister or peel (flaking). This is an
indication of trouble, especially if it shows prematurely on
a recently painted house. If there is an outside chimney, is
it snug against the house wall? Or is a crack developing between the chimney and house? Chimney separation can indicate serious structural trouble.

A crawl space under the house should be inspected.
Crawl in with a flashlight. Is it dry? Is the wood sub-struc-
ture free of rot and condensation? What about termite evidence? There should be insulation under the house floor or
around the inside walls of a closed-off crawl space *and* a
vapor-barrier material over the crawl-space earth. The underside of porches and outside stairs should be inspected in
the same way.

Inside, the living quarters. Does the kitchen conform to
the work-triangle principle? Is there adequate space for
complete modernizing, if necessary? Or for adding new
equipment such as a dishwasher? Inspect metal cabinets
for rust and corrosion, wood ones for warping, both kinds for
ease of operation. Check the sink for chipped enamel, rust
stains, and scratches. Try the faucets for quick hot water
and adequate pressure. Look under the sink, a crucial place,
for signs of water leaks, rust, and rot. Is there a kitchen
exhaust fan, and is it properly located (in ceiling or high
on the wall over the range).

Open and close all windows and doors. Look for ease of

opening and closing, and for weather stripping around window and door frames.

Small wall cracks generally are inevitable, especially in plaster walls. Serious cracks are usually deep ones that start at a corner of a room, or are deep gashes at the joint where the ceiling and wall meet. If in doubt about a suspicious wall, sound it with a careful, well-placed pound of your fist. It should feel solid.

The fireplace. You should see light when you look up the chimney from the fireplace (with the damper open, of course). Every fireplace should have a workable damper. Every chimney should be lined with flue tile—i.e., you should not see the bricks inside. Absence of chimney lining can be serious but is correctable. How well the fireplace works usually can be judged by lighting paper in it. If smoke pours back into the room, the fireplace is probably defective.

Bathrooms. Are the fixtures of adequate design and in good condition? Is the bathtub under a window? It should not be. Check the joining of the tub with the floor and wall for a good waterproof seam. What about the condition of wall and floor tile? An interior bathroom without windows should have an exhaust fan that turns on with the light. Two decided drawbacks are an old-fashioned bathtub with legs (which is almost impossible to clean under), and the lack of a tile floor or full wall tile around the bathtub and shower. You will very likely want to correct both.

The attic. Is it easily accessible by means of stairs or a pull-down staircase ladder? If you can reach it only by setting up a ladder, this will be a terrible nuisance, particularly if the attic is used for storage. Are there attic-ventilating louvers? These are essential, the bigger the better. Or there should be screened windows at each end (kept partly open in winter). Is there insulation at the floor? How much? (Insulation should not be under the sloping roof rafters of an attic unless the space is finished off for living.) Look for moisture condensation and wood rot. If present, condensation usually can be corrected by increasing attic ventilation, but make sure that the condition has not progressed so far that the beams are seriously weakened. In winter, check the insulation for dryness. If it feels moist to the touch, attic ventilation is inadequate. Are there any signs of roof leaks, such as stains or discolorations? A clue to good over-all construction quality, incidentally, is a chimney that is totally self-supporting and independent of house framing. A chimney may be framed into the house, but attic floor joists and beams should not be fastened directly into the brickwork; i.e., the house should not lean on the chimney.

Miscellaneous. Is redecorating or new paint needed? Are there screens and storm windows and doors or will you have to buy them? Do appliances come with the house? How old are they? What about their operating condition? Will your car fit in the garage? What about the condition of driveway and sidewalks?

Classifying House Flaws

Flaws can be graded according to the trouble and expense they represent. The lack of a safety valve on a water heater is serious, but one can be had for small cost and be installed in jig time. This is therefore a minor flaw. To help you appraise a house, you can use the following grading system, based on the type of flaw and cost of correcting it.

Class A Flaw Minor importance	Anything that costs less than $100 to correct and does not indicate a serious fundamental defect. Examples: Not enough electric outlets (if main electric board is large enough to handle more); broken roof shingles.
Class B Medium	Anything that costs $100 to $500 to correct. Examples are: worn roof on a small house; new exterior wall paint needed (with old paint failing in a normal manner, not because of peeling); or no insulation.

Class C Serious	Anything that costs, say, from $500 up to about $1000 to correct. Examples are: bad heating plant; low water pressure due to clogged plumbing pipes. These flaws also can disqualify a house unless it is otherwise a real bargain.
Class D Major flaw	This rules a house out. Examples are: badly rotted structure; bad wet-basement condition; chronically bad septic-tank system.

An Actual Buying Example

The sixty-six-year-old Victorian house mentioned at the beginning of this chapter is a typical illustration of how to spot a bargain buy; it also illustrates how to avoid a common buying mistake which could be disastrous. The chief advantages of the house were large living space including five upstairs bedrooms, an excellent room layout, location in an established neighborhood, and the sweeping river view.

Its major flaws included typical ones already mentioned: an old, inadequate wiring system, obsolete gravity furnace, no wall insulation, and no downstairs bathroom. Extra money for correcting these flaws was allowed for on top of the house price. The total cost of the house plus repairs and improvements still came well under the cost of a comparable new house.

One major flaw, however, was overlooked at first. It showed up shortly after the buyer and his family moved in, during a heavy rainstorm. Making a casual trip to the basement, the new buyer was confronted with the unhappy spectacle of rain water literally cascading down one of the foundation walls into the cellar. Though it looked and was quite serious, fortunately this wet-basement trouble was later amenable to correction. The buyer was lucky. He realized that he should have had an expert check out the *entire* house before he bought it and he should not have relied on his own judgment just because he happened to be an engineer and a writer who wrote a lot of articles about how to buy houses.

In other words, the moral of this little true story is that even if you think you're good, you should still hire the kind of expert mentioned in Chapter 15 for checking a house you may buy. So says the buyer of this particular house who is also the author of this book.

The Vintage-Year Theory

Like wine, an old house sometimes can be rated according to the year in which it was made, according to Long Island professional engineer and builder, George Silverburgh. Many houses, however, do not conform to average standards for the year they were built. So do not condemn one just because it was built in a bad year. But knowing the year of its birth can serve as a helpful guide in spotting flaws peculiar to that year.

According to Silverburgh, the 1920s were not good vintage years, by and large. Houses built then were structurally sound but mechanically poor (poor heating, plumbing, and wiring, though these flaws may have been corrected by owners in later years). Houses improved in the 1930s, particularly after the FHA was created in 1934. "By the end of 1939," he says, "automatic heat, copper and brass pipe, and rock lath were being used more and more." Houses built in 1940 and 1941 were even better—"the best vintage years, even though many modern products were still to come." Houses built in 1940 and 1941 reflected the availability of many good materials and skilled labor at low cost.

Cross off most houses built during World War II years because they were intended for temporary housing only. Nineteen forty-six had acute material shortages and was not a good vintage year. But 1947 and on were better years, "except for many houses with radiant heat. Every time a leak occurs the slab has to be torn up." Silverburgh rates houses built since 1920 in this way:

1.	1941 and 1940	5.	1946
2.	1939	6.	1934 to 1936
3.	1947 to 1960	7.	1930 to 1933
4.	1937 and 1938	8.	1920 to 1929

Some experts, it also should be said, dispute these ratings. For one thing, many a fast-built, shoddy development house went up following World War II, but the 1947 to 1960 group is nevertheless put in third best position. For another, Silverburgh's theory does not give full value to the extra size and space you get with many older prewar houses. Facts like these temper his ratings and should be kept in mind.

Summary

The purpose of this chapter has been to cite the possible troubles that *may* be encountered in any house not new. It may inadvertently sound as if a frightening number of flaws are to be expected. This is not true. Almost all houses require a few repairs or remodeling. But a good many are in surprisingly good shape. Small and not so small deficiencies also crop up in many new houses. A good idea is to set aside perhaps $500 to $1000 to pay for them. Don't put all your money into buying the house. This also applies, of course, when you buy a new house.

It may be reassuring to know that by and large old houses require less annual upkeep expense than new houses. According to a survey by Allied Home Owners Association, new house buyers spend an average of $335 a year for improvements and repairs, versus an average of $150 a year spent by used-house buyers. This may be largely because new-house buyers, caught almost at once in a space squeeze, are forced to add new finished living areas or increase storage facilities, two limitations that are much less likely in an old house.

It may also be because many new-home buyers, dissatisfied with certain features, feel compelled to change things, improve the kitchen or bath, as well as plant trees, buy storm windows and screens, and in general go about remedying the usual limitations of a new house. And it is because some owners want to keep the house in mint condition. Like a new baby, many essential needs of a new house are never realized until after you take possession. And like cars, all houses require continual maintenance and upkeep. Neglect is the chief enemy of houses, new or old.

CHAPTER 19

BUYING A NEW HOUSE

First and foremost consideration is the reliability of the builder.

One man bought a $35,000 house that developed a serious wet-basement problem a few weeks after the house was finished and he had moved in. Like many other new houses, this one ostensibly was guaranteed against defects for a year. But the builder would do nothing, so the owner took him to court. The judge ruled that the builder would have to pay $6100 for correcting the defect. Nevertheless, the owner was still out of luck.

The builder had just about liquidated his building corporation; it had no money left. Ironically, the very same builder had started a new batch of houses directly across the street with a new corporation. Legally, there was nothing the owner could do, despite his court victory and despite seeing full-speed-ahead work on more houses across the street every day by the same builder.

This is how many a quick-buck builder gets in and out, making a fast profit and then moving on to greener pastures. He feels no responsibility. This is also characteristic of many a non-builder speculator—lawyers, carpenters, or anybody else with a hankering to make a killing in houses. They operate with impunity. When the last house is finished, the corporation profits are divided up, the company is disbanded, and the owners move on to another project.

A reputable builder does not resort to corporation switching. His firm is in business for life. So before you buy, find out how long the builder has been in business with his *current* company name and look up some of the other houses he has built.

Main Advantages of a Development House
Roughly three out of four new houses are built by devel-

opment builders. A good development builder saves on quantity production so he can offer houses at prices 10 to 20 per cent lower than the same size houses by small builders. Hence a $20,000 development house would cost you as much as $24,000 to $25,000 if built by a one-at-a-time builder. The biggest savings, however, can be expected only from a good production builder who builds at least fifty to a hundred houses a year.

Buying a development house also involves risks. You buy from a model house, signing a contract that calls for delivery of a house that is "substantially similar." You can't examine the exact house until it is finished. You may not even see your lot beforehand, since it may not be staked out when you sign your contract. It may be only a numbered plot on a plan as steep as a mountain or flat as a pancake. Buying a development house therefore calls for a special set of rules in addition to the usual design and structural standards for judging a house:

1. Don't be deceived by a glittering model house. It is usually shrewdly furnished by professional decorators with furniture of small proportions so the rooms will look large. (This is a decorating trick which you can borrow for your own use.) So don't expect a huge thirty-foot living room, though it looks that large in the model, when it measures only twenty feet.

A builder will also spend $1000 to richly landscape the model house but allow only $50 to landscape your house. The model may be done with $5-a-roll wallpaper but you get the 60¢-a-roll kind. And the eye-opening kitchen may be loaded with appliances not included with the house; you pay extra for each. Naturally the builder wants to make his house look like a knockout, but, like that of automobiles, the base price is for the stripped-down model. You must pin down exactly what comes with your house and what does not.

2. Complete specifications on what you get should be spelled out in the contract. This should include the amount of landscaping, the exact construction specifications such as exactly how much insulation in walls and ceiling, amount of

wiring, type of heating, waterproofing, termite protection, and so on as given earlier. It should also include the kind of wallpaper, paint, the kitchen and laundry appliances. In all, you need a list of complete construction specifications just as if you were building a new house.

3. Who pays for street paving, water and sewer lines, and sidewalks? Are you certain that the builder does? The town or village may require these of the builder, and he must post a bond to insure completion of such work. But not always. Then you may be hit with extra assessments. Your contract should verify that the builder provides them or know the reason why.

4. Don't accept a lot sight unseen. It may be too rocky for grass, or railroad tracks may practically cut through your back yard. Check the site in advance. Are you satisfied with its size, terrain, and orientation? If you want to save the trees, this also should be written in the contract (location of each tree spelled out). Otherwise the bulldozer approach may level your site like so many others. Also remember, however, that a few trees can be expected to die. Excavating for a house inevitably damages some roots.

5. What about the local zoning? Is the neighborhood zoned for residential use only? If not, you may well wake up some morning to find a factory going up where once there were lovely woods. Don't take anybody's word on the zoning. Go direct to a local zoning-board official for authentic information. Knowing the zoning rules will also help if you plan to expand your house later or add a garage. (Buyers in one development passed up an optional garage with the model house. They figured on adding it later. They discovered too late that not enough space was left alongside their houses for the garage plus adequate clearance to the lot line required by the local zoning code.) Is your lot big enough and so proportioned that you can add to the house in accordance with the zoning rules?

6. Specify the final date of completion in your contract. Two completion dates can be given in the contract: the nominal completion date which is usually not met, and the

final, irrevocable "outside completion" date. This last generally is not included unless you insist.

Now building houses is a tough business and time must be allowed for delays due to bad weather, union troubles, and innumerable other difficulties that plague builders. On the other hand, protect yourself against undue delay in moving in, particularly if you have sold your old house or your apartment lease will soon expire. The inclusion of a definite "outside completion" date will release you from the contract if the house is not completed within a reasonable time, and permit you to look elsewhere.

7. Total sales price should be specified in the contract. It is best not to have an escalator clause permitting a builder to raise the price in case of future cost increases. However, a builder has little control over price increases occurring during construction. If he insists on an escalator clause, recognize his point of view. Then the right to raise the price should be subject to special conditions clearly stated in the contract. If costs fall, the house price should drop, too.

8. The contract should specify the "extras" that come with the house. As already noted, all those shiny kitchen appliances you saw in the model may or may not be standard equipment. What about decorating? Is it included or not? If so, each should be spelled out.

9. Check the construction while the house is being built. Visit the site regularly with a rule and set of plans. The carpenters may locate a closet improperly or frame a doorway where it is not supposed to go. Errors happen. Catch them early and they can be easily corrected.

But don't expect the builder to make major changes at no cost because you've changed your mind. Changes are extremely costly, particularly by development builders whose production is geared to a set schedule. Changes from the standard plan should be brought up in advance and put down in writing. If you must have something altered later, get a firm price in writing before it is done; and be prepared to pay extra for it.

10. Make a final inspection of the house just before you take title (closing day). Jot down all unfinished work,

structural complaints, lack of landscaping, or the omission of special features that were to be included. Check all equipment, including windows and doors for proper operation. A major defect or incomplete work should be cited at closing time. This is your last chance. Your lawyer then can arrange an escrow agreement to guarantee that the work will be done. Some of the money due the builder is withheld by the bank until the work is done, or else the money is later made available to have the work corrected by somebody else.

11. Get all necessary documents when you take title. The builder should give you: 1) A certificate of occupancy, issued by the local building department, which officially states that the house has been inspected and is deemed safe to live in; 2) certificate from the health department approving the plumbing and sewer installation; 3) warranties from the dealers or manufacturers of the equipment and products used in the house—e.g., heating warranty, appliance warranties, and necessary service and warranty papers for roofing, hot-water heater, range, refrigerator, washer, drier, and so on. Keep all this information in one file for future reference.

12. Get a copy of the house plans, including plot plan and location of the septic tank.

13. And have a lawyer check the sales contract.

Custom-House Features at Development-House Prices

The materials and equipment in most new houses are generally of minimal quality, passable stuff just good enough to get by FHA's minimum construction rules. Development houses are often notorious in this regard. We have noted earlier that a top-grade water heater costs only about $20 more than the poorest kind, that first-rate wiring costs no more than $50 additional in the average house compared with skimpy, borderline wiring. The time to substitute good, quality products for questionable stuff is *before* your house is started, and preferably before you sign anything.

Development-house builders often are quite willing to make changes. Not all people realize this. They accept a new house as is, look hard at its limitations, and as soon as they move in launch a crash program to change and modify it. It makes sense, therefore, to talk over desired changes with the builder in advance. It's also cheaper and easier. Many builders have a standard "Changes and Additions" list of the special features available and the cost of each. You can have the kitchen sink changed to a different location, closets added, or a patio or fireplace installed.

Some features, on the other hand, cost no more to do later than if done during construction. If a development house, therefore, comes with a finished recreation room, say, you could trade this for a second bath and finish the recreation room yourself later at no more cost than before (except for running heating and wiring lines). Unlike wall insulation, attic insulation usually can be added any time after completion at no more cost than during construction.

Try your luck at substitution. Substitute features you consider non-essential for those you need. Trade window shutters, which do no functional good and generally add little decorative value, for double glass windows or storm sash and screens. If necessary, open up and offer extra money for features that obviously will cost a builder more than his base price can absorb.

It also should be said that not all builders tolerate changes, particularly many large production builders. Their construction is tightly geared to the mass production of a standard house with no individual variations permitted. But by and large most builders do permit reasonable changes, provided you bring them up in time, preferably before the house is begun.

CHAPTER 20

BUILDING A HOUSE

"We thought we were smart when we chose a building contractor. We made the poor man show us the houses he had built. We peered at mitered casings and scrutinized the workmanship. Everything looked fine, but we forgot to take the owners aside and ask them privately what they thought of the builder. Like them, we had to camp on the builder's doorstep to get our house finished months after it was supposed to have been completed.

"One other thing hurt, too. The builder told us not to bother with an architect . . . he could draw up the plans himself and save us the outside fee. We didn't know then that we could have an architect design the plans, tailor-made to our specifications, if that's all we wanted. Or that architects not only design plans but they know about the best materials and they inspect the house while it's being built to make sure things are going right.

"We finally got our house finished, all right, and it's fairly well built. Having a builder design it may have given us strong walls, but the floor plan is a nightmare. We also ended up with a twenty-four-inch wide door from garage to kitchen that requires a side-moving contortionist to slip through with groceries, and a breakfast-room window at just the right height for looking out if you are eight feet tall. We could mention a few other things, too. . . .

"Building a house can be stimulating and enlightening, even if downright maddening at times. It was an experience we wouldn't have missed. But we should have been fore-warned about a few things."

So says a man who with his wife decided that the only way to get the house they really wanted was to have it built for them. His words emphasize advice for anybody who builds.

Two Fundamental Rules

First, use an architect if at all possible. Architect-designed houses can make all the difference in the world. But there are architects and architects. Like other professions, architecture is not immune to incompetent nincompoops, or opinionated bossy types who inflict their total views on you regardless of what you may like. Talk to a few beforehand. See houses they have done, and talk to the owners (privately). Choose one who shares your likes and dislikes, one you have rapport with. Or at least use architect-designed plans. For a few hundred dollars you can get working blueprints of a Frank Lloyd Wright house, for that matter.

Second, choose a truly reliable builder. Here again, apply the same old advice: Get the names of people he has built houses for and take the time to call them. Talk to bank officials, real estate brokers, and others familiar with local builders. These things take only a few hours of time in the beginning, but they can save you months of endless trouble later. And, by the way, it's best not to be your own general contractor unless you are a contractor.

Building a house is recommended only if you cannot find what you want in a ready-built house or an existing one. Building, on the other hand, is about the only sure-fire way of getting a well-designed house fitted out with everything you and your family want in a house. What's more, it need not be much more expensive than the usual speculative-builder house. A really good architect, for example, can save you big money by careful advance planning. At the other extreme, of course, there is the artistic architect who doesn't believe in spending $75 for a perfectly good (and attractive) kitchen counter top when he can give you a hand-made tile job by a local artisan for $750. In a case like this you must lay down the law.

Building Costs

Building costs vary from about $10 a square foot of living area in parts of the South up to $15 to $20 a square foot in the North. A 1000-square-foot house may cost you about $10,000 plus land in Georgia, up to $15,000 in Chicago. These are approximate costs for new, speculative-builder houses of small to medium size. Custom houses will run $20 per square foot or higher. Sometimes, though, a good architect will bring in a custom house at a lower price per foot than a builder, which will more than pay his fee.

Costs of Special Features

Size in square feet should be tempered by other considerations. A custom house is more expensive partly because of higher-quality materials and workmanship compared with the usual speculative-builder house. The number of appliances and "extras" should be figured in. If you are comparing, say, a house with a basement and garage versus another without, here are *approximate* figures on how much you should credit such features in the $15,000 to $20,000 house price range:

Unfinished basement is worth	$1000 to	$1250
Carport	500	750
Garage		1000
Fireplace (less if prefabricated)	600	750
Roofed-in porch of 200 to 250 sq. ft.		1000
Exterior brick		1000

To estimate what total construction cost of a typical house should be: Add for carport, garage, fireplace, porch, according to figures given. Add $500 to $750 for additional bathrooms, depending on size.

Other features such as wood paneling, de luxe kitchen equipment, built-ins, two-car garage, can raise the price from $500 to $2500 and must be priced locally. *Not* included in the above figures are the cost of land, water and sewer pipes, driveway, and special landscaping, which require individual estimating. An improved lot with water and sewer lines today may cost from 15 to 20 per cent of total house price, according to builders. This cost formerly accounted for about 10 per cent of house price before the price of suburban land near cities began skyrocketing dur-

Fig. 26 COMPARATIVE BUILDING COSTS IN THE UNITED STATES

Chicago	29%	Sacramento	−1%
Cleveland	21%	Jacksonville	−1%
Springfield, Ill.	20%	Providence	−1%
Reno	17%	Burlington, Vt.	−1%
Charleston, W. Va.	16%	Topeka	−2%
Buffalo	16%	Portland, Ore.	−2%
Des Moines	12%	Boston	−3%
Sioux Falls	10.4%	Newark, N. J.	−3%
Milwaukee	9%	Kansas City, Mo.	−4%
Cincinnati	9%	Little Rock	−4%
Pittsburgh	8%	Los Angeles	−5%
St. Louis	7%	Albuquerque	−5%
Miami	6%	Richmond, Va.	−5%
Columbus, Ohio	6%	Washington, D.C.	−6%
Fargo	6%	Birmingham, Ala.	−6%
Salt Lake City	5%	Portland, Maine	−6%
New Orleans	5%	Jamaica, N. Y.	−6%
Detroit	5%	Camden, N. J.	−6%
Shreveport	5%	Wilmington, Del.	−7%
Minneapolis	5%	Philadelphia	−7%
Grand Rapids	5%	San Antonio	−8%
Indianapolis	5%	Lubbock, Texas	−8%
Hartford, Conn.	4%	Manchester, N. H.	−8%
San Diego	3%	Tulsa	−8%
Billings, Mont.	3%	Atlanta	−9%
Baltimore	2%	Tampa	−9%
Albany	2%	Charlotte, N. C.	−11%
Casper, Wyoming	2%	Houston	−11%
Louisville	1%	Phoenix	−13%
Omaha	1%	Memphis	−14%
Seattle	1%	Fort Worth	−14%
San Francisco	1%	Dallas	−15%
Denver	1%	Columbia, S. C.	−15%
Boise	00%	Knoxville	−16%
Spokane	00%		

ing the 1950s. Start with an average base building cost of $12 per square foot of floor area. It will be higher or lower according to building costs in your area, 29 per cent higher in Chicago, 16 per cent lower in Knoxville, as shown by the accompanying chart of comparative building cost figures from FHA. Adjust your base figure accordingly.

Deduct 10 per cent from base price when it is a 1½-story, two-story, or split-level house (since you get more space for less floor and roof).

Add 10 per cent for: unfinished basement, brick veneer outside walls; 5 per cent for central air conditioning.

Building Procedure

The steps in building a house are: getting a lot, buying plans and specifications, signing a construction contract with a builder, getting a building permit, and the actual construction, including inspections.

As mentioned earlier, an architect should evaluate your land before you buy it. He can often spot subtle characteristics that can make or break you, in other words, advise you about its feasibility for building, point out advantages and drawbacks. The lot also should be evaluated in advance by your mortgage lender, usually a bank. This is crucial. A bad lot in the view of the lender can wreck the financing plans for the whole house. And will the bank accept the paid-up lot as the equivalent of a down payment on the house?

The Contract

You will need a lawyer. Every detail of the structure should be spelled out, including the materials and construc-

Fig. 26 Basic building costs in the United States *average* about $12 a square foot of living area. This is for a typical house but does not include the cost of special features (noted in text). Actual costs vary higher or lower than the base cost, as shown in this chart based on FHA figures. Thus, costs range from a high of 29 per cent above the $12 average in Chicago (nearly $16 a square foot), down to a low of 16 per cent below in Knoxville (about $10 a square foot). You can figure approximate base cost in your area according to the percentage given for the nearest city.

tion methods. Normally, you make partial payments as the work progresses, when the foundation is in, the roof is on, when plumbing, wiring, and heating are completed, and then final payment when the house is completed and you receive the certificate of occupancy. Before making each payment to the builder, the architect should certify that each step is properly done and complete. For certain parts of the house, such as lighting fixtures and wallpaper, the builder will allow you a fixed amount of money and you pick them out and buy them.

Lien Protection

Even though you have paid the general contractor in full when the house is finished, a sub-contractor, plasterer, or electrician, say, may not have been paid. He can turn around and file a lien against the house—i.e., against you. This has happened when a contractor went broke, or skipped town with somebody's wife. For protection against liens, it is customary for the contractor to break down each partial-payment bill into the various sub-contracting work it covers. Then you write a series of checks payable jointly to the contractor and the sub-contractors involved. Their endorsements constitute acknowledgment of payment. For further protection, insist on signed receipts from each sub-contractor for the value of work done up to the date of each partial payment to the contractor.

When will the house be finished? A completion date should be specified in the contract together with a penalty clause if the builder doesn't meet it. But give the builder plenty of leeway in time. After all, the weather, workmen's whims, and union problems are beyond human control. However, he should deliver the house within a reasonable time.

Completion Bond

The builder should post a completion or surety bond. It will cost about 1 per cent of the total construction cost. A bond by itself indicates that the bonding company thinks enough of the builder's ability to back him. If the contractor breaks his leg or for any number of unforeseen reasons he cannot finish the house, the bonding company will arrange for another builder to finish up at its expense. Be generous. Tell the contractor you will pay for the bond, if necessary. All you want him to do is post one. If he cannot get a bond, this is the time to find out why.

Insurance

Fire insurance is mandatory. It is common sense. The owner generally pays for enough to cover 100 per cent of the house's insurable value.

The contractor should have both workmen's compensation and liability insurance coverage. The first protects both you and him against damage to other people or other property as a result of work performed on your house. However, a neighbor or passer-by struck by a falling brick could sue you as well as the contractor, particularly if the contractor has limited coverage. Therefore you need a liability policy, too. Double-check the amount of coverage in the contractor's policies. If it's skimpy, tell him to get more, even if you must pay the extra premium yourself.

Avoiding Disputes

One of the most widespread causes of disputes in custom building stems from changes in the plan when the house is going up. What may appear to be a trivial change to you will often necessitate a major alteration by the builder.

A classic example occurred when Mr. Blandings built his dream house. He got an unexpected bill from the builder for "changes in closet . . . $1247." It was for an alteration by the builder after the house was two thirds complete. Mrs. Blandings had seen four pieces of flagstone left over from the porch when she was visiting the site. "All I did," she plaintively explained later, "was ask Mr. Retch [builder] if he wouldn't just put them down on the floor of the flower sink and poke a little cement between the cracks and give me a nice stone floor where it might be wet with flowers and things. That was absolutely every bit of all I did."

To accomplish this little extra, the builder first had his carpenters rip up new floorboards. He then chopped out the underlying beams to provide a wood cradle to hold the cement which in turn would hold the flagstones. Then a lally column was required for extra support. For underneath the floor he had to call back: 1) the plumber to relocate the main hot- and cold-water pipes; 2) the electrician to rip about sixty feet of armored electric cable which also had to be relocated; 3) the heating man to wrestle a heating duct into a new location because it blocked the lally column; 4) the plumber once again to install a floor drain. The builder then had to change the pitch of the entire floor so that it would drain properly (if flower water was spilled); and since this in turn prevented two closet doors in the room from opening, the doors and closet had to be taken down and rebuilt, the doors being sent back to the mill for reworking ("because the builder liked to do things right"). Toss in a few other minor and not so minor related expenses and that's why the total bill for "changes in closet . . ." came to $1247.

This is an extreme example to be sure, and Mr. Retch should not have ordered his men full speed ahead before warning Mr. Blandings of the extra cost involved. But even more bizzare incidents happen all the time when people building a house ask for a seemingly minor change *during* construction.

Asking for changes during construction is natural. It is to be expected. Your wife may want extra kitchen cabinets, or the bedrooms cry out for more closet space. It's a simple matter to ask the builder to make the change. But to avoid a future dispute, draw up a *change order*—exactly what is to be done and the extra cost. You and the contractor sign it. This will forestall an explosive misunderstanding later.

For Successful Builder-Client Relationships

Co-operate with your builder. It's his job to provide a satisfactory house, and there is nothing he wishes to do more than get the job done fast and well. The longer it drags out, the more it costs him. Assume that your builder is honest and conscientious. Don't treat him with suspicion, as if he were a rogue bent on swindling you. (The time to check his character and credit is before you hire him.) Get one you can talk with. But don't talk to him incessantly.

Plans should be finished and everything down on paper before the work starts. Don't leave any items vague or agree "to work it out on the job later." This lights a fuse for future trouble. And don't be a back-seat driver, hanging around the job giving orders to workmen. If you don't like something, take it up with the builder or architect. By all means, make a regular inspection of the work progress. But stay out of the way of workmen. After all, they have their work to do, too.

CHAPTER 21

A PREFABRICATED HOUSE
The pros and cons

In 1947 some 37,000 new houses in the United States were built with factory made parts—they were prefabs made by home manufacturers. By 1960, the home manufacturers, growing every year since the war, were accounting for about one out of every nine new one-family houses, a total of 126,000 put up and sold in that year.

Almost every one of them, especially the latest, is indistinguishable from a conventionally built house. They are being built in nearly every part of the country. The chances are that a few at least are being built in your town every year. You may pass some every day and not know that they are prefabs.

In short, the factory-built house has come a long way since World War II days when tens of thousands of them were hurriedly built in slapdash fashion chiefly for temporary housing. They were just that—flimsy, temporary boxes that became blots on the landscape and gave a tainted reputation to the term "prefab house."

Today, however, the average prefab house is as sturdy and strongly built as the average conventional house. In many cases it is a better-built house. And it often offers special advantages that make it a better buy than a conventionally built new house. This depends, however, largely on where you live; though factory-made houses are now turned out by over 400 manufacturers, only a few brands are available in most states, and there are still various parts of the country where they are not available.

You can buy a factory house for less than $6000 or more than $50,000. In fact, there are even a few prefabs that sell for over $100,000 to well-heeled families who get a large lavish home at 10 to 15 per cent less cost than the same size luxury house built by conventional methods.

What Is a Prefab House?

The Home Manufacturers' Association, the industry's trade group, gives this official definition:

"It is a house whose components have been built in a factory and trucked to the site in pre-assembled parts and sections. The house package usually consists of exterior walls with windows and doors already installed, roof and floor systems, interior partitions, exterior siding. Kitchen cabinets, appliances, heating and plumbing are usually included. Although the degree of factory fabrication varies with manufacturers, the trend is toward more complete house packages, often containing everything except cement, in order to eliminate costly on-site labor."

In non-official language, a big trailer truck drives up from the factory with a bundle of precut wood, wall panels, floor, roof, and partition sections, packages of roof shingles, nails, kitchen cabinets, and just the right quantity of nearly everything else needed to erect and complete the house. The house foundation, of course, is prepared in advance. The floor, walls, and roof construction is by and large the exact kind of construction used for conventional houses. The big difference, though, is that the manufactured structure is put together in the factory in sections or panels designed for quick assembly at the site of the house.

Not all makers, however, provide a complete or nearly complete package of house parts. Many of them prefer not to include such crucial parts as heating, plumbing, and wiring in order to avoid local code problems with each. They prefer that these be installed by local contractors.

Some so-called home manufacturers are merely glorified lumber yards who merely furnish the bare bones of the house: precut lumber, doors, windows, and perhaps interior partitions—and that's all. Everything else is bought and installed at the house site. The larger and better-established manufacturers go a lot farther. They provide a complete package plus the paint and finishing materials needed to

complete the house. In some cases they also can provide
heating, plumbing, and wiring systems, provided your
town's building code does not arbitrarily ban such prefabricated systems (which can be every bit as dependable and
safe, if not more so, than locally made systems).

Finally, a few manufacturers also provide an absolutely
complete, all-factory-built house. The entire house is built in
the factory and shipped in two or three separate sections,
as if it were sliced cleanly down the middle. The sections
are delivered by truck, one following the other, and then
clamped together, in effect, over the foundation. Outside
water, sewer, and electric lines are connected up, and you
can move in almost at once. This is the newest twist in prefabs and is considered in some quarters still in the experimental stage. (For this reason, it is difficult to judge how
much of a bargain this kind of house package will be, and
how well each brand is designed and built. Again, you have
to judge by your fundamental guides: the amount of house
you get per dollar, total price versus price of other houses
nearby with the same features, and quality of the individual
parts and components.)

What Are the Advantages of a Prefab House?

The prefab proponents cite six main advantages:

1. Variety of choice. You can sit down and choose among
a large variety of basic models, and different architectural
styles, from Cape Cod and colonial to ranch and contemporary houses. You can generally order countless changes
and variations in the size, colors, style, and type of materials
used in each basic plan. Each change generally can be
worked out at a fixed price to you; you know exactly what
everything will cost.

2. Construction quality. The manufacturers make a big
point of "precision engineering under factory-controlled
conditions." The countless small and large pieces of lumber
and boards, nails and other parts, usually handmade at the
site, are cut, sized, and preassembled into a few large components in the factory where there is much less chance of
error, compared with working at the site of a house. Though

the basic structural systems used are generally identical with conventional building systems, some companies use new prefabricated systems that represent significant advances over traditional building methods. Plainly then, there is far less chance of mistakes and errors. Most manufacturers also use top-grade, kiln-dried lumber (or their expensive, high-speed, woodworking machinery would be knocked out of kilter by warped or knotty green wood). And in general, the other materials provided with the house package—doors, windows, paint, roofing, etc.—are of equal or higher quality than the comparable materials bought and installed by the average local builder.

3. Architectural design. Most prefab houses, by and large, are designed by architects (which is not true for most conventionally built houses). What's more, many packaged houses are designed by top national architects. There is even a line of expensive prefabs designed by the late Frank Lloyd Wright.

4. Speed of construction. This is undeniably one of the biggest advantages offered. Once your lot is staked out and the foundation prepared, the packaged house can be delivered and erected in a matter of weeks. Starting from scratch, in fact, the structural frame of the house often can be erected and roofed over in a day or two.

5. Easier financing. This is often easier to obtain when you buy a factory house, particularly with an FHA or VA home loan since the FHA and VA are usually familiar with the house design and specifications. They have reviewed the same house before, thus there are fewer processing delays. And some manufacturers are set up to provide you with a mortgage or arrange for you to get a conventional mortgage locally.

6. Lower house cost. The manufacturer obviously saves money by making bulk purchases of lumber, roofing, appliances, and so on. He also saves through the use of assembly-line production methods in his factory compared with the cost of the same work done by expensive hand labor at the site of a house. And there is far less material waste. As a result, the finished house generally will cost

from 5 to 20 per cent less than a comparable conventional house, excluding land and foundation cost.

You will not always get this much of a break on the price, however. It depends on the particular brand, on various local conditions, and also on the dealer who sold it to you and who will put it up for you. Sometimes the dealer pockets the extra savings and prices the house at or near the price level of a comparable, conventionally built house. And sometimes, particularly in highly competitive metropolitan areas, the going prices for conventional construction are kept so low by competition that there is little difference between them and factory house prices. (In these cases, however, the factory house is often the better buy because of inherently better construction; the same stiff competition among local builders that keeps prices down also leads to frequent corner cutting and inferior workmanship.)

The price of a factory house also depends on its shipping distance from the factory, since shipping can get expensive. For this reason most makers find it uneconomical to sell and ship their houses farther than a 500-mile radius of their factories. A few maintain that they can ship up to 1000 miles away and still provide a lower-cost house than you can build locally.

How Do You Buy a Factory House?

Almost all of them are sold through a local builder-dealer who represents a particular manufacturer. He sells you the house, and then he handles the siting of the house on your lot, excavation and foundation work, and then delivery of the house package and its erection. In many cases, he was formerly a conventional builder who turned to factory houses. You choose a house from plans and pictures or from actual models. You contract for it almost exactly as you would for a conventional new house.

Some dealers will put up the house on your lot. Others will provide the house and lot. Still others specialize in putting up entire sub-divisions of factory-fabricated houses like a regular large-scale, tract builder. The difference between the two is that one puts up factory-made houses in volume;

the other builds his own houses in volume, each one starting from scratch. The factory house, sub-division builder generally offers a greater value per dollar, and a better house. He benefits from mass production savings twice, once in the factory, the other in land development and the over-all sub-division savings inherent with building many houses at one time. He also offers a greater variety of houses; you can choose virtually any style and type of house provided by the manufacturer. If you don't want to live in a sub-division, you might be able to contract with the same dealer to put up one of his models on a lot you will provide elsewhere.

Sometimes you can buy a house package from the factory and put it up yourself. But this is not done by most factories, nor is it recommended. For one thing, the building process is not so simple as it may strike you at first. For another, professional building skill and experience is required to avoid blunders that can botch the entire job. For this reason, most manufacturers will not sell direct; they sell only through dealers with building experience.

One exception is the Vacation House package, a growing trend among the manufacturers. This smaller, simpler house "kit" is provided chiefly for the summer-house market. These generally can be ordered straight from the factory and you handle the house assembly. (There are also shell houses, as opposed to factory-made houses, which are sold directly to buyers for completion by the buyer.)

How Do You Find a Good Factory-House Dealer?

Look in the yellow pages of your phone book under this heading, or under "Buildings—prefabricated," or look for the name of the particular manufacturer whose house you may want. The larger manufacturers advertise regularly in such magazines as *The American Home, Better Homes & Gardens, House & Garden, House Beautiful,* and in the semi-annual house-building manuals such as *New Homes Guide, House & Garden's Book of Building,* and *House Beautiful's Building Manual.*

Write to the Home Manufacturers Association, Suite

1117, Barr Building, Washington 6, D.C., for a list of their manufacturers. The HMA members include over fifty of the leading prefabbers in the country (but not all top firms are members). By and large it is best to stick with a manufacturer who is a member of the HMA. Some 100 of the total of more than 400 producers are listed in a prefab directory of the December 1957 issue of *House & Home*, a building trade magazine which is available in many libraries. Or call the nearest Home Builders Association chapter (listed in the phone book) or the real estate editor of your local newspaper.

How Do You Judge the Quality?

Although many prefabricated houses are constructed with top-grade lumber and embody some of the latest and best construction techniques, they nevertheless require the same thorough over-all checking as a conventionally built house. Like conventional builders, house manufacturers sometimes tend to use a certain amount of minimal quality equipment and products—i.e., minimal insulation, lowest-cost bathroom and kitchen fixtures, and wall surfaces. For that matter, there is often little difference between the plumbing, heating, and wiring, among other things, installed in a factory house, and those of conventional houses, since these particular things are so often bought and installed locally. Hence, the same fundamental design and construction standards, noted throughout this book, apply to factory houses as well as to conventional houses. And the reputation and reliability of the manufacturer's builder-dealer is all important. You should investigate his credentials just as thoroughly as you would a conventional builder. Check his qualifications with such people as bankers and building officials, and talk to other people who have bought homes from him.

What About Availability?

Unfortunately factory houses are still not available in every part of the country. Their strongholds are in the so-called Midwest Triangle (embracing Ohio, Indiana, Illinois, and portions of the bordering states), the Southeast, and Middle Atlantic states, parts of New England, the west coast, and the Northwest. But the Southwest and Rocky Mountain states are still fairly barren of them.

Here are some of the biggest manufacturers (though this listing does not mean endorsement by the author or publisher, and it does not mean that these are the top manufacturers in product quality and reliability. Other manufacturers not listed may well offer houses of equal, or in some cases better, quality):

Admiral Homes, Inc., West Newton, Penna.

W. G. Best Corp., Effingham, Ill.

Ivon R. Ford, Inc., McDonough, N.Y.

General Homes, Fort Wayne, Ind.

Harnischfeger Homes, Inc., Port Washington, Wis.

Hodgson Houses, Inc., Dover, Mass. (maker of what is believed to be the first prefab of all in 1892)

Inland Homes Corp., Piqua, O.

Kingsberry Homes, Fort Payne, Ala.

Knox Homes Corp., Thomson, Ga.

National Homes Corporation, headquarters in Lafayette, Indiana (largest maker of all with subsidiaries in the East, South, and West)

New Century Homes, Lafayette, Ind.

Page & Hill Homes, Inc., Albert Lea, Minn.

Scholz Homes, Toledo 7, O.

U. S. Steel Homes Division, U. S. Steel Corp., Pittsburgh 30, Penna.

Special mention also should be made of the Techbuilt brand of factory houses which has won a sackful of prizes for its contemporary Techbuilt houses. Its houses are designed by the architect Carl Koch and are available in many parts of the Northeast and some parts of the Middle West as well as in most of New England. All models, including vacation houses, are of exceedingly neat but unabashedly contemporary architectural design, so don't write them if you are strictly in favor of a Cape Cod, colonial, or another traditional house. Their house catalogue can be had for 50¢ from Techbuilt, Inc., 127 Mount Auburn Street, Cambridge 38, Massachusetts.

"Shell Houses"?

These are not prefabricated houses. They are low-cost, unfinished houses chiefly for low-income families who cannot afford to pay more than $50 to $100 a month for housing and who are (or should be) either sufficiently skilled or ambitious to tackle the job of finishing the house themselves.

You get just what the name implies: a shell consisting of a completed exterior house shell (rough flooring, exterior walls, windows, doors, and roofing), but the interior is virtually bare except for interior partition bones and roof supports. The buyer must install heating, wiring, lighting, and plumbing as well as finished flooring, ceilings, insulation, interior wall surfaces, trim, cabinets, kitchen and bathroom equipment. You can do this yourself or sub-contract the same work. Depending on the manufacturer, you can also elect one of several options, in addition to the shell of a house; the price goes up accordingly. These are:

1. Shell plus the materials to complete it—interior wallboard, trim and paint, interior doors, kitchen cabinets, plumbing fixtures (but not pipes), water heater, and electrical fixtures. You provide and install everything else (plumbing pipes, heating, wiring, etc.)

2. Shell, plus the installation of all or most of the second-stage materials just noted above, depending on the particular house and manufacturer. You provide and install everything else.

3. The completely finished house provided and installed by the manufacturer's dealer, except sometimes some of the final trim, finishing, and paint, depending on the house.

The chief appeal of a shell house is low price, no down payment (but you must own your lot, which is the equivalent of a down payment). And it provides an opportunity for people with limited money but some technical skill to do much of the work by themselves. Small shell houses sell for as little as $1000, but more representative are prices ranging from around $1750 for small one-bedroom models up to about $5000 for three-bedroom models. A few makers also offer larger models, including two-story and split-level models for $5000 to about $10,000. These houses may cost another 50 to 100 per cent to completely finish, but you can end up with a house that is worth two to three times the shell price as a result of handling the work yourself.

Shell houses tap a big market of low income families, particularly residents of small towns and rural areas where conventional mortgages are unavailable or the buyers do not make enough money to qualify for an FHA, VA, or conventional mortgage. It is a burgeoning new development that started originally in the Southeast and Florida but is gradually spreading northward and westward.

But Watch Out for Trick Financing

There is, however, much criticism of the shell-house business. Critics charge that the interest charges are exorbitant and, in fact, that shell houses are just another installment-credit racket. The buyer generally pays from about 8½ to 18 per cent true interest on his financing, or considerably more than the usual 5¼ to 7 per cent interest charges for conventional mortgage loans. In addition, the house must be paid off within five to ten years, which means proportionately higher monthly payments compared with those of the more common twenty- to twenty-five-year mortgage term.

Finally, there is much concern over the quality of many shell house brands. They are made by more than fifty different producers, a few of which are regular prefabricators, while most specialize in shell houses only.

Final Warning on Shells

So be particularly wary of buying a shell house for the two reasons just mentioned—stiff interest and time-payment charges, and questionable construction quality, depending on the manufacturer. These two things should be emphasized again and again. Don't be taken in by the no down payment and low monthly payments. These can be misleading. Figure out what your total over-all costs will be (simply by multiplying the monthly payment by the total number of months you have to pay).

And watch out for what is called "balloon" financing. One shell-house maker, for example, sells an unfinished two-bedroom 748-square-foot house for $4340. You can buy this for only $55.66 a month on a five-year plan. That sounds pretty low, but the financing is rigged so that your final, or sixtieth payment, is $3302.25!

In short, after paying off a total of nearly $3000 in fifty-nine months, you still owe $3302.25 because of the stiff carrying charges; you have actually paid off only about $1000 of the original house price, and you then have to refinance the house for another five years, often longer. Your original indebtedness has ballooned sky-high. The purpose of balloon financing is simply to get the monthly payments down as low as possible to lure in the most buyers and sell the most houses. So double-check the financing papers in advance and try to get a regular bank mortgage rather than the usual installment-payment financing.

Checking the quality of shells is also highly important, especially because there are little or no built-in construction safeguards to protect you. At best, very few of them conform to FHA's minimum rules, and because they are designed for sale in rural areas where there are no building codes to protect you, the door is wide open to let in the cheapest and lowest-quality construction.

It also should be said that some shell-house makers offer a good product. But because of the lack of standards, the lack of supervision, and the lack of really good construction controls, you must take special precautions before buying one. Thoroughly check the reputation of the maker and the dealer you buy from. Call the nearest local Better Business Bureau and ask about him. Get the names of other people he has sold to and talk with them. Here again the same old advice may seem tiresome to hear, but nevertheless following it is necessary to avoid getting stung.

PART 6

THE PROCESS OF SHOPPING, BUYING, AND PAYING

Although Americans are becoming more and more bargain-conscious (as evidenced by the rapid spread of discount stores) and we are more and more conscious of quality goods (as evidenced by the growing influence of the consumer-research magazines), most of us are sheer neophytes when we enter the market place for a house. This is particularly true for the process of negotiating and paying. The interest rate for paying off a home-loan mortgage is the lowest interest rate of all consumer installment loans, yet the total interest and other expenses involved with buying a house can be so large that they make all other consumer debt charges seem like peanuts.

This section is therefore a guide to show you how to go about getting a house at the lowest possible cost. It tells you about bidding procedures for an old house; about the importance of shopping for a mortgage; and about closing costs, those inevitable bills you must pay over and above the price of the house which come as an unhappy shock to so many buyers, particularly first-time buyers. And at the end of this section is a glossary of real estate terms you will see bandied about in real estate ads and hear among builders, real estate brokers, and mortgage people.

CHAPTER 22

SHOPPING AND NEGOTIATING

Here is an example of what happens when you buy a house.

A house is put on the market for, say, $28,500. The owner paid perhaps $22,000 for it five years before. He put several thousand dollars worth of improvements into it. Real estate values also increased during his ownership. It is a fairly good house and the owner wants about $25,000 for it. So he prices it at $28,500 to give himself room for bargaining. He also figures on the usual 5 per cent commission off the selling price his real estate agent would earn.

The house goes unsold for a couple of months. The owner lowers his asking price to $27,500. A few potential buyers show up. One offers $20,000 and is flatly turned down. Another offers $21,500 (his first bid) and shows genuine interest in the house. The owner says no but does not close the door. After a few weeks of discreet bargaining back and forth, the potential buyer says he will go as high as $24,000, his final offer, no higher. He figures he would have to put another $750 in it for redecorating and minor improvements. The seller says no but he will come down to $25,000, his final price, he says.

At this point the deal can go in any one of several directions. If the owner has to sell, and no one else is interested and the potential buyer stands firm, the owner will probably come down in price. If the owner does not have to sell, and does not mind holding the house longer, the buyer must meet his price or go elsewhere. The real estate agent may try for a compromise, getting the two to meet halfway at $24,500. Or the owner will turn to the agent and tell him, "Okay, I'll compromise if you compromise, too, and take a cut in your commission. We'll split the difference three ways, each of us making up one third." What happens depends on the people involved.

Like a horse trade, buying a house has no written rules. Practically nobody but the naïve buyer pays the original asking price for an existing house. Sellers generally know this and put their house on the market at a price pegged at least 5 to 10 per cent higher than they want to allow for bargaining. A man in a fashionable suburb put his house on the market one spring for $62,600. His broker confided to a friend, "He'll take $55,000 right now if he could get it. If the house isn't sold next August when his son will be set to go off to college, he'll take $48,000."

This is not true, however, with new houses. A builder will rarely come down in price unless he is closing out a development or sales are so slow that his back is against the wall.

Bargaining is going on more and more today in the used-house market, because the acute housing shortages following World War II are giving way to a buyer's market in houses almost all over. Yet many an old-house owner has a wildly inflated idea of what his house is worth and prices it accordingly.

Thus, the first rule in buying a house is to set *your* value on what it is worth and the top price you are willing to pay. If you seriously want the house and are uncertain of its value, hire a professional appraiser (for $25 to $35) to tell you. Then find out how long the house was on the market. If it has gone unsold more than two or three months, this is a signal to cut your first bid, even more than usual. A variety of other tricks of the trade also enter the picture. But before getting into them you should understand a few other things.

Shopping for the Right House

Houses are sold chiefly through real estate advertising and brokers. Get the newspaper that carries the most real estate advertising. Saturday and Sunday editions have the thickest real estate sections.

Tell everybody you know that you are looking. Be prepared to shop around. Take your time. Don't be rushed into buying. You can always rent a temporary place, if necessary. Indeed, this is often better than buying, especially when you arrive in a strange community. It gives you time to become familiar with the community, its schools and other characteristics. And it forestalls a hasty purchase that could turn out disastrously.

Buying a house takes endurance. You must look long enough to get a good idea of what's on the market and what current values are. Besides, when you give yourself time to shop and are not desperate for living quarters, your bargaining position rises and your vulnerability to a bad buy declines.

Keep a record of the most promising houses you see. A handy 15¢ notebook is all you need. Mark down such things as asking price, location, owner's name, number of bedrooms, size in square feet of floor area, taxes, heating bills, your offhand estimate of its value, and special features pro and con. Without a record you soon will get a blurred picture of those you have seen, particularly the earliest ones. Later you may find that one of the first houses you saw, seemingly not very captivating at the time, abruptly seems like a bargain compared with everything you have since seen. If a house warrants special attention, get a floor plan of it, or make your own by pacing off the room dimensions. Study it at home for zoning traffic patterns, interior circulation, and adaptability for your furniture.

Don't be fooled by phony glamour, shiny new paint, or a well-kept lawn. A seller naturally will tidy up his house to make it look good. But although the kitchen glitters and high-voltage bulbs are used to make things look extra bright, is the house really a good buy? What about the fundamental design and construction?

Negotiating and Bidding

Assume that you have found a house you like. You have determined what you think it is worth, and the top price you are willing to pay. The total floor area in square feet gave you a good idea of its value, based on local construc-

tion costs. You have seen what new houses of the same size
are selling for (considerably more). You have adjusted the
price by such features as the two-car garage, the modern
kitchen, but only one bath, and you have figured in the
approximate value of the land itself, based on $2000 to
$3000, for example for the same size suburban lots nearby.

Your First Offer

Start with a low bid. Brokers say, "It is amazing how
often buyers pay the asking price, yet the seller expected to
come down." For that matter, when the price of a house
for sale is clearly labeled *asking price*, the buyer is tacitly
conceding that this is the price he wishfully would like to
get but he is open to any reasonable offer.

Make a lower bid even if the house is listed at a *firm
price*, notice that the owner will not take less. But you
never can tell. How low to start depends on your judgment
of the house value versus how much swollen value you
think the seller has built into the asking price. Many owners
have mildly exaggerated ideas of their house's value; others
go hog-wild. It also depends on the kind of property, the
demand for such property, and how long it has been on
the market.

If you are in the market for a big country place, the asking price is usually far in excess of true worth today. The
seller may say that $100,000 has gone into his property, yet
he is only asking $65,000. Offer $35,000 and you may well
get it around that figure. (Yes, that low.) The ratio here of
about 30 per cent on investment or 55 per cent on asking
price is not unusual. Because of high upkeep and low demand, big expensive places today are exceedingly difficult
to sell. One exception is a large house in a fashionable old
suburb where you may have to offer 60 to 75 per cent of
asking price before your bid is even considered.

Coming down to more realistic levels, most houses in the
$15,000 to $35,000 bracket may have to be bid at 75 to
80 per cent of asking price before the buyer will even
bother to reject the bid. Start low anyway. A very low bid
may offend the owner, but on the other hand it is often

surprisingly successful. If it offends, it is remarkable how quickly you'll return to grace by raising your bid.

The Importance of Self-Control

The first bid is likely to be turned down. This is to be expected. Hold off a few days. Don't panic. Self-control at this time can be difficult if you really want the house and are anxious to raise. But overeagerness can destroy your bargaining position. Houses do not sell like hot cakes. There is nearly always ample time for additional bids.

There is always the likelihood, of course, that the house will suddenly be snapped up by a newcomer, just arrived, during the very time you are preparing to make another bid. Or that another buyer will grab it at the owner's price. But this is a very slim possibility, particularly with used houses in today's buyer's market. To buy a house at the lowest price you have to risk that small chance.

If you tend toward nervousness and bargaining is distasteful to you, let the real estate broker carry the ball for you. He wants to see a sale made. Or make your first offer a little closer to the asking price (if this makes you feel better and you can afford it). But again, remember, that most sellers figure on coming down at least 5 to 10 per cent, even more on high-priced properties, and have this much cushion built into the price at the start.

Finally, of course, there is also the stubborn owner who won't budge. You have to meet his price or it's no deal; take it or leave it. If his price is outrageously high, you go elsewhere. But if you feel the house is worth his price, you have to meet it or no sale.

If your bid is decisively rejected, you must either quit or raise enough to make a difference. A reasonable increase is 2½ to 5 per cent, at least $500 more on a $20,000 house, or $1000 if you started very low, and then in steps of $500.

Typical Bidding

Say you are interested in a $22,500 house. The owner probably paid around $17,000 for it a few years before. He has sunk money into it, you admit privately. But the house is in a neighborhood of $20,000 houses. You decide you will go up to $19,500 but no higher. If you offer $19,000 or $19,500 for it at first, you leave yourself little room for bargaining. Besides, first offers are almost always turned down as a matter of custom.

You therefore offer $17,500 to start. Pay little attention to the cries of indignation from the broker. He'll say that it is an insult to present such an offer to the seller. Tell him to swallow his pride and deliver your offer. He'll phone back in a few hours and tell you that he told you so, the offer is much too low. The seller laughed at the bid. However, the broker continues, the seller has just decided to let the house go for a mere $22,000, provided it's a quick sale.

Now things are beginning to stir. You answer that you need a day or two to think it over. Maybe you had better take another look at the house. You show more interest now, but now is also the time to check the house thoroughly and bring up *your* reasons why the house may be worth less.

The real estate broker calls to confirm another appointment to see the house. "By the way," he says, "another man is coming out to see it tonight. He's really interested." You are left with the impression that you had better hike your bid fast and act if you want the house.

This is one of the oldest ploys in the business. There are always other buyers in the wings. To be sure, another person is sometimes interested, until he hears that the house costs more than $15,000. Discount this kind of pressure unless you really have good reason to believe it.

In fact, when you return to the house you could casually do a little softening up yourself. "I'm having a hard time deciding," you say offhand. "There's another house on the other side of town my wife and I also like a lot. And, it's somewhat cheaper."

If the owner truly has to sell, he'll suffer a mild case of fright. Within a day or two you're likely to hear that he'll come down another $500. "After all, you have redecorating to do, and in all fairness, this will take care of it." You say $19,000 is the highest you'll go and that's that. You may get a surprising acceptance then and there. Or after a lit-

tle more give and take you get the house at around $20,000
—$500 more than you originally figured, but you were
dead set on the house and no other.

Other Negotiating Tips

Suppose you deal directly with the owner and no real
estate broker is involved. If the house is also listed with
brokers, you know at once that the owner is prepared to
accept 5 per cent below the listed price, or whatever the
customary broker's fee is. That is the net price he would
get if a broker sold it. You should be able to buy the house,
therefore, for the same net price, at least.

Sometimes owners have two prices, one for brokers, one
for people dealing direct. You may never know this. You
have to proceed with discretion. Start with a low offer and
work up.

Sometimes when you deal directly with the owner he will
say that the price mentioned is the "broker's price" or the
"agent's price." This is his way of saying that if you buy
without a broker, you can deduct the broker's commission
from the asking price.

Finally, bargaining is an art. Of course, it can be carried
too far. Make too many low bids, overdo it, and you make
yourself *persona non grata*. It requires tact and a knowledge
of human nature. Outright lying is never necessary—but
you do have to learn to spar, to feint, and to allow the
owner to save face. If you feel incapable of the give and
take, you can simply offer the highest price you are willing
to pay and let that be your firm offer. Better still, make at
least one feeler offer, somewhat lower. You may be sur-
prised at how fast it is accepted. Or deal through a broker
and let him do your bargaining.

The Deposit and Binder

When the seller and you agree on a price, you hand over
a deposit to show good faith. It will be deducted later from
your down payment. But a few days later the seller may
get a higher offer from someone else and return your
money. You're out in the cold, unless the deposit has been

accompanied by an iron-clad contract, sometimes called a binder or "offer to purchase," giving you an unbreakable option to buy the house within sixty or ninety days. Or the deal falls through because you cannot get a reasonable mortgage and your deposit is not returned.

The binder or "offer to purchase" represents one of the most important single acts in the buying of a house. You put into writing your intention to buy. There is no special wording. Sometimes it is called a Preliminary or Conditional Sales Contract, a Deposit Receipt, Offer to Buy, or just plain Contract. It must be signed by both the buyer and the seller. It may be on a mere scrap of old paper and accompanied by no cash deposit or down payment whatever, but once signed by both parties it becomes absolutely binding. You have committed yourself to buy the house, and the seller has committed to sell to you under the terms of the paper you signed. (Once in a while a technical mistake in the wording of the offer-to-purchase contract may provide a loophole for either the seller or you to back out, but this is unusual.)

For self-protection, therefore, don't sign a binder or whatever else it may be called until your lawyer has looked it over. Better still, have your lawyer draw it up. You should clearly understand and be agreeable to everything it says. There is no need for stilted language; you have a right to insist that it be written in clear, understandable English. It should contain specific information and details about the property, the terms of payment, and certain escape clauses for yourself (though not every seller will consent to all you may wish), as follows:

1. That the sale is subject to an appraisal acceptable to you by an independent professional appraiser, or an FHA or VA appraiser. (But try to do this before you give a deposit.)

2. That the sale is contingent upon one or more inspections made for you by a contractor, construction or termite expert (hired by you), or other inspections you may wish. Sometimes the inspection is paid for by the seller, sometimes by you.

3. The approximate date of closing the sale, the day when title is conveyed to the buyer.

4. The date you move into the house.

5. The rent to be charged to the seller if he occupies the house after closing day.

6. A short time limit during which the seller can either accept or reject the offer.

7. Full price of the house, amount of deposit, down payment, and a legal description of the property, including lot number, location, and lot size.

8. The kind of mortgage loan to be obtained, length of time it will run, and maximum interest you will pay. Also specify that you are not to pay any discount premium (as discussed in the financing chapter).

9. The top limit on total closing costs that you are willing to pay, including the cost of title insurance.

10. How much prorating of taxes between you and the seller.

11. The type of deed the seller is to convey.

12. The seller is to furnish an abstract of title (though not customary in all states).

13. Appliances, special equipment, furnishings, storm windows, screens, and anything else that is to come with the house. Get appliance serial numbers, if possible.

How much deposit should you give? As little as possible. Ten dollars is often adequate. You may be asked for a $100, but then $50 is enough. The amount of deposit is actually of small value; *the crucial thing is the contract that accompanies it.*

Choosing a Lawyer

Choose one who specializes in real estate. Not all lawyers are real estate experts. In most states a lawyer will be indispensable for closing the deal. So you won't save money by putting off getting one until after you have made a deposit. An exception is sometimes made in states such as California, in which a bank's escrow department customarily handles real estate transactions.

The Steps (Mostly Legal) in Buying a House

Here is a review of the main steps in buying a house.

Signing a binder or "offer to purchase." This highly important first step must be signed by both parties. It commits you to buy the house (in line with the terms and special conditions of what you sign). It need not be accompanied by a deposit or down payment but usually is. This is, in fact, a binding sales contract, even though the word "contract" may be discreetly omitted.

The down payment or deposit given to the seller along with the offer-to-purchase contract is also called "earnest money," showing that you are in earnest. On the other hand, you may give the seller an impressive $10,000 down payment on a house and he legally may still sell the house to somebody else *unless* there also is an accompanying offer-to-purchase and both of you have signed it. The amount of down payment normally is 5 or 10 per cent of the house price, though the smaller the amount the seller will take, the better.

Whatever the amount, it is credited against the total price of the house. If you renege on the deal, the seller may keep the money as payment for his time and trouble. In other words, it is the seller's consolation prize when a buyer does not fulfill his part of the bargain.

What if the seller reneges, decides not to sell to you, and returns your down payment? He may have found another buyer who will pay more, or he simply may have had a change of heart. You may sue him for damages, but this is generally more trouble and expense than it is worth. You may also sue to force him to go through with the deal, but here the law is generally in your favor. He probably will be ordered to sell to you (provided, of course, that the offer-to-purchase contract has no gaping loophole). It has long been established law to recognize that each individual property may have unique appeal to a particular buyer and no other lot or house is exactly like it.

Morning-after Panic

Shortly after signing to buy a house many people are struck with this psychological depression, particularly the first-time house buyer. Did you do the right thing? Or are you chained to mortgage debt for a house you really do not want? Some people begin worrying about how to get out of the deal, and how to get their down payment back.

Brace yourself and remember that second thoughts like these are common. Many people experience them. Secondly, if you have read a book like this one, or simply used your head, and investigated the entire deal in advance, everything is probably all right. You also know that there is no perfect house. You had better get busy arranging for the mortgage and prepare to move.

Obtaining a Mortgage Commitment

This is that written notice from a bank or other lender saying that it will give you a mortgage to buy the house. The mortgage itself is not signed and sealed until closing day, but before you can set a date for closing you must be assured that you can finance the house—i.e., obtain a mortgage. You will have or should have inquired about a mortgage, of course, before you signed to buy.

After you agree to buy you set in motion your formal request for a mortgage. You fill out a mortgage application, your credit is checked, an appraisal is made of the house, the ownership records (title) of the house is checked at the local courthouse, and when everything is satisfactory the lender sends you the commitment, a simple letter saying that a mortgage will be provided. Then a date is set to close the deal for the house—i.e., closing day.

During the time between the contract and the closing you should also investigate such things as the closing costs you will be charged (Chapter 25). That is, if you hadn't prudently investigated the potential closing-cost charges even before you signed the binder. What will they be?

What should you pay and what does the seller pay? In some states, as noted earlier, the buyer customarily pays for oil left in the fuel tank. And although title insurance is normally paid for by the buyer, it is the custom in some states for the seller to pay for title insurance. It's best to determine all such closing-cost charges before closing, and preferably before you even sign the initial contract.

The Closing

The loose ends are pulled together and you formally buy the house and take legal possession. In some states you and the seller, together with your lawyers and others involved, get together at a specified time and place to carry out a somewhat ceremonious legal transaction. In other states, the same things are done for you and the seller by lawyers or by what are called escrow agents.

At the closing you pay the seller the remaining money you owe him. This is usually the remaining cash to fulfill the total down-payment requirement, and the balance is the money advanced for the mortgage loan you obtain. You sign for the mortgage, pay the closing costs charges, reimburse the seller for any taxes and insurance he has paid in advance, and he turns the deed over to you. This is unless, for example, you are to pay the seller part or all of the price in future installment payments. Then the deed is withheld until you have paid in full.

After the Closing

You shake hands with the buyer, everybody says formal words of congratulations to everybody else, and you arrange to move into your new house. Sometimes, however, the seller may not have moved out or, even worse, a tenant is ensconced in the place and may have no plans for leaving. Here is where you may be confronted with a little problem since possession is nine tenths of the law. Or you may have purchased a new house from a builder but the house is not finished, or the unpaved streets, mired in mud, are far from passable.

Such contingencies should be anticipated. Your occupancy rights should be clearly ascertained before closing day and put in writing. If there is a tenant who has not moved, postpone the closing date until he has. Otherwise the tenant is protected by whatever agreement he had made with the seller. He may have a lease for another year or, worst of all, prior rights to buy the house at a price lower than you paid. Then there is little you can do. So if there is a tenant and a lease, you should insist on seeing the lease before you sign any contract. If it is an oral lease, you should obtain from the tenant a written bill of particulars specifying all pertinent facts of his occupancy.

If you contract for an unfinished house from a builder, it is best to put off the closing day until the house is ready for occupancy. Then stop and see that the house is absolutely complete before you close for it. To protect yourself, the initial contract should specify that the house will be completed and ready for occupancy by a specified date; if not, you should retain the right to invalidate the purchase and have your deposit returned.

CHAPTER 23

SHOULD YOU USE A
REAL ESTATE BROKER?

By all means, yes. Use more than one. At the same time you also can be shopping on your own. First it may pay to scout the houses that are advertised by owners. Then the broker's fee might come off the price if you buy directly.

On the other hand, a good broker can do you much good. But you should know first what a broker can and cannot do for you. He is a clearing center for houses. He can screen houses for you and save you many a wild goose chase. Just as some sellers never will list their houses with brokers, others will put their houses completely in a broker's hands. The houses are not advertised except by a broker.

A good broker can give you general information about a community, tell you about the stores, churches, and schools, and drive you around to see houses in his car. He can help you get financing, and according to a survey of home buyers, brokers provide surprisingly helpful service "in telling buyers in advance about closing costs, and then following up by handling red tape details involved in the sales transaction." They also can act as your middleman for bargaining purposes, as noted in the last chapter.

Surprisingly, though the seller pays the fee, nonetheless, many a broker is on the buyer's side. Not all, of course. But more than you may think. They say: "The buyer is moving into the community. He may be back to sell his house in a few years. Or if we treat him right he sends friends and relatives to us. This is one of our biggest sources of new business."

The broker's commission is usually 5 per cent of the sales price. Sometimes it is 4 or 6 per cent, and ranges up to 10 per cent for farms and houses in rural areas. It is paid by the *seller*, never the buyer. No reputable broker will ask a fee to find you a house. The one exception, occasionally, is if you ask one to locate a special house in a particular location thereby requiring special effort on his part over and above the usual performance expected. The fee should be agreed upon in writing beforehand.

Brokers' Weak Points

Two common complaints about brokers is that they use high pressure tactics, and don't show real interest in showing people the kind of house specified. Much complaint is also made about brokers who glibly tell you that a house is "well built." This brings up a fact to remember:

By and large, brokers know little or nothing about house design and construction. What's more, they're not expected to know any more than a Wall Street broker specializing in electronics stocks is expected to know all about electronics. So don't believe what a broker may say about the design or construction of a house. ("You can easily knock out that wall and make one big room." "It's a terrifically strong house." "Great layout and outstanding design." This sort of thing is largely baloney compounded with nonsense.) A really good broker keeps his mouth shut about such things. It also should be said, though, that some brokers are former builders, or just through sheer exposure to houses year after year, they have developed a sixth sense which in general gives them insight into the kind of construction that stands up best in their area, or they know the houses built by the good builders around. But these brokers constitute a decided minority.

Three Other Common Complaints About Brokers

1. Disputes over deposits withheld. A person gives a broker a deposit on a house. The deal falls through but the broker withholds the deposit. If the buyer merely changed his mind out of fickleness, he does not deserve his money back. The broker did his job and deserves compensation. But more often, the buyer has a legitimate right to his money back. The only way, therefore, to protect your de-

posit is to have an escape clause in writing when you hand it over, assuring you of its return if the deal collapses.

2. Disputes over contract terms. The buyer says that a clothes washer and drier were supposed to come with a house. "It was all arranged with the broker." The owner says not so, and hauls them off with him when he moves. The broker is caught in a cross fire of charges. Moral: Everything that goes with the house should be spelled out in writing, including the serial numbers of appliances.

3. Misrepresentation. A broker says that a house is as solidly built as Gibraltar. His client buys it and then finds the place swarming with termites. Or a broker tells you the schools are great (though actually they are over-crowded), or he withholds a little information about the zoning—the buyer finds out later to his distress that a gas station is to be built across the street.

When troubles like these arise, you have recourse to state authorities. They can suspend or revoke the broker's license. If the broker is a realtor member of the local real estate board you can also complain to the board and some redress may be made. But that's closing the barn door too late.

Brokers vs. Realtors

A broker is a person who is licensed to deal in real estate for pay. All states now require that they be licensed. He is sometimes called a real estate salesman or agent. Salesmen also must be licensed. The broker is usually the person who owns the business whereas the salesman is one who works for him. The term agent has no legal meaning; it is a catchall phrase that is used for brokers, and salesmen, and also for realtors.

There are roughly 500,000 licensed brokers and salesmen in the United States—one for every ten houses! A good many are part-timers—housewives, cab drivers, weekend salesmen out for a fast buck. Others are full-time operators in the worst sense of the word. Still others are hard-working professionals who take pride in their work as do people in any other profession.

Only about 70,000, however, less than 15 per cent of the

total, can call themselves *realtors*. A realtor is a licensed
broker or salesman who is a member of the National Association of Real Estate Boards, and also a member of the
local real estate board (of which there are some 1377 in
the country).

By and large you will do well to deal with a realtor.
He is among the leading brokers of a community, but not
always. In other words, many a non-realtor broker is as
reputable as any realtor.

Choosing a Good Broker

Ask friends for the names of good brokers. Call the mortgage officers of a few banks and savings-and-loan associations. Bankers do business every day with brokers. Read
the real estate ads. Which agents run the greatest number
of listings for the kind of house and neighborhood you prefer? (Brokers tend to specialize in a particular neighborhood. A good man will know just about everything about
his neighborhood, including every house bought and sold
there in recent years and the price of the sale.) When one
or two names recur frequently, you have the best men.

The Multiple Listing Service (MLS)

A warning about the MLS: This is a cross-listing of
houses among many brokers in a community. Each broker
member of the MLS lets the rest know of the houses he
has personally listed. As a result, news of a house for sale
is spread among many brokers. If another broker, other than
the originating broker, finds a buyer for the property, the
originating agent still gets part of the sales commission.

The time to be on guard is when a broker takes you
to a house he heard about through the MLS—in other
words, a house originally listed by another broker. Chances
are that the house is beyond your broker's usual territory,
i.e., it is in a neighborhood that may well be unfamiliar to
him. Be on guard here. You cannot rely on getting accurate
information about the neighborhood from your broker.

A New York editor, for example, ended up buying a
house in a neighborhood that seemed to exude exterior

charm but turned out to be loaded with snobbish, status-conscious neighbors. It was, in fact, a restricted neighborhood, and the editor's family had been secretly approved. But after moving in he found the neighbors so prejudiced and intolerant that he had to move; he would not allow his children to grow up there. The broker should have told him about the neighborhood in the first place, but, being unfamiliar with that part of the county, he didn't know.

So if your broker shows you through a MLS house, check the neighborhood. Talk to the broker who originated the listing. Then make an extensive investigation on your own as you would for any other house you might buy.

Obligations to the Broker

A broker serves an essential purpose. Most work hard for their money. One may spend months showing you houses and then you buy through another broker. If he finds a house quickly, he is begrudged his fee. But often he was able to find and sell the house fast only because of much time and experience invested in his business.

Find a good broker and be honest with him. Help him weed out undesirable houses by telling him exactly what you're looking for, the price you can pay, and special features you want. Don't be vague. He may ask personal questions about your job and income to get a line on how much house you can afford. Tell him.

Be on time for appointments. After all, a broker's time is worth money, too. If you already have seen a house through direct contact with the owner or through another broker and you are taken to it by a second broker, speak up at once. Do not enter it with a second broker, or you leave yourself open to a lawsuit.

Once you've landed on a house you like, don't try to elbow out the broker. Don't call the owner on the sly and try to dicker secretly with him. For one thing, it's dishonest. For another, you may need the broker to help with sales details and financing. If you discuss certain things directly with the owner, do it openly. Let the broker know. And if the owner secretly suggests cutting the broker out and splitting his commission between the two of you, don't do it. It's not only dishonest, but he leaves himself open to a lawsuit and you'll be dragged in, too.

CHAPTER 24

FINANCING
Getting the best mortgage deal

You can get a $20,000 mortgage, say, and over the years pay over $18,600 in interest on it. You can get another $20,000 mortgage that will cost you only about $13,000 in interest.

If you come into a windfall and want to pay off your mortgage all at once ahead of time, you may find, unhappily, that you must pay the bank a stiff penalty fee for this privilege. You discover too late that they would prefer you to pay it off over the long run. Another kind of mortgage, however, will permit prepayment at no extra charge, and with proportionate savings on your interest charges to boot. It depends on the small print.

Like buying a car or even the house itself, getting the best home loan at the best terms requires that you shop around, as well as know a few important points about mortgages. The home-loan mortgage represents the biggest single debt that the typical person ever incurs in his lifetime. Yet most of us automatically assume that a mortgage is a mortgage and let's get it over with quickly. Actually, the kind of mortgage you get and the advantages or small-print hooks can vary greatly from bank to bank.

What Is a Mortgage?

It is a special loan for buying a house. A lender puts up the cash to buy the house. You sign a legal document binding you to pay him back in regular payments plus interest for a specified number of years. You pledge the house and its property as security and promise to pay taxes, keep the house insured, and maintain the property in good condition. If you default on payments the lender has the legal right to take over the property. (Most banks, however, will try to work out a reasonable arrangement in case of a financial crisis before they resort to drastic action.)

There are three main kinds of mortgages in the United States—the VA (Veterans Administration), sometimes called the GI mortgage; the FHA (Federal Housing Administration) loan; and the conventional mortgage.

The VA Mortgage

This is in many respects the best kind to have if you can get one. Even if you are a non-veteran you should know about the VA mortgage because you still can take one over when you buy a house from a veteran. To qualify for a VA loan you must be a veteran of World War II or the Korean War. World War II vets must apply before January 25, 1967. Korean War vets have until January 31, 1975.

Chief advantages of a GI mortgage are lowest interest charges of all mortgage loans, lowest down payment requirements, and certain built-in legal protections for the buyer. As this is written, top allowable interest rate for a VA loan is 5¼ per cent; this may go up or down slightly in future years. Sometimes a VA loan is obtainable with no down payment, but most lenders require 5 to 10 per cent down in cash. The loan may run as long as thirty years and you may prepay any or all of it in advance with no penalty.

The government does not put up the money for the loan (except in the case of VA direct loans, discussed below). It protects the lender against loss by guaranteeing up to 60 per cent of the mortgage up to a maximum guarantee of $7500. There is no limit on the mortgage amount; it could be $10,000 or $100,000.

Before the loan is okayed, a VA appraiser inspects the house and sets an appraisal value on it—i.e., says what he thinks the house is worth. You cannot be charged more than this amount. You get a copy of the appraisal, called a "certificate of reasonable value."

Sometimes the appraisal can lead to subterfuge. This is when the seller wants a higher price for his house than the VA appraisal value. Say he wants $20,000 for his house but the VA appraisal is $18,500. A VA mortgage would be rejected if the house is sold for more. A canny seller then might lower the official price of record to $18,500 but turn around and ask you to make up the $1500 difference under the table. This is strictly illegal and can get both of you in hot water.

Suppose you have signed a sales contract based on buying the house at $20,000. If, however, your contract said that the price was dependent on a VA appraisal you can withdraw from the deal with your money back. Otherwise you may be forced to buy at $20,000 and have to get a less advantageous, non-VA mortgage (which does not put protective limits on house price vs. appraisal value).

GI-Loan Disadvantages

The major drawback of VA loans is simply that they are generally hard to obtain because of their low fixed-interest rate. Not many lenders offer them, since they can get higher interest return for their money on other mortgages. Sometimes, however, you can get a VA loan if you pay a premium for it, in other words pay what is called "points," as explained in a moment.

If you are a veteran living in a small town or rural area and unable to get a VA mortgage, you may apply for a VA *direct loan*. This is the only time the government actually puts up cash for any mortgage. Direct VA loans are made for up to $15,000 and they do not require a down payment (unless the house costs more than $15,000). Direct loans, however, are not available in most metropolitan areas where there are supposed to be enough mortgages available.

To get a VA loan, take your *original* military discharge certificate to the nearest VA office and get a paper called a certificate of eligibility. This is essential. It is needed by the bank or lender making the mortgage. For a direct VA loan, see your nearest VA office.

The FHA Mortgage

Anybody can apply for one. But you must meet certain

income requirements based on house price and mortgage carrying charges. The house itself must also pass certain minimum construction standards laid down by the FHA. This means that the house will be a reasonably well built new house or an old house in fairly good condition.

(It does *not* mean, however, that the house is flawless or of top-grade construction, or a bargain. It also does not necessarily mean that the house is superior to another house sold with a conventional mortgage. In most cases, though, an FHA house is the best assurance that you are getting sound construction.)

The FHA interest is almost always lower than conventional mortgage interest. As this is written, FHA rates stand at 5¼ per cent; you cannot be charged more. On top of this you pay another ½ of 1 per cent insurance service charge, thus a total of 5¾ per cent. This makes an FHA loan more expensive than you may think at first. The ½ per cent service charge may, however, be lowered to ¼ of 1 per cent. Part of this service charge is later returned to you as a rebate when you have paid up the mortgage, or if you have owned the house at least five to six years before selling it.

Another advantage of an FHA loan is its low down payment scale. It is 3 to 5 per cent for houses priced up to $18,000, and then steps up for higher-priced houses. The top limit on an FHA mortgage is now $22,500. You can spend more for a house, but you make up the difference in cash. An FHA mortgage can run as long as thirty-five years.

The trouble with an FHA mortgage is that, like a VA loan, it may be hard to obtain, depending on the mortgage market when you apply. When money is "tight," lenders back away from both FHA and VA mortgages, since they prefer the higher interest rate they can get on conventional mortgage loans. An FHA loan also involves a certain amount of red tape.

An FHA mortgage is actually made by many of the same banks and other lenders who offer conventional loans. Like the VA, the FHA does not put up any money. It just insures the lender against loss if the mortgage is foreclosed. The lender puts up the money. More accurately, it is called an FHA-insured mortgage.

FHA-in-Service

If you are on active military duty, you can take advantage of an FHA-in-Service mortgage which is designed to help military people buy houses. It may permit an even lower down payment than required by a regular FHA loan. Interest rate is the same as for a regular FHA loan. But the maximum mortgage loan obtainable is $20,000, rather than $22,500. The Department of Defense pays the ½ per cent service charge for you as long as you are on active duty (which means nearly 10 per cent lower monthly payments). You must have served at least two years on active duty, though not continuously, and eligibility ceases when you go off active duty or retire. You apply for information and a certificate of eligibility at your local military headquarters.

The Conventional Mortgage

This means any non-government mortgage loan made by a bank, savings-and-loan association, insurance company, or anybody else, for that matter, putting up the money to buy a house. A conventional mortgage loan is generally the easiest kind to get, involves the least red tape, and can be obtained fast, sometimes in a few days. But it generally carries the highest interest rates, the largest down payments, and the stiffest small-print restrictions.

Interest rates range from about 5½ per cent in the East up to 7 per cent, sometimes more, in the Far West and Hawaii. Down payments generally range from 25 to 40 per cent, depending mainly on state laws. New York recently passed a law permitting savings banks to accept down payments as low as 10 per cent but not many banks are willing to go this low so far.

The exact down payment required usually will be less for a new house than for an old house. It also depends much on the house's appraised value (usually less than the selling price), and your credit rating. A conventional mortgage generally runs from ten to twenty years, seldom longer.

By the way, you are generally not informed of the appraisal value figure when you get a conventional mortgage. Ironically, you pay for the appraisal but the report goes to the lender. To find out what it is—a good indication of the house's actual value—you must ask. Don't be shy. After all, who has a better right to know? Remember, however, that the appraisal value of a house is almost always lower than the selling price (except with a VA loan). But if it is sharply lower than the price you are paying, you had better find out why.

Can You Avoid Paying "Points"?

A family named Harvey wanted to buy a $20,000 house. They needed an $18,500 FHA mortgage. They were told, however, that an FHA mortgage could be had only if they paid an extra $740 to swing the mortgage deal. This was in addition to the $20,000 price. It meant that they would end up paying $20,740 for the house.

They would not have to pay a $740 premium if they were getting a conventional loan, but this required a much larger down payment than they could afford. The only way they could buy the house was with an FHA loan. So they were forced to pay the extra $740 to get the mortgage. Even if Mr. Harvey had been a veteran and wanted a VA loan, a "points" premium would almost certainly also have been charged.

The paying of "points," sometimes called a "discount," has been a widespread practice with FHA and VA mortgages. It is a complicated thing and takes a little explanation. It is, in effect, a premium or bonus that is paid on top of the house price, in order to get a low-interest, government-backed mortgage. The amount may vary from one or two percentage points of the mortgage up to a stiff twelve points ($1200 extra on a $10,000 mortgage), sometimes more. The exact charge you encounter varies according to the mortgage money market at any one time and where you live. The tighter the national money market (more demand for mortgages than available money to fill the demand), the greater the points charge.

The reason for a points premium, basically, is that FHA and VA mortgages carry lower interest rates than conventional, non-government-backed mortgages. We have noted that, as this is written, both VA and FHA interest rates are fixed at a ceiling of 5½ per cent. Most banks, however, can make more money, in other words get a higher return, by investing in conventional mortgages with interest rates ranging anywhere from 5¾ to over 7 per cent. The mortgage lender says, "Why should we put our depositors' money into government-backed mortgages when we can make more money in conventional loans?" (One answer is that government-backed mortgages are practically riskless, since the government insures the lender against loss in case of foreclosure. This is not true with higher-risk conventional mortgages. But this argument, unfortunately, carries little weight with lenders.)

But sometimes a lender will say, "Okay, we will take an FHA or VA mortgage loan if you sweeten the pot for us. We'll discount the loan in advance." He then proceeds to give people like the Harveys an $18,500 loan discounted at 4 per cent. He skims four points ($740) off the mortgage, and turns around and gives the seller of the house only $17,760 ($18,500 less 4 per cent). The seller, however, may not want to take it on the chin to the tune of $740. So he tells the buyers that they will surreptitiously have to make up the $740 or they cannot have the house. They need the house, it's the only way they can get a mortgage so they are forced to comply.

Now the buyer has still signed up for an $18,500 mortgage, and over the years he pays off this total amount plus interest. Since the lender, however, only laid out $17,760 for an $18,500 FHA loan at 5½ per cent, he will actually make more than 5½ per cent. His return is carefully figured so that his yield actually will come to just about as much on the FHA loan as it would otherwise be on a higher-interest conventional home loan. This is the key to the whole thing.

Not all banks and other lenders, however, like the idea of "points." That is why many a lender often will not give you an FHA or VA mortgage. They abhor the system and avoid it by dealing only in conventional mortgages. It should also be said that there has been a gradual leveling off in the paying of points since the Kennedy administration took over in 1961. And when mortgages are easy to come by, as is predicted for the 1960s, VA and particularly FHA loans may again be available with little or no points premium required.

Law Forbids Buyer to Pay Points but . . .

Here it should be emphatically said that the government forbids the *buyer* to pay the "points" charge for an FHA or VA loan. The builder or seller may absorb it, but *not* the buyer. Unfortunately, though, what usually happens is that a builder will bury the charge in the price of his houses, or a seller will hike the price of his house enough to allow for absorbing the points charge. Or the buyer will be discreetly but firmly told that he has to pay for it under the table, or under the guise of another name, as happened to the Harveys.

Summed up, you may or may not get involved in "points," depending on mortgage availability when you buy a house. If mortgages are hard to obtain where you live and at the time you buy, you may find points charged for an FHA or VA loan.

What can you do about it, if anything? First call a few banks, real estate brokers, or mortgage brokers to find out if points are customary. If a sizable amount is involved you have a few alternatives. You can try for a conventional mortgage at a higher interest rate and higher down payment. Or you can frankly tell the seller of the house that if he wants a sale the points situation is *his* business. You can afford only an FHA (or VA) loan and that's that. Of course, he may, with a four-letter word, tell you where to go. Or he will bite his lip and accept the deal. Or, if you really want the house and the seller won't budge, you'll probably end up paying the points charge in one way or another.

Paying Points for a New House Mortgage

If you are buying a new house from a builder with an FHA or VA loan, it is often likely, as just mentioned, that the "points" charge is buried in the price of the house. You pay for them but don't know it. Like the man who sold his house to the Harveys, the builder takes it on the chin when *he* gets paid for the FHA or VA mortgages his customers sign up for. The lender financing the houses discounts each mortgage and the builder gets that much less money. At times many builders took such a beating on this that they were forced into bankruptcy. Now, however, most builders, forced to play the game for economic survival, simply rig the price of the houses in camouflaged ways and the buyer pays extra for the privilege of low down payment and low interest on FHA or VA financing.

Ask the builder if his FHA or VA mortgages are discounted. By how many points? Can you get your own mortgage for one of his houses? If so, will he give you a break on the house price equivalent to the points charge he normally would "pay" the bank?

Say, for example, the Harveys were buying their $20,-000 house from a builder who had arranged for $18,500 FHA mortgages. Say further that the builder had to pay four points for these mortgages, so he was actually getting only $19,260 for each house he sold ($1500 down payment from the buyer, plus $17,760 from the bank for each $18,500 mortgage they give on his houses, thus $19,260 net cash). If you provide your own mortgage, will he sell the house to you for this same price? Or for whatever the net price happens to be, depending on the points charge when you buy?

You should also know that FHA and VA do permit a mortgage service charge of up to 1 per cent of the mortgage, regardless of whether you are buying a new or old house. This is perfectly legal. It is sometimes called a mortgage commitment fee, or just plain fee. It is a legitimate charge to cover the expense of procuring and processing the mortgage. And if you build a house with FHA "construction" financing, FHA permits a charge of up to 2½ per cent on the money you borrow for construction. Not all lenders, however, charge the full 1 per cent service fee or the full 2½ per cent construction charge. Some are not that greedy, another reason why it pays to shop for the best mortgage terms you can get. The mortgage service charge, by the way, is part of your closing costs (next chapter).

Where Do You Obtain a Mortgage?

From a savings bank, commercial bank, savings-and-loan association, mortgage broker, insurance company, or from a rich aunt, for that matter. Try each. Try your local banks first, particularly the one where you may have an account. But before accepting its terms, shop elsewhere for comparison.

In general, a savings bank is likely to give you better terms than a commercial bank. A savings-and-loan association specializes in mortgage financing, but, by and large, it prefers conventional loans over lower-interest, government-backed loans. Then try the nearest mortgage broker, and the local offices of insurance companies. These sources, however, can be quite impersonal, and possible complications may arise due to distance. Your own life-insurance company may be inclined to give you preferential treatment, but don't count on it. Insurance companies also have been known to require that you take out life-insurance protection equivalent to the mortgage amount whether you want it or not. This hook can be expensive.

Do not overlook that rich aunt who may be sitting on a tidy nest egg that she'd like to invest. But keep the deal on a firm business level and *your* lawyer should approve the fine print just as if you were dealing with a stranger. Each of these mortgage sources can provide an FHA or VA mortgage as well as a conventional mortgage.

How Much Down Payment?

The minimum down payment required depends on the

loan, as we've seen. But don't let the minimum be your sole guide. The larger the down payment you can make, the better. A large down payment means a smaller mortgage, smaller monthly carrying charges, and less total interest. Say you can afford enough cash down to hold your mortgage to $15,000 instead of $20,000. On a twenty-year 5½ per cent mortgage, the smaller loan would save you a total of $3254 in interest charges.

On the other hand, don't overextend yourself. Don't use all your cash for the down payment. Obviously, you should allow for moving expenses, and the inevitable fix-up, landscaping, and decorating bills. Here is how monthly payments vary for a $10,000 loan at 5½ per cent; monthly payments and interest would be 50 per cent higher for a $15,000 loan, 100 per cent higher for a $20,000 loan, and so on.

TERM OF LOAN	MONTHLY PAYMENTS FOR PRINCIPAL AND INTEREST	TOTAL INTEREST PAID AT END
20 years	$68.80	$6510
25	61.50	8423
30	56.78	10,441

Thus, your choice falls between two extremes: 1) signing up for a long-term twenty-five- or thirty-year loan with the lowest monthly payments, but highest total interest in the end; and 2) a relatively short-term mortgage but with monthly payments that may be too much of a burden. Best compromise is the term with the top monthly payments you can afford now, making an allowance for your additional expenditures for taxes, insurance, and house upkeep. Later when your children are older, or your income has increased, you can make extra payments to pay off your loan in advance (provided you have arranged for a mortgage that permits paying off ahead of time).

A few more words should be said about interest rates. It is not always the specter many people fear. Lenders charge much less interest on home loans than on almost any other typical consumer loan. Compared with renting a house, paying off a mortgage plus interest for a house you buy is almost always cheaper. What you spend for interest is also tax deductible. So don't let interest rate alone determine the kind of mortgage you get. Other features of the mortgage should be weighed one against the other along with what the interest rate will be.

Monthly Payments Required to Repay a Mortgage of $10,000

To help you decide on the best plan, here are the monthly payments including principal and interest for different loan periods at different interest rates.

Maturity	5¼%	5½%	5¾%	6%	6¼%
10 years	$107.30	$108.60	$109.80	$111.00	$112.29
12 years	93.75	95.10	96.30	97.60	98.89
15 years	80.39	81.80	83.10	84.40	85.75
20 years	67.39	68.80	70.30	71.70	73.10
25 years	59.93	61.50	63.00	64.40	65.97

The above figures can be used to compute your monthly payments for any other mortgage amount at the same interest and number of years given. Monthly payments for a $15,000 mortgage would be 50 per cent greater than above; 100 per cent greater for a $20,000 mortgage and so on. For example, a $20,000 mortgage at 5½ per cent paid off over twenty years would require monthly payments of $137.60, exactly twice the $68.80 monthly payment (from chart above) for a $10,000 mortgage at the same interest and the same twenty-year period.

Monthly payments for mortgages up to forty years, and for interest rates in ¼ per cent steps from 4½ up to 6½ per cent, are given in a handy little book, *Improved Payment Tables for Monthly Mortgage Loans;* $1 from Financial Publishing Co., 82 Brookline Avenue, Boston 15, Massachusetts.

Three Special Provisions to Ask For

Not all mortgage contracts contain the following special provisions. Ask for them, or go to another lender.

1. *Prepay without penalty clause* which, as already mentioned, lets you pay off your home ahead of time without a penalty charge. Your monthly payments, however, do not decrease; just the over-all time required to pay off the mortgage and total interest are reduced. Some lenders accept prepayment of up to 20 per cent of the mortgage in any year without penalty. Others charge extra if you prepay. The FHA permits prepayment up to 15 per cent in any year without penalty. The VA is the most lenient; you can prepay any amount with no penalty.

2. A *skip-payment clause* which is comparatively new and can be a boon in a crisis. After about five years it permits you to pass up one monthly payment a year. Your mortgage term is extended by the months skipped and the missed interest is added on. Here again the VA is generous —you can skip up to a year's payments, deferring that much principal and interest. The FHA has no such provision. It is also called an *automatic grace period* provision.

3. A *flexible open-end clause* which permits you to re-open, renew, or even increase your mortgage by as much money as you've already paid off. If after five years, say, you have paid off $1500 and you abruptly need cash to pay a big medical bill or expand your attic, on request the $1500 will be returned to you and the mortgage is extended another five years at the *original interest rate*.

Many people can borrow against a mortgage, but without the open-end clause they pay a steeper interest rate on the borrowed money. The open-end deal is also much cheaper than taking out a personal loan or a short-term modernization loan, both of which carry stiff interest rates. It can also be used for adding major appliances like a washer or drier, provided these are made a fixed part of the house and are not movable. It is sometimes called a *package* provision, and the exact wording and limitations vary for different lenders.

Sales Contract Financing

If you cannot obtain a regular mortgage, the seller may propose that he sell you the house on time. He will make a contract whereby you give him a down payment and pay off the balance in regular payments over a certain number of years. This is sometimes called contract financing. In effect, he gives you a mortgage.

But beware: it can be tricky. The contract terms are whatever you and he agree on. The down payment, monthly payments, and interest rate can vary greatly from small to large. Since there is no one (such as VA, FHA, or a conservative bank) to protect you, sales contracts often carry a variety of hooks to protect the seller. Prepayment may be barred. You may not even be allowed to improve the house without the seller's approval. The usual reason for such contracts is that the house has inherent flaws which rule out an FHA, VA, or conventional mortgage. Avoid one unless you know exactly what you're doing and a good real estate lawyer is protecting *your* interests.

The Second Mortgage

This can be a crutch to help you swing the deal for a house. It also can be highly expensive, and even lead to loss of your house.

Assume you want to buy a $20,000 house but the maximum first (regular) mortgage you can get is $13,000. You only have $3000 for a down payment. Another $4000 is needed before you can buy the house. It is proposed that you obtain a second mortgage for this amount. Tread carefully at this stage.

For one thing, a second mortgage usually carries a higher interest rate than a first mortgage. For another, its term may run only five or ten years, thus with proportionately higher monthly payments. For still another, if you only can get a $13,000 mortgage on a $20,000 house, the house may be wildly overpriced.

When you apply for a second mortgage at the same time you are getting a regular first mortgage for a house you are buying, you should notify the lender giving you the first mortgage (the $13,000 noted above). He generally must approve the second mortgage terms since, naturally, he wants assurance that you can carry the total financing burden, and he also wants to avoid subjecting the first mortgage to foreclosure proceedings.

A second mortgage is almost always limited to a deal involving a conventional mortgage loan. They are not permitted by FHA. The VA allows them only under certain conditions.

There is another kind of second mortgage which you may need when you take over the existing mortgage of a house you are buying. This is a different matter. The existing mortgage may have been substantially reduced over the years by the owner, and you may be unable to make up the difference between it and the house price with cash. You need additional financing—i.e., another loan or "second" mortgage. It usually can be had at much the same interest rate and terms as a regular mortgage. Nevertheless, of course, the total monthly charges for both should be in line with your ability to pay.

Taking Over an Existing Mortgage

A house you buy may have a mortgage on it. Then you may save money by taking it over from the seller, particularly if it has a lower interest rate than prevailing rates at the time you buy. Many existing VA mortgages, for example, carry interest rates as low as 4 per cent, the initial postwar interest rate on such mortgages, and 4¾ per cent as late as 1959. Many FHA mortgages were issued at a rate as low as 4 per cent. In fact, old conventional mortgages also carry lower rates than new loans today. You usually can take over the same mortgage at the same interest rate, even if it is a VA loan and you are not a veteran. In addition to lower interest, closing costs are usually lower, compared with starting fresh with a new mortgage.

The drawback in taking over an existing mortgage is that a high down payment may be necessary. You have to make up the full amount of the mortgage that has been paid off by the seller.

Special Mortgage Help

Suppose you find it exceedingly hard to get a mortgage. If you live in a large city and are repeatedly turned down because you are colored or a member of another minority group, or if you live in a small town or rural area, mortgages are hard to come by. Then you could turn to the Voluntary Home Mortgage Credit Program. It is a joint industry-government group set up by Congress to aid home buyers unable to obtain FHA or VA loans locally. You have to prove that you have been turned down by at least two local lenders. Then the VHMCP will step in and try to locate a home loan for you from co-operating banks, savings-and-loan associations, or insurance companies in nearby cities. Since its inception six years ago, VHMCP has helped about 50,000 people get mortgages amounting to nearly $500 million. VHMCP does this at no cost to applicants. Write to the Voluntary Home Mortgage Credit Program, Washington 25, D.C., for details.

How Long Does It Take to Get Mortgage Approval?

It may take only a week or two, or up to two or three months. VA approval generally takes the longest time.

Your income, credit, and job standing are checked; an expert must appraise the value of the house and its neighborhood. Ownership records must be checked at the local courthouse to be sure there is a clear title.

When all has been done and approved, you receive a paper from the lender called a mortgage commitment. This makes it official. He has committed himself to giving you a mortgage. Then a date is set to close the deal, settlement day. This is when the loose ends are tied together and the deal is formally closed. But be prepared, for settlement day is also the time you are charged for a variety of expenses called "closing costs" (next chapter).

For additional information on mortgages: Write for "FHA Facts for Home Buyers," 15¢, from the U. S. Government Printing Office, Washington 25, D.C.; "Financing the Home," Circular A1.3, 15¢, from the Small Homes Council, Mumford House, University of Illinois, Urbana, Illinois; if you are a veteran write to the Veterans Administration, Washington 25, D.C., for "Loans for Veterans," VA pamphlet 4A-1, no charge.

Mortgage Check List

1. Shop for a mortgage. Don't accept the first acceptance you get. The mortgage market fluctuates from month to month and year to year. At times mortgages are tough to get and you have to shop just to find one. At other times it is a buyer's market. Lenders look for people like you. They soften their requirements and lower their rates, vying with each other for your business. Compare the terms and features offered by each for the best deal. A VA mortgage is generally your best bet, an FHA loan, next best.

2. Interest rate is important, but don't let it blind you to other advantages. A conventional mortgage at slightly higher interest may well be as good or better than a VA or FHA especially if a high "discount" is attached to the government-insured loan.

3. Don't commit yourself to a high down payment and stiff monthly payments that will tax your family budget. Leave enough cash left after the down payment to pay for closing costs, moving, and the inevitable fix-up and improvement expenses (even with a new house). Buy as much house as you can afford—but be certain you can afford what you buy.

4. Check on the special features and restrictive clauses in the mortgage contract. Is prepayment allowed without penalty? Is there an open-end clause? A skip-payment clause?

5. Is there a mortgage you can take over?

6. Avoid a second mortgage.

7. Hire a lawyer to check the mortgage contract in advance, as well as handle the whole transaction.

CLOSING COSTS

On the day you close the deal for a house you are presented with a group of expenses called "closing costs." Sometimes they are called settlement costs. They are *in addition* to the price of the house and can range anywhere from $250 to $1000, sometimes more.

They sometimes come as a shock. You pay them for a new or old house. They vary from city to city and state to state, but wherever you live you pay them or you don't get the house.

Rightfully, they should be figured as part of the house cost. If you know about them in advance, you may get a break by special arrangement with the seller or mortgage lender, by bargaining, or simply by refusing to buy the house unless they are reduced. They fall into three main groups of expenses associated with the transaction of buying: mortgage service charges, title search and insurance, and transfer of ownership charges.

Mortgage Service Charges

As already noted, this is also called the mortgage commitment fee, the mortgage broker's fee, or just a fee. It is a charge for such things as the cost of obtaining a mortgage in the first place, preparing the loan papers, notary fees, and processing it. By itself it will range anywhere from $50 to $300 or more—from ½ to 1½ per cent of the mortgage itself. Buy the house for cash or take over an existing mortgage and you could eliminate this expense.

The size of the mortgage service charge depends chiefly on your mortgage lender. Some lenders only charge about $50 to $75; others a flat percentage of the mortgage—1 per cent, say, a flat $200 on a $20,000 mortgage. You should ask what it will be when you shop for a mortgage.

It is best when the mortgage-fee charges are itemized one by one. Some lenders automatically do this. The total is almost always lower than if you are billed a flat percentage fee. Lenders who do not itemize these charges may tell you that they customarily charge a flat percentage and that's that, take it or leave it. These people are in the driver's seat when mortgages are hard to get, as during the tight-money period of the second Eisenhower administration. But when mortgage money is plentiful and lenders actually solicit mortgages, they will offer inducements for mortgage buyers. Then the mortgage service charges are low or even eliminated. After all, they will be making a steady 5½ to over 6 per cent interest every month on your loan, and when they need mortgages they figure they can give up the thick icing on the cake—additional charges just for issuing mortgages.

Title Search and Title Insurance

This will cost you another $75 to $300, sometimes more, depending on such things as the house price and location. Before you buy a house you naturally want to be sure that you are buying it from the legal owner and there is no question about its ownership. This requires a check of the title records, generally at the local courthouse, a "title search."

A search, however, is not enough. A long-absent heir may turn up and claim that he is the rightful owner. Other snags can develop to jeopardize ownership. Thus a title insurance policy is recommended for most people. The mortgage lender almost always insists on a title policy, in addition to a search. Naturally, if something abruptly turns up to threaten your title to the house, the lender wants to be sure he gets repaid in full for his mortgage loan.

But there are two kinds of title policies. The first is the *mortgagee* policy. It protects the lender only. You pay for it but you get little protection from it. There is also the *owner's,* or fee, policy. This is what you need for title insurance protection. Almost everybody should buy both kinds.

Two policies may seem illogical and totally unnecessary. But for highly complicated legal reasons, coupled with our wildly archaic real estate laws in most states, most of us need two title policies. Now you may pay for a mortgagee policy for the lender—you have no choice if you want a mortgage—but balk at buying a second policy for yourself. Many people stubbornly do this. Unfortunately, though, if a showdown later developed over ownership of your property, you would painfully learn that your stubbornness was ill advised. You could have great legal expense to defend your rights. But if you had an owner's policy, too, the title insurance company would step in and pay for your defense. In other words, defense against cranks and nuisance suits (such as a neighbor who may claim you overlap his property) are as much a benefit of title insurance as the protection you get against outright loss of your home.

Sometimes the cost of a title search and the mortgagee (lender's) policy are lumped together in one charge. The owner's policy should be bought at the same time. The extra charge for this second policy is comparatively low if you get it at the same time, usually closing day, at which the other policy is issued.

Title search and insurance charges are generally lowest when you buy a development house from a builder who has arranged for a batch of title insurance policies on his entire development. This cuts the cost of each individual policy. Some big builders, such as Levitt & Sons, even provide a mortgagee title policy at no charge. An additional owner's policy will cost you about $35 to $50 more, cheap additional protection, if you get it on closing day.

When you buy an existing house title insurance sometimes can be had at a discount if the house had changed hands before within the last five to ten years and a title policy had been issued then. You should then ask about a "reissue policy." Some title firms give a 40 to 50 per cent discount on a reissue policy if they hold the original policy. Others do not. Ask about this. Don't just accept the policy that happens to be sold by the lawyer or bank handling the sale. The seller should produce his title policy for you in advance. Or talk to the bank who holds his mortgage. Ask for the name of the title company who insured his mortgage. A call to their representative should tell you whether or not you can save money.

Transfer of Ownership Charges

This third category of closing costs consists of a variety of small and annoying charges which you generally can do little about. It covers such things as recording the deed ($5 to $15), appraisal fee ($10 to $20, though this is sometimes lumped under mortgage service fee), credit report ($5 to $25), property survey ($40 to $50, though the seller sometimes can provide an old survey), federal and local tax stamps (from $10 to $50), and legal fees. Depending on the lender, you may have to pay for the lender's lawyer (up to $100 or more), as well as your own lawyer; the lawyer's fee should be determined in advance.

Any Other Costs?

Yes, though technically speaking these are not closing costs. You still pay them on closing day, so be prepared. They may include the payment of escrow money (required when you get an FHA mortgage), for insurance. Escrow money is an advance payment for taxes and fire and hazard insurance. It goes into a special fund to protect the lender should you fall behind in your regular monthly mortgage payments.

When you buy an existing house, the property and school taxes are generally paid up for a period after you take possession. You therefore reimburse the seller for what he has paid ahead. Sometimes he will also ask you to pay for the oil left in the tank.

Closing-Cost Summary

The important thing about closing costs is to pin them down in advance. Real estate brokers, lenders, and builders sometimes play them down. They may say, "Oh, figure on two or three hundred dollars." Later you find that they have somehow risen to twice that amount. So:

1. Insist on a complete list of closing-day charges including lawyers' fees before closing day, preferably before you hand over a down payment and sign any contract for the house. Don't be brushed off. Don't take no for an answer. Actually, the exact charges for all the potential bills are impossible to ascertain beforehand. So:

2. Give yourself an out in the contract, an escape clause, by including the maximum amount of closing-day charges that you will pay. If total closing costs exceed what you believe are fair and reasonable, the contract should state that you can call off the deal and get your deposit back. Be specific; put a figure in the contract. For example, "If closing costs, including the cost of an owner's title insurance policy, plus all other charges to be paid by the buyer on closing day in excess of the stated price of the house exceed $—— [specify your amount here], this contract is void and the down payment will be returned to the buyer." This clause will give you strong bargaining power later when the chips are down. Then the mere threat of walking out on the deal will often shake up the seller, the lender, or others involved, and they may well reduce or absorb certain charges.

3. Arrange for reduced closing costs before closing day. Try to get the seller to provide the survey if necessary; after all, he is selling you the property and he should vouch for its boundaries. What does the lender charge for mortgage service fee? If you think it is too high, tell him you are going to another lender. He may or may not come down, depending on how badly he wants your business. Remember that your bargaining position is at its peak *before* you sign the contract. Up to this point the builder or owner eager to sell may be quite willing to absorb certain charges. And don't be afraid to bargain on closing costs just as you should bargain on the house itself. Once you sign the contract your bargaining power vanishes forever.

No stigma is attached to bargaining for lower closing costs or to bidding for a house, for that matter, provided of course that it is done in an honest, straightforward manner and is not offensive. Nevertheless, many of us find it distasteful or, for curious reasons, improper. We may feel that we are acting honorably and that all of the costs presented to us are also honorable and justified. Unfortunately, real estate does not always work this way.

For one thing, the give-and-take of bargaining has been so established by custom that you are often expected to bargain. For another, the original terms asked may be set as high as the traffic will bear and the buyer beware. For still another, certain aspects of your particular house sale, mortgage, or closing costs may legitimately justify lower charges and it is up to you to mention them. It is therefore not only perfectly proper to raise such questions and "bargain," but it is incumbent upon you for the self-interest of you and your family. Far from reflecting on you, such actions will generally earn you respect and a fair deal all around.

CHAPTER 26

GLOSSARY OF
REAL ESTATE AND LEGAL TERMS

ABSTRACT or **ABSTRACT OF TITLE.** A legal paper that cites the history of a property. It lists the chain of previous owners, when each bought and sold the land, and the price paid each time. Its purpose is to show that ownership of the property is clear and uncontested up to the current owner. In some states, the owner retains a copy; in others, it is on file at the county courthouse or state capital. You could ask to see it before you buy a property.

AMORTIZATION. The gradual paying off of a loan, such as a mortgage, in regular payments. The more you pay off, the more the loan is amortized. When 50 per cent of the mortgage is paid up, for example, it is half amortized.

APPRAISAL. An evaluation of a property to determine its value. It is required by a mortgage lender, for example, so that he will know the house value and therefore how much of a mortgage he can give on it. An appraisal is usually a conservative figure. It does not take into account the high prices of nearby houses in an inflationary period, nor does it necessarily take into account replacement cost of a house. FHA and VA both send you a copy of their appraisals, but when you obtain a conventional mortgage you are generally not shown it unless you ask. An appraisal is concerned chiefly with market value—i.e., what the house would sell for in case of foreclosure.

CERTIFICATE OF TITLE. Like a car title, this is the paper that signifies ownership of a house. It usually contains a legal description of the house and its land.

CLOSING COSTS. Sometimes called settlement costs, they are various expenses involved in the transaction of selling a house, changing title, procuring and processing a mortgage, all of which are paid over and above the price of the house at the time the deal is consummated. See Chapter 25.

DEED OF TRUST. This is used instead of a mortgage in such states as Colorado, Delaware, Mississippi, Tennessee, and Virginia. A third party, not the mortgage lender, holds the deed until it has been paid off or defaulted.

DEPRECIATION. A decline in the value of a house as a result of wear and tear, usually from 2 to 3 per cent of total price each year. During the inflationary years following World War II, however, depreciation was greatly offset by rising house values. Now, however, as housing supply catches up with demand, depreciation is reasserting itself and existing house values will probably decline more and more each year.

EARNEST MONEY. The deposit money given to the seller by the potential buyer to show that he is serious about buying the house. If the deal goes through, the earnest money is applied against the down payment. If the buyer whimsically changes his mind and backs out of the deal, the seller generally keeps the earnest money. If a satisfactory mortgage cannot be obtained or the house turns out to be defective, the buyer may legally pull out and get his money back (but this contingency should be clearly written in the offer to purchase).

EASEMENT RIGHTS. A right of way granted to a person or company entitling him to use property that he does not own. A neighbor may have the legal right to use a driveway running on your property as a result of an easement given by a previous owner of your land. Electric companies often have easement rights to erect their poles in front of your house even though you own the property.

EQUITY. The increasing portion of the house that you own as you pay off a mortgage. When the mortgage is fully paid up you have 100 per cent equity in the house, or in other words, own it outright.

ESCROW. Money or papers given to a third party to hold until all conditions in a contract are fulfilled. The driveway or landscaping may be incomplete, or there may be painting still to be done on the day you close the deal for a house. Rather than hold up the transaction, part of your money is withheld from the builder or seller and held in escrow by the bank, say. The bank will later release the money when the work is done or let you use it to have the work done.

MORTGAGE.   A special kind of loan for buying a house.

MORTGAGE DISCOUNT "POINTS."   See Chapter 24.

MORTGAGEE.   The home buyer who signs up for a mortgage loan in order to buy a house.

MORTGAGOR.   The bank or lender who puts up the money for the mortgage.

TAX ASSESSMENT.   A tax for a specific purpose such as providing paved streets or new sewers in a new development. The people who benefit from the improvement must pay the assessment. It may amount to a few dollars, a few hundred dollars, or a $1000 or more.

TITLE INSURANCE.   Special insurance to protect property owners against loss of their property due to any unforeseen occurrence that might place ownership in jeopardy—a legal flaw in the previous ownership, for example. Or a prodigal son who suddenly returns from Australia and claims he, not his stepbrother who sold it to you, is the rightful owner of your property. See Chapter 25.

TITLE SEARCH.   Checking the ownership papers on file at the courthouse or statehouse to see that the ownership of the house is free and untainted; i.e., there are no liens against the house. A title search is usually mandatory before a house is sold. Sometimes its cost is lumped in with the cost of a title insurance policy, sometimes its cost is itemized separately.

PART 7

WHAT'S WRONG WITH AMERICA'S HOUSES?

Why is it so hard to find a good house nowadays? Why are so many new houses so poorly built, so ugly, so awkward to live in, yet so expensive? The way houses are built today makes them unique among all other mass-produced products made and sold in the United States today. Compared with houses, there is far more uniformity in the quality, and far less uncertainty about the purchase, of virtually all other products we buy, from food and clothing to appliances and cars.

We approach the buying of a house often with trepidation and much suspicion. Regardless of how careful an investigation is made of the house, we still cannot throw off the nagging apprehension associated with buying a pig in a poke. This should not be.

To shed light on the reasons why houses are so uniformly low in quality and so high in price, requires probing beyond the builder. The builder, in fact, is hopelessly enmeshed in a tangle of outside restrictions and controls that legislate against better houses and lower costs for reasons that follow.

A prosperous young doctor and his wife, living in a cramped city apartment with a new baby, went shopping for a new home in the suburbs.

They spent nearly every weekend for more than six months driving around countless suburbs before they found a house that came even close to meeting their needs. In all, they inspected and turned down fifty-eight houses. Partly out of desperation, they finally settled for a $30,000 old house—number fifty-nine—even though it required another $5000 worth of improvements.

The doctor and his wife learned the hard way that it is tough to find a reasonably good house today even if you are among the top 3 per cent in annual income and can spend a good deal. For the many millions of other Americans who make less money, finding an adequate house is even tougher, if not downright impossible at prices they can afford.

Construction costs have risen so high that more than half of the nearly fifty million families in the United States have been priced out of the new house market. According to government statistics, the average American family's income after taxes is around $5800 a year. About 45 per cent of all families have net incomes under $4000 a year, and 25 per cent of the total take home between $1000 and $3000.

Yet the average construction cost of a new, one-family house is about $13,500. And as anybody with open eyes can see, a minimal house with two to three bedrooms and elbow room for an average family with children generally costs at least $15,000, if not more. No wonder more than twenty million Americans are said to live in sub-standard, dilapidated hovels that are unfit for human occupancy. No wonder the federal government is forced to come to the aid of low income families with subsidized public housing (which the rest of the populace pays for). In New York City alone one out of every eleven inhabitants lives in a public housing project.

Exploding Demand

What's more, the shortage of good housing today is mild compared with what is likely to come. According to the Census Bureau, our mushrooming population is expected to hit between 260 and 275 million by 1980—an awesome increase of 80 to 95 million people in less than twenty years. We lose as many as 300,000 houses a year from our present stock because of plain old age; they have to be replaced. Thousands of other existing houses are bulldozed over every month to make way for new superhighways. And around the end of the 1960s, our "new family formation rate" (the economist's term for people who get married) is expected to explode as wave after wave of World War II war babies set up housekeeping. These forces put additional pressure on the demand for living space.

America's $18 billion a year home-building industry, beset with horse-and-buggy building methods, is incapable of meeting the demand. The high cost of building houses is one of its basic problems. But even more alarming, according to economist Louis Winnick, is the "terrible, terrible *sustained rise* in building costs."

The big trouble is that building costs have risen considerably faster than our ordinary year-to-year inflation, which, of course, is bad enough. From 1890 to 1950, building costs had risen nearly 500 per cent, or well over twice the 220 per cent average price increase in all general prices during the same period (using constant dollars). This is one of the significant findings of a monumental three-year study made for the National Bureau of Economic Research by Drs. Leo Grebler and David M. Blank, with Dr. Winnick.

The three economists found that the two most flagrant causes of high building costs are the steeply rising prices of building materials (particularly lumber) and stalled labor productivity in the building field. Though they make more money than they used to, carpenters still hammer nails by hand. Masons still lay bricks manually. But whereas a respectable mason used to be good for 1000 bricks a day, you are lucky if his output goes over 500 today. These are only two glaring examples of technical backwardness in an industry which widely scorns the use of mass-production techniques.

What can be done to arrest the cost spiral and head it downward? And while house prices have been steadily rising over the years, it seems as if the quality of new houses has been sliding steadily downhill. What can be done to reverse this trend, too?

When you delve into the basic problems besetting our hapless building industry, you find that each problem reinforces the other, and two and two keep adding up to five and six compounded troubles. Conversely, by attacking each of the three major problems—poor design, low construction quality, and high costs—you find that the reverse can be true. As each individual problem is erased, the cures can multiply, and snowballing advantages can result.

Why Poor Design?

As noted in the beginning of this book, you not only pay a high price for a house today, but the bills keep coming in long after you've bought it. The central problems are low-quality design and construction, examples of which are studded throughout these pages.

The chief reason for poorly designed houses as opposed to poor construction is that few builders employ architects. According to the American Institute of Architects, only 15 to 20 per cent of all development houses are designed by architects (and development houses account for about 75 per cent of all new houses). Most builders shun architects because they would rather save his fee and design (sic) their own houses. Besides, they find that people shopping for houses cannot tell the difference between a well-designed house and a poor one. The builder would rather put his money into snappy-looking kitchen appliances which catch the eye and impress more people than a soundly laid-out floor plan.

Another much-overlooked influence has worked against the use of architects—our obsolete financing and appraisal methods. Nearly all builders require financing. When they show up at the bank, plans and cost sheets in hand, the typical banker cares little whether the house is really well designed. For that matter, some bankers can't tell the difference. As a result a builder will seldom get credit for an architect's fee listed on his cost sheet.

The same goes for appraisers who will rarely give a house extra value for mortgage loan purposes just because it is handsome and well designed. Like bankers, many appraisers don't know the difference. A house may be designed by a world-famous architect (which does enhance its value) but it will get no more appraisal value than the

same size house down the road designed by a local carpenter, unless it is monstrously hideous and misshapen.
Thus, the outmoded view of bankers and appraisers—whose
underlying importance in building is often overlooked—has
been a repressive influence on design and a widespread
reason for mediocre design.

Perhaps the bankers really should not be expected to lift
design quality. After all, their chief function is to safeguard
the investment money put up to finance houses. This in turn
directs their attention mainly to the resalability of houses.
That is to say, they bet their money only on houses that
will easily sell in case of foreclosure. Since most buyers are
unaware of good design and do not demand it, why should
the bankers bother? This has long been the ruling concept
in financing houses. But as more and more people become
aware of good design and construction, increasing pressure
will be put on them to lift their standards.

. . . And Why Low-Quality Construction?

It's easy to blame the builders, or the unions, for poorly
built houses, a widespread parlor game in America. To be
sure, there are gyp builders and crooked union leaders, as
well as many others in the business who are far from blame-
less. But the basic reasons for shoddy heating, skimpy wiring, and slovenly workmanship go deeper.

What are they? For one thing, the building of houses is
a highly complex and technical job. Much technical know-
how is required. Few people by themselves can be expected
to know all there is to know about the different structural
and mechanical aspects of construction. And few builders
can afford the technical staffs that are required.

For another, the builder is caught up in a vicious system
where incredible pressure is put on suppliers and contractors
to cut their prices. Something must give. Inevitably it is the
quality of the materials and the workmanship. A smooth-
talking salesman offers a builder bargain-priced water
heaters, say, at a price $15 cheaper per unit than another
salesman. The builder visualizes $1500 saved on a hundred
houses. The offer is hard to resist. It is his buyers who later

pay for the loss of quality. The builder, even the salesman, may not even realize that the cheaper heaters lack the rugged interior tank coating that is required to stand up against corrosive water. On the other hand, there are undoubtedly some builders and some shyster salesmen who know indeed what they are doing but whose moral standards are roughly equivalent to those of a horse thief.

And for still another reason: so many houses today are built by hand with virtually no construction controls exerted over how well the individual workers do their job. Irrespective of ability and intent, there is much latitude for human error.

The obvious solution for lifting construction quality is clear-cut, national standards for everything that goes into a house. All of the products and materials for houses should be clearly labeled with quality tags, the way beef is graded choice, premium, and so on, or the way building products in the mammoth Sears, Roebuck catalogue are graded "lowest cost, better, and best." This is a fundamental need if construction quality is ever to be improved.

Why High Costs?

Our third major problem, high costs, stems from the enormous waste and inefficiencies inherent in the building industry today. Putting it another way, standardization and mass-production techniques are urgently needed if the spiraling cost of houses is to be arrested and brought down.

The huge cost penalty we pay for houses today, as a result of old-fashioned building methods, can be seen by comparing the cost rise in houses with that of other products since the 1890s. In 1895, for example, bicycles were advertised for $50 to $60, and you could build a big, three-story, ten-room house for $3200. In 1905, bicycles still sold for $50 to $60, you could buy a spanking new Oldsmobile Limited for $1890, but the cost of construction had risen so that you got less house for more money; a typical eight-room house cost about $3500. In the years since, the value of the dollar has diminished, to be sure. We now spend about $2.50 for a bag of groceries that sold for a dollar in

1900. But the makers of bicycles and automobiles, beset by rising costs on all sides over the years, fought back through the introduction of assembly-line methods and mass-production techniques. The prices of their products are not much higher in actual dollar cost today than they were around 1900. Of course, auto prices slid down to well under $1000 in the years since before rising again, but nevertheless Detroit's auto makers have done comparatively well in holding the line, compared with the building industry. By rights, the comparable ten-room house that cost $3200 in 1895 should not cost more than $20,000 today (excluding land). It actually costs at least $40,000 to $50,000, depending on where you live.

The conclusion soon becomes plain: The big sprawling home-building industry is saddled with waste and hopeless inefficiencies largely because so many little parts and pieces still are put together by expensive hand labor at the site of each new house. And the almost total unacceptance of mass production techniques by the industry in the last sixty-odd years, while other industries were introducing technological improvements, has forced the prices of our houses today *twice as high as they might otherwise be.*

The Last Stronghold

In the words of a team of Harvard and Massachusetts Institute of Technology experts who made an intensive study of the "Design and Production of Houses," housing is almost "the last major stronghold of pre-industrial handcraft production." The walls of a typical house, for example, require as many as fourteen long, drawn-out and separate steps of construction. It takes weeks before they are finished. At a tortoiselike pace the 2 × 4 studs are put up; the outside sheathing is then applied, followed (years later, it seems) by the exterior wood or masonry; then insulation inside; a wait for wiring and plumbing pipes to be run through before the inside wallboard and plaster can be applied; and finally two coats of paint each on inside and outside.

Yet the same walls can be mass-produced, section by

section, in a few minutes on a factory assembly line. In fact, the entire shell of a house—floor, walls, ceiling, and roof—already is mass-produced by prefabricators. Delivered to the site of a house, they can be completely assembled and roofed over in less than a day's time. What's more, the resulting structure is usually stronger, better-made, and better-looking than its handmade counterpart.

The same mass-production techniques can also reduce the cost of interior parts of the house. Plumbing, one of the biggest single costs in houses today, can be brought down by as much as $500 a house, sometimes more, by the use of prefabricated plumbing systems. Such savings are already a matter of record where prefab plumbing assemblies are permitted. Similar savings are possible for interior partitions, for kitchen cabinets, for entire bathroom units, for that matter, and for virtually everything else in a house except perhaps for digging the hole under the house and putting up the foundation.

How Much Cost Reduction through Mass Production?

The sheer power of prefabrication coupled with mass production could produce astronomical savings. A few years ago a prefab manufacturer was quoted $45 a bathtub for his houses. An investigation showed that by installing his own 1800-ton press he could turn out his own tubs for a mere $15 apiece, based on producing 40,000 tubs a year for 40,000 houses.

The same prefabber even looked into electrically operated windows, which may sound like the ultimate in labor-saving devices. Wired by hand the way an electrician wires your house, the cost would have come to an extravagant $50 a window. But if the same electric operating mechanism was bought and installed on a mass-production basis for the same 40,000 houses a year, their cost would nose-dive to a mere $3.50 a window!

Carl Koch, a well-known architect, points out that painting a house normally costs from 5 to 10¢ a square foot of surface. "The same surfaces (on panels) can be roller-coated in factories with high-grade baked-enamel finish for way under 1¢ a square foot. And the home buyer would get a more evenly applied paint that is virtually indestructible." You not only would save on first cost of your house; you would save handsomely on maintenance and repainting costs over the years.

The Central Utility Core

Probably the biggest savings as a result of factory-made components and mass production could be made by means of a "central utility core" for houses—a compact, centrally located cabinet which would combine all of the major mechanical, electrical, and other utilities of a house. This means the furnace, hot-water heater, wiring center, main plumbing assembly, prefabricated chimney, air conditioner if desired, and even some of the basic mechanisms for your kitchen appliances. Moreover, one basic heating mechanism could provide heat for cooking and hot water as well as for heating. The entire utility core would be contained in a wall-like cabinet with various plug-in attachments for easy on-the-job hookup. It would be mass-produced on factory assembly lines and would mean that all of the different utility equipment, now delivered and installed separately, could be delivered and installed in one economical swoop. The total savings possible could alone bring down the total cost of our houses by an estimated 10 to 15 per cent.

The Main Roadblock

But no manufacturer in his right mind would today tackle the research program necessary to develop a practical utility core, or any other comparable new product for houses, for that matter. He would be licked before he started. The success of such a product plainly depends on the existence of a mass market for it, and today a mass market is legally impossible: We have more than 2000 different and conflicting building codes in the United States, each with its own differing rules specifying how a house should be built and how the various equipment such as plumbing and heating must be made and installed. Our wildly archaic building codes, in short, are a principal obstruction, the main roadblock, that prevents the use of moneysaving standardization and mass-production techniques in house construction.

In the Minneapolis area alone builders have to cope with twenty-seven different building codes. On New York's crowded Long Island, where more than 25,000 houses a year are built, there are more than fifty different codes. In addition, New York City legislates against the economical use of copper by banning soldered copper joints. Philadelphia, ruled by entrenched brick and masonry interests, sharply limits non-masonry houses. Excessive plumbing restrictions add about $500 apiece to the cost of many houses in the Pittsburgh area. Glue-nailed trusses, a highly promising postwar development, are disallowed in Columbus, Ohio, and dozens of other cities. Also prohibited by obsolete codes are such new, cost-saving products as prefabricated fireplaces, chimneys, and plumbing. Thus, conflicting and outmoded codes not only bar standardization but they also outlaw the use of new methods and materials. If General Motors had to cope with such conditions, its assembly lines would be forced to operate on a maddening stop-and-go schedule to accommodate model changes for individual dealers.

Clearly then, real technical progress cannot be achieved until we have a system of modern, up-to-date uniform codes—i.e., a new national building code for the same reasons we have standard-gauge railroad tracks, and standard 115-volt electricity.

But whenever enlightened building men propose code reforms—and many have tried—they are confronted with instant and violent opposition from a bedrock of entrenched pressure groups. These include local contractors (particularly plumbers), union leaders, and building officials who don't want changes, as well as many old-line suppliers of such products as brick, stone, and steel who have spent years getting codes written their way. There are also opponents in many local officials who, according to architectural expert Burnham Kelly, "have honest intentions but inadequate knowledge."

Of course it is true that building codes are essential to protect the health and safety of home buyers—to prevent, for example, unsanitary plumbing and rickety houses. They should be strict and efficient. But they need not be restrictive and obsolete, too.

The people who keep fighting against a uniform code argue that it will never work, chiefly because of climate variations from state to state. They say, for example, that a house roof in Maine must be built stronger because of the snow load than a roof in Georgia.

The advocates of a uniform code agree that such climate variations require a special approach, but this is a far from insoluble problem. As a matter of fact there is a neat solution: A few modifications can be written into the national code to apply to those parts of the country where climate variations require special construction. But the main construction requirements of a national code would be the same all over. After all, water flows through pipes the same way in St. Paul as in St. Petersburg, and the structural problems of heat, cold, and rain are fundamentally the same wherever you live.

The new single set of building requirements recently issued by the Federal Housing Administration prove that one set of rules, with appropriate regional modifications, is possible. With one sweep of the broom, the new FHA rule book takes the place of twenty-eight different sets of rules with which its officials around the country were formerly burdened. The FHA rule book is, in effect, a single national code. And in Canada, despite great climate extremes across the provinces, housing experts have been at work for several years on the development of a national code, which, by the way, is no easy task.

The Eli Whitney Principle

There is one other need if we are to enjoy the full flowering of benefits possible as a result of a uniform code and the widespread introduction of mass-produced components: the need for standardization. Not standardization of looks, the proponents stress, but standardization of a few key dimensions in houses so that the same mass-produced components may be used by all builders and in all houses.

Putting it another way, we need *interchangeable* components based on one measuring stick in the same way that the multitude of nuts and bolts in Detroit's cars all use the standard threads. This is not so in housing, where dimensional standardization is as much needed today as it was when Eli Whitney's principle of the interchangeability of parts revolutionized factory mass-production methods over a century ago.

Bathroom sinks, kitchen cabinets, and heating units come in a bewildering number of sizes and shapes. A window manufacturer has noted that there are 2500 different kinds and sizes of steel windows on the market. A top architect points out that Sweet's Construction Catalog—the building industry's Bible—requires fourteen volumes, contains over 17,000 pages, yet offers only a selected list of the better companies' products.

As a result, the dimensions of our houses and the rooms within vary in such helter-skelter fashion that design chaos is the rule of the day. A variation of an inch or two in window or door sizes can throw an architect's entire plan out of kilter. Japanese houses, on the other hand, are a marvel of intelligence and sophistication. Everything has been based on the size of their traditional Tatami floor mats, about 3 × 6 feet in size, for over 500 years. Doors and windows may be one of one-and-a-half one mat wide, and one mat high. Rooms may be three, four, or eight mats in size. Even their lumber is cut in the mill to predetermined mat lengths (which also must cut costs for the Japanese equivalent of our do-it-yourself homeowners). Such standardization is surprisingly flexible, and it has given rise to what experts call the simplest and most efficient building industry in the world.

We need not standardize via floor mats (though maybe it's a better idea than we think). But settling on a few basic starting dimensions for houses, as imaginative architects have long urged, can bring about a huge simplification of nearly everything in houses. Take the kitchen, for example.

Not long ago, Westinghouse introduced a line of packaged kitchen components with 250 different cabinets. The base cabinets for under the sink alone had to be made in fifteen different widths because of varying kitchen sizes. "The production scheduling problems that result are a nightmare," says Will M. Kline, Jr., manager of Westinghouse's kitchen department. But if all kitchens were standardized on a module such as one foot (so that interior dimensions would be an even multiple of one foot), Kline says they could reduce the number of cabinet sizes made and stocked by a significant 60 per cent *with no loss of design variety or flexibility*. The cost of kitchen equipment, sinks, range, and oven, as well as cabinets, could be shaved by a good 15 to 20 per cent.

Merely by standardizing the windows of one of its houses, a big builder could cut the price of screens to buyers by $56 a house. A prefab house maker who formerly stocked seventy-six different window sizes for his different houses cut down to sixteen sizes, and he affected savings from stock room to delivery.

Architectural Forum has pointed out, in fact, that standardized sizes would result "in incalculable large savings on the cost of distribution and stocking of excessive numbers of component sizes." The entire process of building a house could in one fell swoop simplify down, in effect, to the dropping of its various preassembled component parts neatly into places with little sawing, fitting, or waste. The same efficient process could extend over to the remodeling or expansion of your present home with comparable reductions in cost. A top building executive estimates that such standardization by itself could save home buyers about 10 per cent at least on house costs, or $2000 off the price of a $20,000 house.

Standardizing on a few basic dimensions after the war enabled Great Britain to put up 175 new schools in record time. Much of the speedy reconstruction of war-torn Germany is credited to the adoption of the same modular idea for their building. But in the United States the chaotic lack of a standard measuring stick for our houses imposes a deceptively large hidden-cost handicap on builders and manufacturers. It is one of the much overlooked forces that push up the cost of houses as well as making it tough to achieve the economies inherent in mass-producing standardized components.

One other block to efficient construction techniques and lower house costs should be mentioned, and this is the practice of many cities and towns of adopting rigid licensing laws. These laws require that certain parts of the house—chiefly heating, plumbing, and wiring—be installed by local licensed workers. At first thought this may seem to be a good safeguard against shoddy work by hack workmen, and they are so represented by the local building trades and contractors who push them through.

As a result, however, preassembled components are barred by law even though they are factory-engineered and put together by highly skilled workmen. Local workmen must do the installation from scratch by extravagant hand methods at the home building site. You pay the extra bill.

It is as if your town barred new automobiles unless local mechanics assembled all of the parts. Imagine what your next car would cost if *this* became local law.

Avoiding Look-Alike Houses

The technological twins, standardization and mass production, may seem to support the idea of even more lookalike houses. But on the contrary, mass-produced components hold out the promise of far greater diversity in houses than ever before. A few basic mass-produced parts with co-ordinated dimensions can, like a child's set of blocks, be put together in a huge variety of different sizes and shapes.

The exterior surfaces of the wall panels can be varied in texture and color so that you would never know that the same facilities are inside. And what's the difference if we all use the same mass-produced plumbing, wiring, and heating cores inside of our houses, so long as they are well made? As a matter of fact, one leading prefab manufacturer offers one of his house packages in three different styles—Cape Cod, traditional, and contemporary—yet each consists of identical floor plan and virtually the same parts throughout. You could look at the three "different" houses next to each other and never know they are basically identical triplets except for deceptively varied exterior clothes.

We'll Get Higher Quality, Too

The icing on the cake with mass-produced, preassembled components is that they will mean higher quality and better workmanship almost everywhere in the house. We have noted the high durability of factory-applied finishes. Other examples abound. Prefabricated fireplaces, engineered in the factory, give you a foolproof design (which will work right and not smoke like so many of their handmade counterparts). Prefabricated chimneys are more efficient than even the thickest brick chimneys (thus reduced fuel bills).

Factory-made kitchen cabinets can get a hot lacquer furniture finish that is impossible to impart in the field. And experience shows that windows factory-set in their wall panels are tightly fitted and calked to a degree that is unrealistic to expect from carpenters doing the same thing on the job. A similar step-up in quality can follow nearly everywhere else in houses, following the introduction of preassembled, factory-made component parts.

At the same time, the nature of prefabrication sharply reduces the possibility of on-site errors and mistakes, it reduces material waste, and reduces the opportunity for pilferage (a much-overlooked and highly expensive problem that has long plagued builders).

Savings in Remodeling

The cost savings of fixing up and remodeling houses also should be mentioned, since these jobs are even more painfully expensive and troublesome than building a new house. The availability of prefabricated wall and ceiling panels, matched to the same dimensional system of your existing rooms, would enable almost anyone to quickly add rooms to his present house at rock-bottom cost. You would, of course, have to provide a new foundation yourself, but after that, the limitless possibilities of standard-size components such as wall sections (you call the signals on color, texture, and particular type) would permit the introduction of remodeling kits for adding on to your present house quickly and far less expensively than ever before.

The Biggest Bargain

How much reduction in costs could we expect as a result of the standardization and mass-production economies that would go hand in hand with a national code? The answer is as much as 40 per cent or more, if the bargain-priced houses now being built by the country's most publicized builder, Bill Levitt, are any indication. Consider, for example, his latest housing development in Matawan, New Jersey. Chiefly because of the sheer efficiency of his mass-production techniques, his houses are priced just about 40 per cent under the same size houses by typical builders. His amazingly large three- and four-bedroom houses range in selling price from $16,500 to $24,990. You get from 1,500 up to 2,350 square feet of floor area, plus a garage. The same size houses by other builders generally cannot be duplicated anywhere else in the North for less than $23,-000, and closer to $40,000 for the largest models.

Levitt's operation is so efficient that he can also afford to throw in at no extra charge a small truckload of kitchen and laundry appliances, central air conditioning and fifteen to twenty young trees and shrubs planted outside; you also benefit from Levitt-installed city water and sewer lines, paved streets, community swimming pools and playgrounds, and Levitt-built schools. Some strict architectural critics may charge that the design and appearance of Levitt's houses fall a bit short of what they could perhaps be. But in sheer total space and value given for the money a Levitt house is clearly the biggest bargain on the market.

Levitt can offer such a bargain because, first of all, he is building in a rural area where he is not hamstrung by conflicting codes and punitive municipal restrictions. Only one code applies. But before he starts his first house an incredible amount of design and planning is done in advance. Virtually all parts of all of his houses are standardized so that each can be prefabricated and then installed, one after the other down the line, with clockwork precision. This, of course, requires the same sort of planning and mass purchasing that is standard procedure for any large, successful industrial corporation launching a new product. But only a few thousand families profit from Levitt's efficiencies each year.

It is therefore probable that the mass-production economies achieved by a Levitt are extremely small compared with the ultimate savings possible with real standardization and mass production in home building on a nationwide scale. National manufacturers could mass-produce key assemblies for houses by the tens of thousands a year. This is already being done on a comparatively small scale in the case of the trailer, the home builder's much-overlooked competitor. Even Levitt could not duplicate the volume price of any one of a number of different trailer brands.

What About Research?

If we are to realize the full benefits of mass production, we will need much more fundamental research. There have been so few major advances in house construction chiefly because of the appalling lack of research. Economist John K. Galbraith has commented that very little research is ever done in industries "where the firms are numerous and small." Housing is the classic example. None of the nation's close to 100,000 different builders has the means of a du Pont or an A T & T. Nor are the more than seventy-five different trade associations and the hundreds of building-product manufacturers either capable of or inclined to sponsor fundamental research of the kind that discovered nylon or developed the transistor tube.

But that is precisely the tonic required to develop such long-needed products as a practical utility core, termite-proof plastic beams to replace wood, a permanent paint, a low-cost lifetime roof shingle, a cheap chemical for individual house sewage purposes that would relieve our cities of making the increasingly large outlays needed for expanded sewage facilities.

Besides the urgent need for basic research, building people constantly mention other pressing problems:

1. The financing dilemma—mortgages for houses are hard to get which coupled with stiff interest rates are a basic reason why low-income families cannot afford new houses;

2. The lack of good long-range land planning and well-designed housing developments;

3. Our exasperating real estate laws and practices, including exorbitant closing-cost fees and high-priced title-insurance policies;

4. The country-wide need for accurate housing statistics on such questions as exactly how much housing and what kind are most needed.

The Code and the Center

Some of these problems will take a long time to solve. But a big start can be made toward solving the overriding problem of high housing costs by a central attack on two of its fundamental causes: the archaic codes which defy technological progress, and the cheap and badly built houses which drain literally billions of dollars a year from family budgets. Several cures are almost self-evident:

1. A National Building Code Commission should be formed to work out a uniform building code for houses. Its acceptance by the states should be voluntary, just as cities in New York can voluntarily adopt the state's pioneering building code. (After more than ten years on the books, the New York State code has been adopted by about half of all municipalities with more than 5000 people.) But model code legislation should be written in advance to allow quick acceptance by each state's legislature, and thus forestall changes by pressure groups.

2. A National Housing Research Center should be established to do for housing what the National Bureau of Standards now does for government agencies and sixteen

different branches of private industry. An NHRC is essential not only for carrying out basic research on new methods and products, but also to set up quality standards (so consumers can protect themselves against shoddy construction). It would also provide the technical expertise and facilities to implement the administration of a national building code.

3. The adoption of standard modular dimensions for all building to eliminate the huge design chaos that exists as a result of the many different measuring yardsticks in use today.

There is already a source of money to underwrite the first two proposals. Additional handouts from the Congress are not necessary. The money could be borrowed from the more than $800 million of unspent surplus reserves held by the Federal Housing Administration. The amount needed to get things under way would require less than 5 per cent of the FHA's reserves—less money than it takes to get one Atlas missile onto the firing line at Cape Canaveral ($37 million).

Inevitably, of course, objections will be raised against using FHA money. But one of FHA's "chief purposes," according to the original Housing Law of 1934 is ". . . to encourage improvement in housing standards and conditions." No greater improvement could be made than a modern national code and, for the first time in our history, some real research for housing.

Some of the same vested-interest groups who bitterly fought the creation of the FHA in 1934 have long fought against reforms such as a national code and government-sponsored research. Unfortunately, the big, sprawling, and contentious housing industry consists of diverse and vocal groups who are often fighting loudly among themselves, each one violently bent on advancing its interests. It is time they were firmly reminded that the most important interests of all are those of the American house owner and his family whose lives and well-being depend so much on the place in which they live.

What You Can Do

All of us can help to speed the acceptance of such urgently needed reforms as a uniform national code and a National Housing Research Center. When your local building code is to be changed you should urge the adoption of a *performance* code, not the hidebound and restrictive *specification* code that prevails in so many places. When the issue of a uniform code is brought up in the Congress— it is sure to come—you should act in concert with friends and neighbors and let your congressman and senators know that you are behind it.

When you build, buy, or remodel a house, you can pointedly ask the builder if he is giving you the benefit of the new laborsaving, preassembled components that are already on the market. And as more and more dedicated leaders in and out of the building industry speak up and advocate an end to old-fashioned building methods, all of us should also speak up. Public opinion, expressed by those of us who live with the consequences of the stalemate, can help prod our public servants.

PART 8

CHECK LIST FOR BUILDING OR BUYING A HOUSE

This check list can be torn out or copied and taken with you when you look at houses. It is a summary of the main points of this book.

Choosing house price, size, and neighborhood

1. What is the maximum-price house you can afford, based on what you can pay for monthly mortgage charges and housing upkeep expenses? . . . . _____

2. What is the maximum down payment you can afford? Does this leave money for moving, new appliances, furnishings, redecorating, and improvements (for a new house as well as an old house)? . _____

3. How large a house do you need (in total square feet of finished living area as well as number of rooms)? . . . . _____

4. Are there nearby stores, shopping centers, schools, churches, and public transportation? . . . . . . _____

5. Is the neighborhood attractive? . . . . . . _____

6. Is the neighborhood zoned for single-family houses only? Did you call the zoning board? . . _____

7. Will you like the neighbors? . . . . _____

8. How good are the local schools? . . . . . . _____

Interior design: the floor plan

9. Are the living, working and sleeping areas properly zoned from each other? . . . . _____

10. Is the family entrance close to the kitchen? . . _____

11. Does the main entrance have a foyer and clothes closet? . . . . _____

12. Is the kitchen centrally located? . . . . . _____

13. Is there good room-to-room relationship? . . _____
14. Is there good indoor-outdoor relationship? . . _____
15. Is the outdoor terrace or patio near the living room? . . . . _____
16. What is the total floor area in square feet (excluding garage and basement)? . . . . _____
17. What is house price per square foot of living area? . . . . _____
18. If the price per square foot is higher or lower than average, is it compensated for by special features (or the lack of them)—e.g., garage, basement, expensive land, high-quality materials, fireplace? . _____
19. Are there any glaring design flaws? Can you correct them or live with them? (For example, front picture window, no front foyer, broken-up walls that limit furniture placement.) . . . . _____

Kitchen
20. Is the work triangle (refrigerator to sink to range) in proper order, and between twelve to twenty feet? . . . . _____
21. Does the kitchen have a good exposure? . . _____
22. Are there adequate windows, lighting, and ventilation? . . . . _____
23. Is there adequate counter-top surface? . . _____
24. Are counter-top surfaces rugged and will they stay attractive? . . . . _____
25. Are good-quality kitchen cabinets used? . . _____

Other rooms
26. Is the living room large and pleasant? . . _____
27. Is it free of cross traffic? . . . . _____
28. Can living-room furniture be properly located? . . . . _____
29. Is there a fireplace? . . . . _____
30. Is there living-room storage for books, card tables, records, fireplace wood, and magazines? . _____
31. Is there dining-room storage for linen, silver, and dishes? . . . . _____

32. Is there a "family" or recreation room? . . _____

33. Is the family room large enough and properly located? . . . . _____

34. Are the bedrooms large enough? . . . . . _____

35. Do bedroom windows let in enough light and air? . . . . _____

36. Are bedroom closets large enough? . . . _____

37. Is the bathroom large enough? . . . . . _____

38. Is the lavatory large enough? . . . . . . _____

39. Is the bathtub under a window? (It should not be.) . . . . _____

40. Are the lavatory, toilet, and bathtub of good quality? Are they stamped with the name of a well-known manufacturer? . . . . _____

41. Is the master bath located where guests can use it? . . . . _____

42. Does the shower nozzle clear your head? Are there soap racks, hand grips, water shut-off valves? . . . . _____

43. Is the laundry large enough? . . . . . . _____

44. Is there ample space for a washer, drier, and ironing board? . . . . _____

45. Is there a place for iron, soap, and laundry necessities in the laundry? . . . . _____

Storage

46. Are there storage places for trunks, boxes, sleds, bicycles? . . . . _____

47. Is there storage space near the outside for summer furniture, mower, and garden tools? . . . _____

48. Does the basement have a thirty-six-inch wide door to the outside? . . . . _____

49. If storage facilities are limited, is space available in the right location for you to add them—i.e., is there good storage potential? . . . . _____

50. With no basement, is there a "basement equivalent" above ground for storage as well as for laundry and utility space? . . . . _____

One-, 1½-, two-story, or split level?

51. Are bedroom, living, and work areas of a one-story house well zoned and separated from each other? . . . . _____

52. Do doorways provide easy access to outdoor patios and play areas? . . . . _____

53. The 1½-story Cape Cod: Is the second-floor space really worth the money or would a two-story house be better? . . . . _____

54. If the attic is to be made into rooms, is the heating plant large enough for them? . . . . _____

55. Are heating ducts and plumbing pipes installed for the second-floor expansion space? . . . . . _____

56. Is the attic well insulated and ventilated? . . _____

57. The two-story house: Is this your best choice if if you have or will have infants (who necessitate much stair climbing)? . . . . _____

58. Is there a first-floor bathroom? . . . . . . _____

59. Are the living room and dining room convenient to each other? . . . . _____

60. The split level: Is there good circulation from room to room? . . . . _____

61. Are heating and insulation adequate, particularly at lowest level and above garage? . . . . . . _____

Outside design

62. Is the house well located on its lot? . . . . _____

63. Are the service, public, and private zones of lot well planned? How much grass to cut? . . . _____

64. Does the house have a simple shape (few jogs, breaks, and offsets)? . . . . _____

65. Do windows line up neatly on the outside of the house? . . . . _____

66. Does the house look attractive? . . . . . . _____

67. Is the roof line straight with few or no breaks? . . . . _____

68. Are there wide roof overhangs over the walls? . . . . _____

Orientation

69. Does the house have good orientation (exposure) in relation to the sun—i.e., are the large windows and main living areas open to the south sun in winter? . . . . _____

70. Will south, east, and west windows be shaded in summer? . . . . _____

Lot and site

71. Is the house properly located on its site (small public-area front lawn, short drive, maximum private outdoor area shielded from public view)? . . . . _____

72. Are there trees and adequate landscaping? . _____

73. Is the site high enough to shed rain water? . _____

74. Does it have good drainage characteristics? If it is a steep, sloping site, are there retaining walls to prevent washouts? . . . . _____

75. Is the site on solid ground or is it filled-in? . . _____

Heating: Warm Air

76. Was the heating installed by a reputable dealer? . . . . _____

77. Is the furnace guaranteed for ten years? . . _____

78. Does the furnace have a belt-driven blower? . _____

79. Can the air filter be removed easily for cleaning? . . . . _____

80. Does the duct system look well designed? . _____

81. Is the furnace adjusted for Continuous Air Circulation? . . . . _____

Hot water and steam heat

82. Is the heating boiler cast iron or steel? . . . _____

83. If it is a steel boiler, does it have a Steel Boiler Institute (SBI) seal? . . . . _____

84. Are modern baseboard radiators used? What kind: cast iron or non-ferrous? . . . . _____

85. If baseboard radiators are used, do they have an IBR (Institute of Boiler and Radiator Mfrs.) seal? . _____

86. Which is cheaper locally, gas or oil heat? . . _____

87. If oil heat is used, is the equipment one of the new high-efficiency "forced draft" brands? . . . _____
88. If electric heat is used, what will it cost? . . . _____

Insulation

89. Are all parts of the house insulated—walls, ceilings, concrete floor, crawl space, walls between garage and house? . . . . _____
90. Is the insulation an approved kind? . . . . _____
91. Is the insulation at least two inches thick for floor and walls, three inches to six inches over ceilings? . _____
92. Are doors and windows weather-stripped? . _____

Wiring

93. Is the electric service at least 220 volts and 100 amperes? . . . . _____
94. Are there at least eight to ten individual electric circuits (fuses or circuit breakers)? . . . . . . _____
95. Are there enough electric outlets and light switches? . . . . _____

Termite and decay protection

96. Does your location require termite protection? . . . . _____
97. What kind of termite protection has been provided? . . . . _____

Faucet hot-water heater

98. Is the heater tank capacity forty gallons or more? . . . . _____
99. What kind of tank: galvanized iron, ordinary glass, good glass, aluminum, copper? . . . . . . _____
100. How long is the hot-water heater guaranteed? . . . . _____
101. If the hot-water heater is part of the regular heating boiler, does it have adequate capacity? . _____
102. Does it have an IWH (Indirect Water Heater) stamp? . . . . _____

Structure

103. Is the foundation on solid ground or on filled land? . . . . _____

104. Is the basement properly waterproofed? . . _____

105. If there is a concrete floor, is there a vapor barrier and an adequate gravel bed underneath? . _____

106. If there is a crawl space, does it have adequate vents? . . . . _____

107. Is there a vapor barrier over the crawl-space earth? . . . . _____

108. Is there cross bridging under the floor (of a basement house)? . . . . _____

109. What kind of floor cover is used in each room? . . . . _____

110. What kind of interior wall material? . . _____

111. Will the outside walls require periodic painting, or is it a permanent wall surface? . . . . . _____

112. If walls are painted, is a top-grade paint used? . . . . _____

113. Are top-grade windows used? What brand? Do they fit snugly, open and close smoothly, and feel solid (shake them)? . . . . _____

114. Are top-grade doors used? How well do they fit? . . . . _____

115. Is insulating glass (such as Thermopane or Twindow) used, or are there storm windows and doors? . . . . _____

116. Is a good-quality roof cover used? What kind and how long will it last? . . . . _____

117. What color roof? Does it blend well with the house? . . . . _____

118. Are roof gutters installed for carrying off rain water? . . . . _____

119. Has the structure been inspected by a *structural* expert? What are his credentials? . . . . . . _____

120. Is a special inspection necessary for termites, septic-tank condition, and heating? . . . . . _____

121. Does the house conform with FHA's minimum property requirements? . . . . _____

122. Is central air conditioning included or are provisions made for its future installation? . . . . _____

123. Have you investigated the reputation and reliability of the air-conditioning contractor? . . _____

124. Is the air-conditioning equipment a top national brand? Does it carry the approval seal of the Air Conditioning & Refrigeration Institute (ARI)? . _____

125. Is the equipment of adequate capacity to maintain your house at 75 degrees and 50 per cent relative humidity during the hottest summer weather? . . . . _____

Buying a used house

126. Is there adequate wiring capacity? Enough circuits and outlets? . . . . _____

127. Is the structure straight and true, not knocked out of kilter as a result of settling or structural failure? . . . . _____

128. Have you had a termite inspection? . . . . _____

129. Is the heating plant in good condition? . . _____

130. The plumbing: Is there adequate water pressure at the highest level? . . . . _____

131. Is the hot-water heater in good condition? . _____

132. Is insulation present in walls, ceiling, and floor (of a non-basement house)? . . . . _____

133. Are the roof and gutters in good shape? . . . _____

134. Is the basement dry? Even if apparently dry-looking, are there any signs of wetness—i.e., stains, streaks, flakiness, mottled-looking beams? . . . . _____

135. How much painting and redecoration are needed? . . . . _____

136. Is there a modern kitchen, or is it large enough for adequate remodeling? . . . . _____

137. Is bathroom remodeling required? Is a new bath or half-bath needed? . . . . _____

138. Do the driveway and walks require repairs? . _____

139. What is the fire-insurance coverage on the house? . . . . _____

140. When was the house built? What does this indicate about possible structural defects? . . . _____

Buying a new house from a builder
141. Was the house designed by an architect? . . _____
142. Does the builder have a good reputation? . . _____
143. How long has the builder's firm been established? . . . . _____
144. If it is a development house, who will provide street paving, other utilities? . . . . _____

Building a house
145. Were the plans designed by an architect? . . _____
146. Have you chosen a reputable builder? . . _____
147. Has the builder provided an adequate completion bond, liability and workmens' compensation insurance? . . . . _____
148. Does your contract clearly spell out *everything* that goes in the house? Has it been approved by your lawyer? . . . . _____
149. Have you made provisions in the contract for protection against sub-contractor liens? . . . . _____

Building or buying a prefabricated house
150. Have you thoroughly checked the design and construction (just as you would a conventionally built house)? . . . . _____
151. Does the manufacturer have a good reputation? What is his Dun & Bradstreet credit rating? . . _____
152. Have you investigated the reputation of the builder-dealer you are buying from? . . . . . _____

Shopping and negotiating (chiefly for an existing house)
153. Are you dealing with reputable real estate brokers? . . . . _____
154. What is a fair current price for the house (based on space per square foot, extra features, prices for comparable new and old houses nearby)? The highest price you can pay? . . . . _____

155. How long has the house been on the market? . . . . _____

156. How much should the owner deduct from his price to allow for repairing defects or a run-down condition? . . . . _____

157. Do any special features make the house more valuable than a comparable house nearby? (A few examples: exceptional design by an architect, modern kitchen, particularly good location, central air conditioning, etc.) . . . . _____

158. According to the real estate agent, how low a price will the owner accept? . . . . _____

159. If you are dealing directly with the seller (no real estate agent involved), can you deduct an amount equal to the agent's fee from the owner's asking price? . . . . _____

160. What is the minimum deposit acceptable? . . _____

161. Is the deposit accompanied by an iron-clad binder or "offer to purchase"? Does it contain escape clauses that assure return of your money in case the deal falls through? . . . . _____

162. Has your lawyer approved the binder agreement? . . . . _____

Financing

163. Can you obtain a GI or FHA mortgage? . . _____

164. Who are the best sources of mortgages where you live? . . . . _____

165. Have you shopped for a mortgage, comparing the advantages and limitations of one against the other? . . . . _____

166. Does the mortgage contract contain prepay-payment, skip-payment, and open end clauses? . . _____

167. Will the mortgage lender discount the mortgage by a certain number of "points"? By how much? Who pays it? . . . . _____

168. What is the total of all other charges you must pay for obtaining and processing the mortgage (service charge, commitment fee, etc.)? . . . . _____

169. Would these charges be much lower with another lender? . . . . ._____

170. What is the mortgage interest rate? Is this the best the lender offers? What about other lenders? . _____

Closing costs

171. What will total closing costs be? . . . . ._____

172. Can you negotiate lower closing costs (or call the deal off)? . . . . ._____

173. If the house has changed hands previously in the last ten years, should you get a discount on reissue title insurance? . . . . ._____

174. Is it local custom for the seller to pay for title insurance? . . . . ._____

175. Will the seller provide or pay for property survey and other necessary items required to complete the sale? . . . . ._____

INDEX